After Sherlock Holmes

W9-DFD-313

ALSO BY LEROY LAD PANEK
AND FROM MCFARLAND

---

*Before Sherlock Holmes: How Magazines and Newspapers
Invented the Detective Story* (2011)

The Origins of the American Detective Story (2006)

*Reading Early Hammett: A Critical Study of the Fiction
Prior to* The Maltese Falcon (2004)

The American Police Novel: A History (2003)

EDITED BY LEROY LAD PANEK AND
MARY M. BENDEL-SIMSO

Early American Detective Stories: An Anthology
(2008; paperback 2014)

After Sherlock Holmes

*The Evolution of British and
American Detective Stories,
1891–1914*

LeRoy Lad Panek

McFarland & Company, Inc., Publishers
Jefferson, North Carolina

LIBRARY OF CONGRESS CATALOGUING-IN-PUBLICATION DATA

Panek, LeRoy.
After Sherlock Holmes : the evolution of British and
American detective stories, 1891–1914 / LeRoy Lad Panek.
p.   cm.
Includes bibliographical references and index.

ISBN 978-0-7864-7765-4 (softcover : acid free paper) ∞
ISBN 978-1-4766-1810-4 (ebook)

1. Detective and mystery stories, English—History and
criticism.   2. Detective and mystery stories, American—History and
criticism.   3. Doyle, Arthur Conan, 1859–1930—Influence.   I. Title.
PR830.D4P336 2014   823'.087209—dc23   2014023685

BRITISH LIBRARY CATALOGUING DATA ARE AVAILABLE

On the cover: detective (© 2014 sodapix/Thinkstock)

Printed in the United States of America

McFarland & Company, Inc., Publishers
Box 611, Jefferson, North Carolina 28640
www.mcfarlandpub.com

For Augie

Table of Contents

Preface

The detective story has had a continuous existence in Britain and the United States since the late 1830s. For the first fifty years, however, it went relatively unnoticed, even by a lot of literary people: Poe, after all, had a hard time peddling his stories, and the rage for sensation novels, not the detective stories in them, made *Bleak House* and *The Moonstone* into transatlantic best sellers. Beginning in the late 1880s and early 1890s, however, things happened. For one thing, Sherlock Holmes happened. But even if Conan Doyle had not created him—or if he had not switched to short stories in 1891—someone else would have probably domesticated and popularized the character of Poe's great detective. It is not my purpose, however, to say very much about Sherlock Holmes and thereby invite the wrath of the Baker Street Irregulars and my friend Langdale Pike. It's what went on around Conan Doyle that has interested me for the past several years, and what follows is a result of trying to ask the right questions and to assemble materials relative to the detective story at the turn of the twentieth century, a time during which the modern detective story began in Britain and the United States.

It's not that the period has been totally ignored. The detective story, after all, is the first form of popular literature to have people interested both in reading it and in investigating its history. Significantly, the interest in the form's origin and development began at the close of the nineteenth century when pieces about the history of the genre appeared both in the popular press and in the occasional academic publication. Then Ellery Queen and Howard Haycraft enthusiastically took up the history of detective fiction in the middle of the twentieth century. Unlike other popular literary forms, moreover, libraries collected and cataloged detective stories—often because of the donation of collectors' personal libraries—and the advent of the OCLC database and its access to worldwide resources in 1967 gave readers unprecedented access to these collections. Publishers' reprints of detective writers in the 1970s, including E.F. Bleiler's editions of Victorian detective stories from Dover and Hugh Green's four Rivals of Sherlock Holmes volumes from Penguin, signaled and facilitated renewed interest in the history of detective fiction. And then there was Google Books.

1

One result of the critical/historical interest in detective stories is that we know a great deal more about books—from the recovery of forgotten novels like *The Dead Letter*, assembled collections of dime novels, and reassessments of best sellers like *The Moonstone* and *Bleak House*. For most if not all of the nineteenth century, however, the majority of detective stories did not appear in books. And until the 1870s most were not novels. In fact, for half a century most detective stories were ephemera, short stories or sometimes serials printed in newspapers or magazines. And that included Poe's tales of ratiocination. At the end of the century the ephemera business changed. Poe underwent a revival. Just as importantly, in the United States and Britain newspaper syndication made fiction, especially new kinds of detective serials, part of their efforts to entice and keep readers. And the publishers of the new illustrated magazines, publishers like George Newnes, made short stories, frequently detective short stories, standard parts of their efforts to do the same thing. From there it was an easy step to print collected short stories in books and preserve them for ... well, for us.

As the principal form of the detective story at the turn of the century, the new short story solidified the plot invented by Poe in 1841 and it slowly changed the subject matter of the Victorian sensation novel cum detective story. The rediscovery of Poe in the 1880s made writers realize the importance of reason/argument and surprise in the detective story, and it supplanted the old notebook format based on a detective's narrative of saving the innocent and righting wrongs. Further, the short story helped to change the tone of the detective story. Sensation novels concentrated on sentiment and pathos—chiefly in showing the suffering of women: thus, for example, the central roles of Lady Deadlock and Esther in *Bleak House* and the sisters in *The Leavenworth Case*. While plots inherited from sensation novels persisted—the missing heir, the stolen inheritance, the guilty secret, etc.—there is very little room in an 8,000-word short story to embellish poignancy the way Collins did in the three volumes of *The Woman in White*. In addition to reducing the room for sentiment, the new short detective stories in the late 1880s and 1890s edged away from the traditional theme of murder will out that emphasized the role of Providence in human justice explicit or implicit in accounts of crime, and concentrated on what human intelligence can do to solve mysteries. In this regard, one of the elements that still needs to be factored into that change was the repercussions of the Jack the Ripper crimes of the fall 1888. Remaining unsolved, they were both testimony that murder demonstrably will not out, and that the public was intensely interested in following the clues and the investigation of the crimes.

In addition to being the first popular form to have its own history attended to, detective stories were one of the most emphatically transatlantic forms of literature. Poe's rediscovery by Scotsmen gave a second start to the detective story, and readers in the United States ensured the popularity and permanence of Sherlock Holmes—a fact of which Arthur Conan Doyle was well aware. Indeed it was not only Conan Doyle who realized that there was more money to be made in the United States than back home, other British writers, from Chesterton to Freeman, published in both countries, sometimes appearing in New York before London. And, going the other way, American writer Jacques Futrelle booked his passage on the *Titanic* at the conclusion of a marketing trip to England. While at the turn of the century some American writers, like their British counterparts, enthusiastically copied Sherlock Holmes when creating their genius detectives, some of them began to voice very different views of the police than their British counterparts and they made corporate and political corruption their villains versus disinherited black sheep nephews.

Therein, of course, lies a tale. And the following is how I have told it. First comes a chapter with a thumbnail sketch of the history of the detective story ending with the celebrity of Arthur Conan Doyle and Sherlock Holmes. Chapter Two presents what contemporary critics thought detective stories were supposed to be and to do for readers. Chapters Three and Four present surveys of detective fiction, first writers from 1891 to 1901, and then writers up to the beginning of World War One. I have covered very few novels in these chapters, in part because the short story was the preferred medium and in part because most novels of the time do not even come in sight of mediocrity— Queen's Quorum includes very few novels in its list of important turn of the century detective stories. Chapter Five centers on gentleman crooks who appeared in what amounted to reverse detective stories: tales of clever crimes completed, not detected. Chapter Six treats master criminals, Napoleons of crime, a character type that made a sporadic start during the period but had a significant impact on popular fiction after the war. All of this ends with brief concluding remarks.

The following, then, is my attempt to shed some light on the history of the detective story at the turn of the last century. It is the result of sorting through as much contemporary fiction as I could find. For the few books unavailable online or through interlibrary loan I have relied on contemporary notices to provide as full a picture as possible. As noted above, I have skimped on novels, written little about specific pieces of newspaper fiction, and have entirely neglected what was happening on the stage—someone, I hope, will take up that area of detectives in literature. The same applies to juvenile literature: too little is known about penny papers and boys' magazines where sensational detective stories flourished, especially stories featuring struggles between detectives and master criminals. This has been a handicap in Chapter Six because of the lack of demarcation about audiences in some of the master criminal tales that made it into regular bindings.

Reading through a lot of detective fiction I have become acquainted or reacquainted with a number of well-crafted, absorbing, and delightful books.

A few of them, however, were inept, repugnant, mind-numbing twaddle, unfit to be read by adults or children. But they are part of the history, and testimony both to the truth of Raymond Chandler's observation about the undiscriminating publishing of detective stories and to the public's enthusiasm for them.

Eva Zinreich, Anna de Jesus-Acosta, and Ross Donehower have ensured that I have been able to finish this book, for which I emphatically thank them, and pronounce them "real doctors." My thanks, too, go to the extended clan, tribe, fellowship, and coven that is the McDaniel College English department. Above, below, and beyond all else my thanks to Chris Goldenheart.

1

In the Beginning

Looking back from the 1920s, its so-called Golden Age, the detective story as a literary phenomenon was hardly new. It began in earnest almost a century earlier in Philadelphia where several publishers picked up pieces by or about the life and works of an actual French detective, Eugene François Vidocq, and put them into print. First, Cary and Hart printed Vidocq's *Memoirs* in 1834, and then William Edward Burton published two of his own detective stories ("The Secret Cell" [1837] about L—"the head of the private police of London—a body of men possessing rare and wonderful attainments" and "The Cork Leg" [1838] about a French detective). These he followed with nine stories featuring crimes solved by Vidocq published in the same year in his *Burton's Gentleman's Magazine*. These pieces about the French police detective as well as a fascination with ciphers, enigmas, and jokes, layered on his own romanticism led Poe to "The Murders in the Rue Morgue" which he wrote in 1841, shortly after leaving his post as *Burton's* editor. In "The Murders in the Rue Morgue" and his other tales of ratiocination—"The Mystery of Marie Roget," "The Purloined Letter," "The Gold Bug," and "Thou Art the Man"—Poe created the character of the eccentric genius detective, the use of embedded clues, the focus on reasoning, the surprise ending, the employment of the obtuse narrator, the contest between detectives, and most of the other devices that were to become the conventions of a certain kind of detective story. That was step one.

Step two started in Britain. Among the fruits of the early Victorian reform movement were changes in criminal law regarding capital punishment, recognition of defendants' rights, and changes in the definition and use of evidence—changes that also were linked with accumulating discoveries in chemistry and biology that would combine to create modern forensic science. Coincident with and related to these changes were reforms in law enforcement—notably the establishment of London's Metropolitan Police in 1828, the formation of a detective police division in Britain in 1842, and the creation of police forces, public and private, in the major cities across the United States. Magazines and newspapers played a significant role in shaping the public opinion that led to and sustained these reforms by publishing fact and fiction about the law's abuses. Thus narratives centered on the real abuses of capital punishment and circumstantial evidence were common in British magazines before mid-century. And relatively quickly these media turned to fiction as a means of promoting new optimistic views of the police and judicial processes, as well as previewing a secular view of the causes of crime and the nature of punishment: seeing crime as sin was slowly displaced in fiction by motives explained by psychology, and the traditional theme of "murder will out" was displaced by the obligation of individuals and the state to examine and detect crime and criminals. By the 1850s fiction about the ways, means, and successes of lawyers and detectives passed off as excerpts from "Diaries" or "Notebooks" became standard features of *Chambers' Edinburgh Journal* and Charles Dickens' *Household Words*. In 1852 a New York publisher pirated the stories about a detective printed in *Chambers'* and published them as *Recollections of a Policeman*, and this became the first collection of detective stories. Then it was off to the races. A number of publishers' house writers in both countries churned out detective stories about finding clues and saving innocents which were promoted as autobiographies of real detectives: thus the 1860s saw books such as *The Diary of an Ex-Detective, The Detective's Note-Book, The Experiences of a Real Detective, The Autobiography of an English Detective, The Revelations of a Private Detective, The Female Detective*, and *Secret Service: Or, the Recollections of a City Detective*. There being no international copyright law at the time, American newspapers began to filch individual detective stories from the British "Notebooks"—and eventually to print their own original stories to fill what was becoming an insatiable need for copy. And so from 1860 to the 1890s detective stories with titles like "Unexpected Evidence," "The Left Handed Thief," "Detecting a Murderer," and "A Detective's Success" became standard features in magazines and newspapers in both Britain and America. Rather than being laid down on Poe's foundation, however, they were narratives of wrongs righted, satisfying readers' curiosity about how detectives operated and how justice prevailed. Some were simple melodramas; some focused on the minutiae of blood stains, foot prints and even finger marks; some featured points of law; some portrayed detectives from other countries; some centered on hunting and chasing. Missing and altered wills, counterfeiting, embezzlement, robbery, murder—detective stories in magazines and newspapers in the last third of the nineteenth century reflected a wide variety of interests and tastes. They appeared in every kind of publication. In the U.S. these ranged from the journals of publishing houses like Harpers, Putnams, and Scribners to newspapers from coast to coast—from *The Bangor Whig and Courier* to *The Puget Sound Herald*.

Around the time of the American Civil War, story papers—tabloid-sized publications containing a miscellany of fiction which were promoted and sold with Barnum-like zeal—became the latest new thing. With circulation occasionally approaching one million, the most important of the story papers (*The New York Ledger, The Flag of Our Union*, and *The New York Fireside Compan-*

ion) quickly discovered the detective story. Story paper detective fiction, however, was a mixed bag. Occasionally one can find at least a hint of originality in the short stories and serial novels, but many of the story papers' detective stories were manufactured articles. Thus in 1891 Ormand G. Smith, of the publishing house of Smith and Street, discoursed on the way fiction was processed for one of their story papers:

> We always read manuscript that is sent to us, but it is rarely that any is accepted. We have our own writers, to whom we suggest plots and leave them to elaborate them. For detective stories we do not pay so much as for love stories, which must contain more or less of facts. There must be a certain air of probability about a love story, you know, while you can put almost anything into a detective story. We find that stories have to appeal to the masses, and represent scenes from every-day life. "What do we pay for our stories?" Well, for a detective story of 80,000 words, $200. That is for good work, of course. We keep a big scrap-book, and when the newspapers print a story about a crime of any special interest, it is clipped and goes into the book. These clippings are worked over by our writers into detective stories. In regard to the love stories, or novels having love as the central element of interest, we often give to our writers the plot and the chapter headings, as well as the title, but ask them to make any suggestion that will be improvements on those of our editors. We have half a dozen writers who cannot fill our orders for love stories, and yet it is difficult to get new men who would be satisfactory to us. We pay as high as $500 for a good love story of 80,000 words. Some of our writers can turn out such a story in a week, or again it may take two weeks, and then again, a longer time. The writer we pay $500 to writes three of them a year, but he is also employed by us on other work ["Literary News and Notes," *The Author*, May 15, 1891].

About the same time that magazine, newspaper, and story paper detective stories took off in Britain and the United States, Charles Dickens and then his friend Wilkie Collins made the detective a significant literary character and the surprise solution to a crime problem one, but only one, of the prominent features of their novels, the most significant of which are *Bleak House* (1853) and *The Moonstone* (1867). Part of this came from Dickens' enthusiasm about and energetic promotion of the newly created detective police in articles in his journal *Household Words*, part was related to the traditional techniques of the serial novel devised to pique and maintain readers' interest, and part was due to the spirit if not the letter of Poe's detective tales. Dickens transformed actual detective Charles Frederick Field into Inspector Bucket in *Bleak House*, creating a character who would, with Poe's Dupin, provide a model for generations of succeeding detective heroes. And Collins' *The Moonstone* (along with his earlier *The Woman in White* *[1859]*) established a fad shortly after mid-century for what came to be known as sensation novels—i.e., long novels based on secrets and the suffering of women, with detectives in them that ended with a surprise revelation. Published almost simultaneously in Britain and America in magazines and then in book form, Dickens' and Collins' sensation novels became widely popular, and the character of the detective, amateur and professional, shared the spotlight. Inevitably linked by reviewers with Collins, for the rest of the century, popular sensation novels increasingly centered on crimes and their solution with the character and techniques of detection and detectives often added. The most celebrated writers among them in Britain were Mary Elizabeth Braddon with her *Lady Audley's Secret* (1862) and Ellen (Mrs. Henry) Wood with her *East Lynne* (1861). While still basically sensation novels, by the last quarter of the century books by Frenchman Emile Gaboriau, and Americans Lawrence Lynch (Emma M. Van Deventer), and Anna Katherine Green were advertised not as sensation novels but as detective stories: Gaboriau's *Monsieur Lecoq* (1869), for example, was promoted as "A New, Entertaining and Intensely Dramatic Detective Story" (*The Literary World* August 14, 1880); Lynch's *Shadowed by Three* (1879) was "a detective's story of murder and other sensational crimes" (*The Publishers' Weekly*, December 6, 1879); and a piece titled "Miss Green's Detective Stories" in *The Literary News* (January-February 1880) announced that

> another edition of "The Leavenworth Case" has been published by Messrs. G. P. Putnam's Sons. The popularity of this remarkable book is constantly increasing. It is conceded to be the best "detective" story hitherto written in our language, and we can call to mind no book of its kind in which the mystery is so well sustained to the end, and in which the climax is so unexpected. It is not merely a story of plot, for the characters are admirably drawn and skillfully constructed. All who have not read the book have a genuine pleasure in store for them.

While newspapers and story papers continued to print fiction about detectives and crimes solved that were designed to appeal if not to the elite nevertheless to a broad readership—adults, children, men, and women—in the last quarter of the nineteenth century, writers and publishers began to spin off publications about detectives directed toward boys—an enterprise related to the spread of compulsory education laws in the United States beginning with that of Massachusetts in 1853. In the U.S., the appeal of detectives to this new audience was led off with Horatio Alger's urchin hero acting as a detective in *Ragged Dick* (1867) and then later with his full-blown detective character, Detective Lynx, in *The Store Boy* (1887). Then came detective stories in story papers specifically targeted at youths:

> The adventures in the adult papers were not beyond the capacity of the boys; but one, and then another, conceived the idea of conciliating their especial interest by making a paper for them, till this branch, with its Boys' Journal, Boys of New York, Boys of America, Boys of the World, Young Men of New York, Young Men of America, has become rather the larger of the two. The heroes are boys, and there are few departments of unusual existence in which they are not seen figuring to brilliant advantage. They are shown amply competent as the Boy Detective, the Boy Spy, the Boy Trapper, the Boy Buccaneer, the Boy Guide, the Boy Captain,

the Boy Robinson Crusoe, the Boy Claude Duval, and the Boy Phoenix, or Jim Bledsoe, Jr., whose characteristic is to be impervious to harm in burning steamboats and hotels, exploding mines, and the like ["Story Paper Literature," *The Atlantic Monthly*, September 1879].

In Britain there were the boys' papers like *Half Penny Marvel, Union Jack* (both of which in time would run tales about detective Sexton Blake) and *Boys' Own Paper* (one of Conan Doyle's early publishers). While detective stories directed at adult readers continued to appear in sensation novels and, increasingly, in newspapers, the new class of fiction directed at boys ramified in several directions. One direction was focusing on the emphasis on observation and problem solving in the detective story and distilling it into a game. Thus there were games like Shadow Buff and The Thief and Detective:

> SHADOW BUFF.—A white sheet is suspended from the ceiling and stretched by weights at the bottom, to form a screen. The "detective" sits on one side of this screen, and the company one by one pass before it on the other side. A strong light is placed beyond them so that while passing, the *shadow* of each will fall upon the screen. The detective must try to name the person correctly by looking at the shadow. Of course each one of the company while walking before the screen will endeavor to alter his gait and general appearance. When one is correctly named by the detective, he must take the place of the latter until he can detect some other party ["Two Lively Indoor Games," *The American Agriculturist*, 1865].

> THE THIEF AND DETECTIVE PUZZLE: The puzzle shown in the accompanying cut has been patented by Mr. Oscar Beisheim, of New York City. It consists of a shallow box, which is divided by thin partitions into a series of streets and squares, whose arrangement will be seen in the illustration. All the partitions are perforated to allow passage from one street or square to another, the perforations being of two sizes to match the sizes of two balls which are supposed to respectively represent a detective and a thief, the thief being able to traverse all the streets and openings, the detective being restricted to movement in a predetermined path [*Scientific American*, May 30, 1896].

Far more popular, however, was placing the detective hero into a simplistic action-adventure story published in an inexpensive format directed ostensibly at youths but also genial to any undiscriminating reader looking for excitement. So in the late 1870s and 1880s there came to be a rapidly growing number of slim novelettes about detectives, detectives like Old Sleuth, King Brady, Cap. Collier, and later Nick Carter. Many began in story papers but soon spread to thinly disguised serial publications called "libraries" which picked up the label of being "dime novels." In the United States these publications employed the detective hero in a peripatetic plot reminiscent of that developed in popular frontier and western stories, featuring a virtuous and "manly" hero, implacable and powerful enemies, and hunting and chasing amid exotic scenery—whether rural or urban (cities being as exotic for many American readers as another planet). In Britain a parallel detective story for boys exhibiting manly virtues triumphing over obstacles in exotic places drew from the popularity of "muscular Christianity," the sports story, and the so-called "imperial romance"— i.e., novels of Rider Haggard like *King Solomon's Mines* (1885), Anthony Hope's such as *The Prisoner of Zenda* (1894) and even Conan Doyle's *The White Company* (1891). In the U.S. these kinds of publications were called "dime novels"; in the U.K. they were "shilling shockers."

While detective stories continued without a lot of comment as staples in bookstores and newspapers, during the last quarter of the century, stories directed at boys, and story papers and dime novels in particular, received a great deal of attention. This ranged from moral censure to complaints that they reflected Gresham's law in literature, bad books driving out good books with their simplistic characters, non-stop action, and lack of reflection. Carl Snyder in "What do the American People Read in *The American Journal of Politics* (April 1894) gives figures for the tide of scrofulous detective fiction inundating the United States:

> There is one class of popular literature that will be set down without dissent as not only baneful, but in many cases directly a crime-producer. That includes what was once known as the "dime novel," the blood and thunder detective story, and the illustrated journals of crime. How great are its proportions and how wide must be its influence, I doubt if many are informed. From a careful personal investigation, I am convinced that the literature of a criminal or debasing tendency reaches, in this country, an average of more than 1,200,000 copies per week, or upwards of 60,000,000 copies per year; that is to say, an average of about five copies for every family in the country.

Robert M. King, in the same year, paints a frightening picture of hollow eyed zombie children spawned by detective stories roaming America's cities:

> The effects of such reading became so noticeable that the attention of the public was generally drawn to the danger of literature of this class. In various cities were unearthed dens of youthful depravity in vacated cellars and garrets—the rendezvous of young criminals who were often children of respectable families, and were led away by the glamour with which pernicious literature invested criminal lives. Railway conductors began to report numerous cases of young runaways who had started to the West to kill Indians. Crazed boys wandered about the streets, hatless and forlorn, and able only to say, in response to inquiries, "I am Willie, the Boy Detective," or "I am the Terror of the Plains" [*School Interests and Duties*, 1894].

While criticism and the efforts of zealots like Anthony Comstock may have temporarily driven detective stories out of "literary" magazines (common at mid-century, detective stories disappear from journals like *Harpers'* and *Atlantic Monthly* in the 1870s), they had no real effect on the explosion of detective stories at the turn of the century. Forces were abroad that would make detective fiction an unstoppable juggernaut.

Part of the impetus for that juggernaut was the beginning of scholarly and academic interest in Edgar Allan Poe and his detective tales. Hardly lionized during his life, after his death in 1849, Poe's reputation suffered at the hands of Rufus Griswold who made himself Poe's literary executor and in 1850 published *The Works of Edgar Allan Poe*. In the last quarter of the 1800s, however, real interest in Poe, his life and works, began in earnest. First, Scotsman John Henry Ingram undertook a self-imposed mission to restore Poe's reputation with his four volume *The Works of Edgar Allan Poe* (published in Edinburgh when Arthur Conan Doyle was about to enter university) and his biography *Edgar Allan Poe: His Life, Letters and Opinions* (1880). These were followed by Stoddard's six-volume *The Works of Edgar Allan Poe* (1884), and biographies by George Edward Woodberry in 1885 and 1909, and James A. Harrison in 1909. During the same period Brander Matthews, a professor of literature at Columbia University, strove to make Poe and his detective stories a standard part of the American literary canon beginning with his analysis in "Philosophy of the Short Story" (1885).

Another part of the building momentum of detective fiction resided in changes newspapers were undergoing in the last quarter of the century. Before the Civil War, with only meager contact with the outside world, news was the smallest feature in the daily or weekly papers of most towns. Four or six pages long and filled with advertisements, short stories—stories under 4000 words— became a part of many papers in the U.S. A lot of them were detective stories. Serials, the form in which most long detective fiction existed at the time, rarely appeared in papers before the 1870s—except for single chapters of serials from story papers distributed by publishers for free to newspapers to act as teasers and inducements for readers to buy the *Ledger* or the *Fireside Companion* and read the rest of the installments. Toward the end of the century burgeoning population, emigration to cities, changes in transportation and communication, as well as savvy entrepreneurs remade the newspaper business. First came syndication. Tillotson's Newspaper Fiction Bureau, the Northern Newspaper Syndicate, A.P Watt's literary agency, and W.C. Leng sold writers' works to a number of papers and thus made serial fiction a feature of British newspapers in the 1870s, and in America S.S. McClure's syndicate, founded in 1884, distributed serials, including detective stories, to newspapers across the U.S. Thus newspaper readers, now literally tens of thousands of them, in the 1880s read serials like *189-H the Tale of a Bank Note*, *The Diamond Button*, *The Strange Footprint*, *The Mystery of a Hansom Cab*, *The Great Bank Robbery*, and lots of others. Syndication, however, was only part of the transformation of newspapers at the end of the nineteenth century. Detective stories played a role in the battles for circulation of the so-called newspaper wars of the last decades of the century. Symbolized by the competition between Hearst and Pulitzer for readers in New York City, in the late 1880s and 1890s publishers of big city newspapers across the U.S. and in Britain aggressively sought means of increasing their revenue by attracting more readers. This led to the creation of comic pages, the beginning of sports pages, the innovation of the Sunday supplement, and even the manufacture of news itself, like Nellie Bly's reporting on her recreation of Jules Verne's fictional trip around the world in 80 days. Increasingly serial detective novels replaced the short detective fiction that had been a staple of the newspaper since the 1860s. One of the tactics of publishers in the newspaper wars was the recruitment of celebrity writers to produce serials about detection. Nellie Bly herself wrote *The Mystery of Central Park* (1889), but the serial novels of Nathaniel Hawthorne's son Julian and Australian Fergus Hume made a much bigger difference. Beginning with *The Great Bank Robbery* (1888) Hawthorne wrote a series of novels subtitled "From the Diary of Inspector Byrnes." These introduced a fictionalized version of Thomas F. Byrnes, chief of the detective bureau of the New York City police—inventor of the photographic mug shot and popularizer of the third degree—whose character presides over the solving of actual crimes embellished with sensation novel elements. A contagious best seller that spread from Australia to England to the United States, *The Mystery of a Hansom Cab* (1888) with its allusions to earlier detective writers (Braddon, Green, Gaboriau) established the self-reflective world that would come to characterize a certain class of detective fiction.

By the late 1880s the detective story was one of the most popular genres in the English-speaking world. And people talked about its popularity: clergy inveighed against dime detectives and librarians debated the propriety of shelving detective novels. Literary people talked about them too. In 1886 a piece in *The Saturday Review* spoke to the popularity of the form and lamented the lack of native British contributors:

> If the abundance of supply affords any accurate test, the demand for the detective novel is great and increasing. Novels of this class must surely be counted amongst the greatest successes of the day. It is book-stall success, so to speak; that achieved by extensive, sometimes phenomenal, sales at low rates, and meaning a widespread dissemination far exceeding anything the circulating libraries could accomplish. The truth, too, of this substantial approval has been accorded to literature of foreign importation. So far native talent has not scored, save in the comparatively rare instances where the writer treats topics with which he is perhaps officially familiar out of the fulness of his own experience. The detective stories apparently most popular with the British public are of French or American origin. The enterprising publishers who have inundated the market with not always irreproachable translations of Gaboriau and Du Boisgobey have made their selection from too limited a field; but they have been wise in their generation, and they must have had their reward. Equally satisfactory must have been the reprints of Miss Green's stories, *The Leavenworth Case* and *A Strange Disappearance,* while another American novel, *Shadowed by Three,* yields to neither in its thrilling and well-sustained interest, however ludicrous and long-winded it may at times appear ["Detective Fiction," December 4, 1886].

Seven years later a writer for *The Speaker* reported his informal survey of British reading habits by interviewing a clerk at a W.H. Smith's bookstall:

> He began by assuring me it was a baffling study. After an experience of twenty or thirty years (I forget which), he would not undertake to prophesy the success of any book outside the limits of detective fiction. Any detective story, whatever its merits might be, he could sell from morning till night; and the strength or weakness of its plot made no difference whatever. This seemed a little odd. Nobody would ask the public to value grace of language in such tales; indeed, it is worse than valueless, being but misplaced decoration. But seeing that by their plots they stand or fall—seeing that they are all plot —we should expect some discrimination here. The clerk assured me that, except for cheapness, the public has no preference. "I want a detective story, please," is the formula. "They leave the rest to me; and if we sell more copies of a good story than of a bad one at the same price, it's because I'm naturally inclined to pick out the good one first. Otherwise it's a toss-up" [October 7, 1893].

When *Beeton's Chrisman Annual* published *A Study in Scarlet* in 1887, detective stories flying off the shelves was hardly a new phenomenon. Sensation novels with detectives in them had been around since the 1860s. Mary Elizabeth Braddon and Ellen Wood cranked out novels until the 1890s, and Anna Katharine Green and Emma Murdoch Van Deventer (writing as Jack Lynch) just hit their stride in 1890. In the 1880s when publisher Henry Vizetelly's attempt to establish a line of literary translations bombed, he made up his losses (and then some) by pushing shop-worn French detective stories:

> Finding that works of a high literary character did not take, we bethought ourselves of the favorite novelist of the Paris concierge, namely, Gaboriau. With his books we were more fortunate, and in the course of a few years sold some hundreds of thousands of volumes. Before, however, we exhausted this Gaboriau series, we produced several of Du Boisgobey's works in the same bright scarlet covers to which the public had got accustomed. We commenced with *The Old Age of Lecoq, the Detective*, to keep up the connection with Gaboriau, whose *Monsieur Lecoq* was one of the best selling of his books. We advertised both series very largely, with the result that we frequently received single orders from large buyers for from two thousand to five thousand volumes at a time [*Current Literature*, September 1888].

Continuing this retrospective marketing of old detective fiction, the thirty-year-old collection of detective stories from *Chambers' Edinburgh Journal*, collected as *The Recollections of a Policeman*, was reprinted several times in the 1880s, and terms like "diary" and "notebook" turned up in a number of detective story titles in the 1880s. Thus Julian Hawthorne subtitled his books "From the Diary of Inspector Byrnes." Dick Donovan's (J. E. Preston Muddock) stories in the late 1880s and early 1890s carry the same tags: *The Manhunter: Stories from the note-book of a detective* (1888); *Caught at Last! Leaves from the Note-Book of a Detective* (1889); and *A Romance from a Detective's*

Case-Book (1892). Indeed, in the early 1890s *The Strand* carried a run of "Stories from the Diary of a Doctor" as well as Dick Donovan's "A Romance from a Detective's Case-Book." But it wasn't just the titles that were old fashioned. Contemporary reviewers picked up on the fact that Donovan's content was also moss covered. Thus

> *Caught at Last* is a collection of some of those detective stories which the railway reading public owes, in the first instance, to the writer who called himself "Waters," and who, about thirty years ago, contributed his "Recollections of a Detective" to *Chambers's Journal* [*The Academy*, March 23, 1889].

By the late 1880s the detective story as it had come to be practiced for the past forty years—as sensation novels or putative "autobiography"—had become at least frayed around the edges and changes began to appear.

There were, moreover, forces afoot that changed who, how, and what people read. Changes in literacy, occasioned by the advent of universal education in the United States and Britain, broadened the numbers of readers. Magazines and newspapers arose in both countries to appeal to these new readers. Contemporary observers attributed the enthusiasm for magazines like *The Strand*, the new interest in short stories, and the rage for detective stories in part to the advent of a new kind of reading—railroad reading. Thus this classification of *The Crime of Christmas Day* made in a review in *The Overland Monthly*:

> It is a very fair imitation of a brief and light French detective romance, and is pleasant and satisfactory train or waiting room reading [April 1885].

Another detective story elicited the same kind of comment in *The Literary World*:

> The book pretends to be no more than it is, and it will while away a railway journey or a tiresome afternoon with a good deal of effectual interest [August 25, 1893].

And railroad reading even became the topic of satire in *Punch*:

> That a purblind public should prefer a Shilling Shocker for railway reading when for a modest half-guinea they might obtain a numbered volume of Coming Poetry on hand-made paper [July 21, 1894].

Entertaining, clever, absorbing stories, stories that did not require overt reflection or contemplation, stories that avoided controversial topics of the day—those were the requirements of railroad reading, requirements which detective stories were able to fulfill. Increasingly in the 1890s, if it was going to be popular, a book had to be short. Thus in some measure the 1890s became the age of the short story. Brander Matthews wrote a paean on the short story (and the short detective story) in 1891:

> The short story is like the lyric—it is a little thing; but only the foolish confuse bigness in bulk with genuine greatness. As Hawthorne told us, there is "no fountain

so small but that heaven may be imaged in its bosom "; so the short story can body forth that impression of life which, after all, is all that literature can give us. And it can do this quite as directly as the longer novel and sometimes quite as forcibly. There is no detective story of Wilkie Collins or Gaboriau, whatever its length, equal in interest to Poe's Gold Bug; and many a three-volume novel fails to give as sharp an outline of London society or of the American girl abroad as is focussed into the vignettes which Mr. James called An International Episode and Daisy Miller ["On Certain Recent Short Stories," *Cosmopolitan*, September 1891].

Writing about short stories—and telling people how to write them—became a literary fad at the turn of the century, witnessed by titles such as Sherwin Cody's *Story Writing and Journalism* (1894), Charles R. Barrett's *Short Story Writing, A Practical Treatise* (1900); George H. Nettleton's *Specimens of the Short Story* (1901); Alexander Jessup's *The Book of the Short Story* (1906); Evelyn M. Albright's *The Short Story its principles and structure* (1907); and Joseph B. Esenwein's *Writing the Short Story, A Practical Handbook* (1909). And they all talked about detective stories as a separate genre. Here's some of what Albright says:

While the ingenious plot with a reversal or surprise—the hoax-plot—cannot be counted among the highest, there is one form of the ingenious plot which deserves a higher rank. The detective story is a real study in plot construction, involving the presentation of a situation and the reduction of that situation to its causes. It differs from other plots in that it presents a mysterious situation and then works *backward* to its solution. The solution is the end. The detective plot is a puzzle solved. A few masters have given it masterly treatment. Poe and his disciple, Doyle, have set themselves apart by their treatment of this plot form. The interest of "The Gold-Bug" and "The Murders in the Rue Morgue" is not, however, to be confounded with that of the lurid "literature" so delectable to the romantic minded youngster.

In contemporary reviews of detective fiction size began to matter very much. As early as 1886 detective novels were occasionally labeled "long winded." In 1889 *Punch* took publishers to task for promiscuous prolixity.

No book sells better than the volume of short stories, or the collection of essays and descriptive papers, and yet for years past publishers have refused to let us have them, and have dosed us with three volumes of twaddle or unreadable polemical novels. It is a satisfaction to find the providers of literary food are beginning to see the error of their ways, and to be convinced that the British public must, before anything else, be amused.

And this same view carried over to reviews of new detective novels. Thus in January 1892 *The Review of Reviews* pronounced that Zangwill's *The Big Bow Mystery* was "a detective story with an ingenious plot, but the reader is wearied by its length. As a short story it would have been most excellent." And *The Writer* in its January 1892 review of *The Diamond Button* lists "brevity" as one of the criteria of the detective story: "its merits were such as might have been easily predicted: directness, lucidity, brevity, a racy detective story, well-told, with characters real, even if not noteworthy."

The new kind of reading, then, had to be short and entertaining. And in Britain it was George Newnes' mission to supply, and to justify, literature as entertainment. Newnes became one of the leaders in the field of what he called "new journalism":

> "There is one kind of journalism," he said, "which directs the affairs of nations; it makes and unmakes Cabinets; it upsets governments, builds up Navies and does many other great things. It is magnificent. This is your journalism. There is another kind of journalism which has no such great ambitions. It is content to plod on, year after year, giving wholesome and harmless entertainment to crowds of hard-working people, craving for a little fun and amusement. It is quite humble and unpretentious. That is my journalism" [Friederichs, *The Life of Sir George Newnes*, 1911].

This view led Newnes first to publish *Tit-Bits*, a miscellany magazine subtitled *"from all the interesting Books, Periodicals, and Newspapers of the World"* which included fiction and puzzles created by Henry Dudeney. And the success of his approach to publishing as "wholesome and harmless entertainment" in *Tit-Bits* led Newnes to create a new illustrated magazine in 1891, *The Strand*, the aim of which he described in his introduction to the first issue: "The past efforts of the Editor in supplying cheap, healthful literature have met with such generous favour from the public, that he ventures to hope that this new enterprise will prove a popular one." It was, then, this new view of journalism (and literature) as entertainment which led Newnes and his editor Herbert Greenhough Smith to accept "A Scandal in Bohemia" for publication in the new magazine. It is worth remarking, however, that Newnes (and Smith) were on the lookout for detective stories in 1890 and that "A Scandal in Bohemia" was not the first detective story published in *The Strand*. B. L. Farjeon's "Three Birds on a Stile" (which turns on a "real" detective unmasking a con man playing a detective) came out the month before Conan Doyle's story.

In the busy literary world before 1891, most comments about the works of Arthur Conan Doyle centered on his novel *Micah Clarke*, or his miscellaneous contributions to contemporary journals. But his two novels about Sherlock Holmes, *A Study in Scarlet* (1887) and *The Sign of the Four* (1890) did receive some notice—the majority of which came in American publications. *The Sign of the Four*, after all, was published by Lippincott's, an American publisher. Rather than being innovations, however, most reviews placed them in the context of contemporary detective fiction. Thus

> LIPPINCOTT'S MAGAZINE has introduced an agreeable diversity in its department of fiction by engaging some stories from popular English novelists, who are also widely known upon this side of the Atlantic. The February number contains a

complete novel, "The Sign of the Four; or the Problem of the Sholtos," by A. Conan Doyle. The author of that remarkable novel "Micah Clarke: His Statement," which has created such a sensation both in England and here, needs no introduction to American readers. Mr. Doyle's last story is even more powerful and brilliant than "Micah Clarke." The scene is laid in London, and the hero is a detective, whose marvelous ingenuity in solving a seemingly insoluble mystery is portrayed with so graphic a pen that Conan Doyle must take rank as a leader in the line of such writers as Poe, or Gaboriau, or Anna Katharine Green. Among detective stories "The Sign of the Four" is bound to become a classic [*The Educational Journal of Virginia*, February 1890].

And

Messrs. Ward, Lock and Co. forward the two first issues of a bright healthy magazine, *Lippincott's Monthly*. It is not a magazine of particular interest to the antiquary, but the principle of a complete story in each issue seems a good feature. "The Sign of the Four," in the February number, by A. Conan Doyle, is a fascinating, weird tale, and reminds us of Wilkie Collins at his best [*The Antiquary*, January 1890].

And

"A Study in Scarlet" by A. Conan Doyle, (J. B. Lippincott Co.), a brightly written novelette, on a plan which is rather distressingly familiar. It is another story about a marvelous detective, a kind of an amateur on the model of Poe's analysts, who "succeeds when all others fail," as the quack advertisements say [*The American National Journal*, April 12, 1890].

Thus while some had good things to say about Conan Doyle's craft, contemporary reviewers saw nothing particularly new in either *A Study in Scarlet* or *The Sign of the Four*. They were simply mercifully slimmed down sensation novels about suppressed grief, danger, and guilty secrets set in exotic locales with a hero who does the same things as other "familiar" detective heroes did.

But then in January 1891 the *Strand* magazine hit London's streets. On the lookout for new things to write, in 1891 Conan Doyle decided to reshape his Sherlock Holmes stories to fit the format of the new magazine. First, he decided to move from short novels based on the sensation school patterns to short stories. Additionally, while writers had certainly featured detective heroes in series of stories before Conan Doyle's Sherlock Holmes—Dupin and, more recently, Anna Katharine Green's Mr. Gryce, for instance—it was not the norm. So a continuing hero in a series of short stories was Conan Doyle's big new idea:

Considering these various journals with their disconnected stories it had struck me that a single character running through a series, if it only engaged the attention of the reader, would bind that reader to that particular magazine .... Looking around for my central character, I felt that Sherlock Holmes, who I had already handled in two little books, would easily lend himself to a succession of short stories [Arthur Conan Doyle, *Memories and Adventures*, 1924].

Six months after it began publication, on July 1891, *The Strand* published "A Scandal in Bohemia," the first of the stories that would be collected as *The Adventures of Sherlock Holmes*. Thirty months and twenty three stories later, in the December 1893 issue of *The Strand*, Conan Doyle stopped writing about Sherlock Holmes and didn't return to the detective story for eight years.

Conan Doyle temporarily quit writing about Sherlock Holmes just as the world was beginning to make him a household word. And American S.S. McClure had more than something to do with that. Having syndicated detective stories in American newspapers in the late 1880s, McClure first came in contact with the Great Detective while traveling in Britain:

> Mr. McClure said he was visiting Andrew Lang at St. Andrews University, in Scotland. Mr. Lang said: "There is a young man named Dr. Doyle who has written a capital shilling shocker (which is British for dime novel), and who is about to have a novel published by Longmans, and this man has a future."
>
> "On my way back to Edinburgh," said Mr. McClure, "I purchased a copy of the shilling shocker, which proved to be one of the earliest and greatest of the famous Sherlock Holmes stories. I read it with unbounded delight. It was more than a shilling shocker. It was a great story, and, although a detective story, it certainly was a piece of literature" [*Medical and Surgical Reporter,* March 7, 1896].

So delighted was he that McClure bought the American syndication rights to the short stories Conan Doyle was about to publish in *The Strand* for $60 each. And in the same month that "A Scandal in Bohemia" appeared in *The Strand* it also appeared in *The Washington Post* and in newspapers in every major city in the United States—and a lot of minor ones as well. The pieces that would comprise the second series of Holmes stories, *The Memoirs of Sherlock Holmes,* moved up the literary pecking order and came out in the American version of *The Strand*, in *Harper's Weekly*, and McClure's new magazine. And in 1903 the stories that would comprise *The Return of Sherlock Holmes* came out both in *The Strand* and in the aggressively marketed American magazine *Colliers*. New fiction about Sherlock Holmes would continue to appear for over five decades: thus *A Study in Scarlet* 1887, *The Sign of the Four* 1890, *The Adventures of Sherlock Holmes* 1891–1892, *The Memoirs of Sherlock* Holmes 1892–1893, *The Hound of the Baskervilles* 1901–1902, *The Return of Sherlock Holmes* 1903–1904, *The Reminiscences of Sherlock Homes* 1908–1913, *The Valley of Fear* 1914–1915, and *The Casebook of Sherlock Holmes* 1921–1927.

Published in newspapers, magazines, and then in book form in both Britain and America, the Sherlock Holmes stories very quickly gained supersized popularity on both sides of the Atlantic. By 1894 Philadelphia's *Literary Era* noted that

> pretty well everybody reads Mr. Conan Doyle; and none of those who agreed in the general verdict that the "The Adventures of Sherlock Holmes" were unsurpassed of late years as stories of detective ingenuity will wait for recommendations

to read the final "Memoirs" of the same supersubtle unraveller of mysteries [January 1894].

And in the U.S. "everybody" meant even people who could not read English who read *A Study in Scarlet* (*Späte Rache*) and *The Sign of the Four* (*Das Zeichen der Vier*) as serials in their German-language newspaper in Milwaukee.

Recognizing as did British writers going back to Dickens that the population of the United States was almost double that of Great Britain, and finding American promoters eager to recruit English notables for their lecture circuits, in 1894 Conan Doyle undertook a literary tour of America. While the purported topic of the talk that he gave to audiences large and small was contemporary British literature, what Americans really wanted to hear about was his Sherlock Holmes. It was Holmes and the detective story that reporters wanted to hear about when Conan Doyle arrived in New York:

> "Now weren't you influenced by Edgar Allan Poe when you wrote 'Sherlock Holmes?'" asked the reporter.
> A hush fell over the room. It could be heard as distinctly as if the string of a violin had snapped, but Dr. Doyle liked the question and replied to it at once, impulsively:
> "Oh, immensely! His detective is the best detective in fiction."
> "Except Sherlock Holmes," said somebody [*New York Times*, October 3, 1894].

And in recognition of the importance of the detective story to him, Conan Doyle even traveled to Buffalo to meet the reigning American queen of the detective story, Anna Katharine Green.

Very quickly—even before he decided to kill Holmes off in "The Final Problem"—Conan Doyle became a media darling. *The Strand*, of course, played a role in creating his celebrity. *The Strand* did not simply publish the Sherlock Holmes stories; it very much participated in making the author a star. In the same issue as "Silver Blaze" *The Strand* published a seven page, photo illustrated article "A Day with Dr. Conan Doyle" which ended with a picture and a letter from Dr. Joseph Bell. And this kind of publicity took off on both sides of the Atlantic. In 1893, somewhat oddly, Conan Doyle was featured in *One Hundred Modern Scottish Poets*. Physicians were particularly proud that one of their own had made good—thus "The Original of Sherlock Holmes" in *The Medical and Surgical Reporter* (February 1894). Conan Doyle's trip to the United States in 1894 gave rise to biographical articles about the author in *The Book Buyer* ("The Original of Sherlock Holmes," March 1894), *Ladies' Home Journal* ("The Creator of Sherlock Holmes," October 1894), and *McClure's Magazine* ("Real Conversations: A Dialog between Conan Doyle and Robert Barr," November 1894). In biographical pieces, as in his reply to a reporter's shouted query, Conan Doyle invariably mentioned Poe, even including a complimentary reference in "The Resident Patient"—and contemporary commentators quickly picked up the link. Thus the fundamental principles of construction that underlie such stories as Poe's "Murders in the Rue Morgue," or Conan Doyle's "Sherlock Holmes" series, are precisely those that should guide a scientific writer. These stories show that the public delights in the ingenious unravelling of evidence, and Conan Doyle need never stoop to jesting. First the problem, then the gradual piecing together of the solution [*Nature,* July 26, 1894].

In addition to Poe, contemporary reviewers compared Doyle to Gaboriau—with the advantage going to the Englishman:

He [Sherlock Holmes] is a subtler detective than Gaboriau ever imagined, he is omniscient upon all subjects that relate to his profession, and his creator has provided him with experiences so varied that we can only wonder at the fertility of invention displayed. "The Adventures of Sherlock Holmes," now published, deals with a dozen episodes—most of them unfamiliar to us—in the career of this acute tracer of criminals and disentangler of intricate complications [*The Dial,* November 16, 1892].

It is in the unfolding of this mystery that Mr. Doyle shows us that France is not the only country which can produce a Gaboriau. And then Mr. Doyle, unlike Gaboriau, is never tedious. He does not prolong the agonies either of his readers or of the victims of the plots it is his business to unravel. The result is a volume which may be safely commended to all who like sensational stories of the best class, ingenious in plot, graceful in narration, and absorbing in interest [*The Speaker,* November 25, 1892].

An awful lot of the contemporary ink on Conan Doyle's life and works, however, centered on the connection with Dr. Joseph Bell, and the novelty of the application of routine medical practice (noticing and understanding symptoms leading to a proper diagnosis) to problems of crime.

While Conan Doyle took a sabbatical from his detective, Sherlock Holmes remained before the public with reprintings of the stories in newspapers and books, literary parodies, and, importantly, on the stage. A character in plays since the 1863 with Tom Taylor's Hawkshaw the detective in "The Ticket of Leave Man," detectives were relatively common in dramas and melodramas by the 1890s. But they became more so when William Gillette, one of America's most famous actors, took on Sherlock Holmes. With Conan Doyle's permission, Gillette combined bits from *A Study in Scarlet*, "A Scandal in Bohemia," and "The Final Problem" to form his play *Sherlock Holmes, or the Strange Case of Miss Faulkner* in 1899. From the start it was a hit. Thus this review in *The New York Times*:

In his new detective drama Mr. Gillette is as original as he has been in all his plays from "A Legal Wreck" to "Secret Service." He has taken his hero (audacity, humor, eccentricity, alertness of mind, and all) directly from Conan Doyle, from whose detective sketches he has also derived certain incidents that serve as well in their way as any other incidents would. But the play is Gilette's, in its deft and novel use of time-honored theatrical contrivance, in its defiance of cherished laws of stage-craft, in its peculiar and characteristic smartness [November 12, 1899].

As Sherlock Holmes Gilette wasn't just a hit in 1899, he continued to reprise the role for three decades and in 1916 he made a silent movie of his Sherlock Holmes play.

It, moreover, was not only the reprints and Gillette's performances that kept Sherlock Holmes in the public's eye during Conan Doyle's sabbatical from writing about the great detective. Unlike earlier fictional sleuths, with this detective readers could remember what the hero looked like. By yet another lucky coincidence, Conan Doyle turned to magazine writing precisely when the technology for printing photographs and drawings was perfected and the illustrated magazine came very much into fashion. Newnes made a point of this, in fact, with the subtitle of *The Strand* as "An Illustrated Monthly." The publisher was so proud of the illustrations in *The Strand* that he put them on exhibition:

The original drawings of the illustrations in this Magazine are always on view, and for sale, at the Art Gallery in these offices, which is open to the public without charge [*The Strand*, September 1908].

The lead off Holmes story in *The Strand*, "A Scandal in Bohemia," contained ten illustrations—compared with only four illustrations in Conan Doyle's first novel, *A Study in Scarlet*. And it wasn't just that the pictures accompanied the stories, the artist had an influence on the public's view of what Sherlock Holmes (and by extension all detectives) looked like. When casting about for an illustrator Newnes and Smith had the popular Walter Paget in mind to illustrate the Sherlock Holmes stories in *The Strand*—he had illustrated editions of *Robinson Crusoe, Treasure Island*, the *Arabian Nights,* and *King Solomon's Mines*, as well as working for *Illustrated London News*. Having forgotten his first name, however, they wrote to him as "Mr. Paget the illustrator." Walter's brother Sidney, who was also an illustrator, opened the letter, took the job, and created what became one of the most recognized of all literary icons.

Along with their popularity with the reading public, Conan Doyle and his character intensified interest in the history of the detective story, and turn of the century readers witnessed a new, broader and deeper interest in the history of the genre. Even before "A Scandal in Bohemia" in 1891, a discussion of Poe, Dickens, and other writers appeared in "Crime in Fiction" originally published in *Blackwood's* and then picked up by *The Eclectic Magazine* in the United States. American academics in particular took an interest in the detective story. Brander Matthews enlarged on his earlier essay on Poe and published "Poe and the Detective Story" in *Scribner's Magazine* (September 1907). His colleague on the faculty of Columbia University, Harry T. Peck, included a chapter on the detective story in his *Studies of Several Literatures* (1909) which begins with a defense of the genre:

SUPERCILIOUS persons who profess to have a high regard for the dignity of "literature" are loath to admit that detective stories belong to the category of serious writing. They will make an exception in the case of certain tales by Edgar Allan Poe, but in general they would cast narratives of this sort down from the upper ranges of fine fiction. They do this because, in the first place, they think that the detective story makes a vulgar appeal through its exploitation of crime. In the second place, and with some reason, they despise detective stories because most of them are poor, cheap things. Just at present there is a great popular demand for them; and in response to this demand a flood of crude, ill-written, sensational tales comes pouring from the presses of the day. But a detective story composed by a man of talent, not to say of genius, is quite as worthy of admiration as any other form of novel. In truth, its interest does not really lie in the crime which gives the writer a sort of starting point. In many of these stories the crime has occurred before the tale begins; and frequently it happens, as it were, off the stage, in accordance with the traditional precept of Horace. The real interest of a fine detective story is very largely an intellectual interest. Here we see the conflict of one acutely analytical mind with some other mind which is scarcely less acute and analytical. It is a battle of wits, a mental duel, involving close logic, a certain amount of applied psychology, and also a high degree of daring on the part both of the criminal and of the man who hunts him down. Here is nothing in itself "sensational" in the popular acceptance of that word.

Weightier than either Matthews or Peck, Frank W. Chandler's *The Literature of Roguery* (1907) contained both a chapter on "The Literature of Crime Detection"—a historical essay which also included a list of eighteen contemporary writers and their work along with a discussion of the Sherlock Holmes stories—and a page-long bibliography.

But it was not only academics who displayed interest in the history of detective stories. Also at the turn of the century Julian Hawthorne made himself into an advocate for the detective story and assembled and published two collections of detective fiction which emphasized its historic, international, even universal appeal. The first, *The Library of the World's Best Mystery and Detective Stories: One Hundred and One Tales of Mystery by Famous Authors of East and West* (1907), was a six volume collection divided into (1) American, (2) French, Italian, Etc., (3) English and Scotch, (4) German, Russian, Etc., (5) English and Irish, and (6) Oriental, Modern Magic. Two years later Hawthorne published another, larger collection, *The Lock and Key Library: Classic Mystery and Detective Stories of All Nations*. Available by mail-order, this new collection had a different collection of categories: North Europe, Mediterranean, German, Classic French, Modern French, French Novels, Old Time English, Modern English, American, and Real Life. The Modern English volume contained stories by Kipling, Conan Doyle, Egerton Castle, Stanley J. Weyman, Wilkie Collins, Robert Louis Stevenson, and Anonymous; the American volume, to which Hawthorne contributed an essay on "Riddle Stories," featured tales by F. Marion Crawford, Mary E. Wilkins Freeman, Melville

D. Post, Ambrose Bierce, Edgar Allan Poe, Washington Irving, Charles Brockden Brown, Fitzjames O'Brien, Nathaniel Hawthorne, and Anonymous. *The Lock and Key Library,* however, was not a conspicuous success: within several years ads promised remaindered copies at half the original six dollar price for the collection. The history of the detective story, however, had a continuing appeal to newspaper editors and (one presumes) their readers—from time to time at the turn of the century the popular press in the United States and Britain took up the history of the genre. Thus in the U.S. "Who Influenced Poe? He was the Originator of the So-Called Detective Novel" appeared on May 1, 1896, in the *Oakland* [California] *Tribune; The Washington Post* ran "Imitators of Poe. American Author the Father of the Present Day School of Detective Stories" on July 27, 1903; "The Detective Story, Origin and Growth of the Clever Amateur Sleuth. Voltaire was his Creator" appeared in the *Indiana* [Pennsylvania] *Weekly Messenger* on March 13, 1907; and on June 13, 1909, "Detectives in Fiction. Some of the Forerunners of Sherlock Holmes and their Methods" came out in *The Washington Post.*

Looking back, then, in 1891 when "A Scandal in Bohemia" appeared in *The Strand,* detective stories were hardly new: they had been around for fifty years and were arguably one of the more popular forms of reading in both Britain and the United States. Even before Conan Doyle's switch from short novels to short stories, however, detective stories were changing. They were both slimming down from lengthy sensation novels and bulking up from thirty five hundred word newspaper stories. They were leaving pseudo journalism about crime and detectives and beginning to look back to Poe for models. They were beginning to be sought out by editors of the new illustrated magazines and, therefore, were becoming a form to which writers turned. They were beginning to be taken seriously—in part because they now were starting to acquire their own history. With all this going on, it was the right place and the right time and Conan Doyle had the good fortune both to be there and to possess gifts as a story teller. And his meteoric rise to what can only be called literary stardom magnified and accelerated everything that was going on. It made even more editors look for detective stories, and it made even more writers try their luck at creating characters and plots about detectives. In fact, during the decades between "A Scandal in Bohemia" and the First World War, Britain and then the United States were awash in detective stories. They all began (and some ended) with Sherlock Holmes—but some of them took the character of the detective hero and the form of the detective story in new directions. But that's something to be taken up later. The more immediate thing about Sherlock Holmes and the stories written in response to his popularity was that almost immediately critics begin to think about and, of course, write about what detective stories did for or with or to their readers and how and why they did what they did. And that's the matter of the next chapter.

2

What Is a Detective Story?

In the beginning, way back in the early 1840s, Poe's Dupin stories had little to do with how real detectives detected, or with crime and justice, or with guilt and innocence. He conceived them as games, as jokes, maybe even as pranks. Recall the less than serious purpose of his "The Balloon Hoax," and all the discussion of playing games at the beginning of "The Murders in the Rue Morgue." This, however, was the road not taken by Poe's immediate successors. They actually did want to focus on how real detectives detected, and about crime and justice, and about guilt and innocence. In the 1850s, after all, professional detectives were still in the process of being invented in Britain and in America. So were changes to the law, the beginning of the science of forensics, and evolving rules of evidence. Writers, then, chose to write fiction about detectives partly in order to portray the new socially useful role they played—even in stories in which that role was secondary, even incidental, to the traditional blandishments of sentiment or action and adventure. And people wanted to read about detectives. That's why publishers, beginning in the 1850s, tried to pass off their stories about detectives as autobiographies. Hence at mid-century (and well into the 1890s) titles containing tags such as Diary, Revelations, Note-Book, Recollections, Experiences, and even Autobiography appeared and partly defined—perhaps even justified—the genre for many readers.

But Poe's kind of detective story crept back in with the problem solving or search and rescue plots threaded through long narratives about women's suffering breathlessly presented in sensation novels—especially Wilkie Collins' sensation novels. Some critics at mid-century, however, did not take altogether kindly to adding Poe's brand of fiction—approaching writing and reading about detection as a game—to the corpus of "legitimate" literature. This critique of *The Moonstone,* for example, suggests that making or enjoying fiction as a game trivializes it:

> Mr. Wilkie Collins's new book is very suggestive of a game called "button," which children used to play, and probably play now. A number of little folks being seated in a circle, each with hands placed palm to palm in front of him, one of the party, who holds a button, comes in turn to each of the others, and ostensibly drops it into his closed hands. Of course, but one of the party can receive it, but in each

case the same motions are gone through with; and having made his rounds, the principal performer enquires, "Who's got the button?" Each one, including him who has it, but who intentionally misleads the rest, guesses at the puzzle, and he who guesses right carries the button at the next trial. The "Moonstone" riddle is so like in its essential features to this child's-play, that it might very well have been suggested by it. Mr. Collins's art consists, in this particular case, in converting the button into a yellow diamond, worth thirty thousand pounds; in calling the players Hindoos, detective policemen, reformed thieves, noble ladies, and so on, and in thus more effectually distracting his reader's attention from the puzzle itself, which turns out at last, like most of Mr. Collins's mysteries, to have no vital connection with his characters, considered as human beings, but to be merely an extraneous matter thrown violently into the current of his story. It would perhaps be more correct to say that there is no story at all, and that the characters are mere puppets, grouped with more or less art around the thing the conjurer wishes to conceal until the time comes for displaying it. These books of his are, in their way, curiosities of literature. The word "novel," as applied to them, is an absurd misnomer, however that word is understood. There is nothing new in Mr. Collins's stories, if the reader has ever read a book of puzzles, and they serve none of the recognized purposes of the novel [*The Nation*, September 17, 1868].

By the turn of the new century, however, a lot of things changed. To begin with, for the first time stories with detectives in them came to be classed as a separate kind of fiction. By the 1880s, instead of being included with all other general fiction, both publishers and reviewers routinely began talking about detective stories as a distinct category of literature. Further, the moral opprobrium associated with writing and reading about crime and criminals which had become attached to dime novels disappeared, and reading about detectives and crime was accepted as a variety of entertainment:

> For, after all, the fascinating part of a detective story is not the murder or the theft, but the methods of the detective; not the poetical justice at the close, but the steps by which it has been reached. In a word, the fascinating thing about a detective story is the search [*The Living Age*, December 1906].
>
> But, first of all, let us dissociate the real horror felt at a real murder, from a murder plot used as a peg on which to hang the absorbing puzzle meant to enthrall the intellect. People who say, "How can you enjoy reading about such a revolting subject as murder?" are unable to discern the difference between a realistic newspaper story and a carefully planned romance [Carolyn Wells, *The Technique of the Mystery Story*, 1913].

And reviewers and critics began to try to define those things that made a story a detective story—other than it was a story with a detective in it. Almost everyone agreed that presenting and solving problems was the bed-rock upon which the form was based. Thus

> it is not difficult to account for the steady popularity of the detective story. The pleasure to be had from a good one is of a unique and satisfying kind. The reader

is invited to take part in a mathematical demonstration, in which the symbols are men and women, with just enough of the background of life to give them reality. The problem to be solved is one of human conduct, and the solution is reached when one has found X, the unknown quantity—usually the criminal [Burton Stevenson, "Supreme Moments in Detective Fiction," *The Bookman*, March 1913].

And the word problem came close to being universal in period detective fiction. It, to be sure, loomed large in the Sherlock Holmes canon. Thus this minuscule sample:

> Sherlock Holmes was a man, however, who, when he had an unsolved problem upon his mind, would go for days, and even for a week, without rest, turning it over, rearranging his facts, looking at it from every point of view, until he had either fathomed it, or convinced himself that his data were insufficient ["The Man with the Twisted Lip"].
> Holmes laughed. "It is quite a pretty little problem" ["A Scandal in Bohemia"].
> "It is quite a three-pipe problem, and I beg that you will not speak to me for fifty minutes" ["The Red-Headed League"].

By the 1890s fictional detectives proved their mettle by understanding and dealing with problems by reasoning. And writers made a point of writing about it. They began to seed in associated words (reason, logic, etc.) as well as mini discussions of aspects of reasoning and, more importantly, built denouements on reprising the steps in the detective's solution to the central problem in the story. Possessing and using brains as a characteristic of the detective hero became a frequent subject for comment:

> It was a point which deserved the most thorough investigation, and only a lawyer's, or a detective's brain, was fitted to the task [Helena Gullifer, *A Fool for his Pains*, 1883].
> Detective-Sergeant Reuben Smart stood in an attitude of respect before his superior officer, Inspector Frisner, but so shifted from one foot to another, in his anxiety to keep pace with the rapid working of the celebrated detective's brain, that the latter out of respect for his nervous system—very highly strung, as with most deep-thinking men and women—was perforce obliged, in defiance of discipline, to tell the sergeant to take a chair [Henry Curties, *The Queen's Gate Mystery*, 1908].

"Deduction" became something that was even retrospectively remarked upon in Gaboriau's heroes:

> Nothing shows more the extreme care of Gaboriau's workmanship than his development of the "systems" he attributes to the Tabarets and Lecoqs. In the reflection in the fiction of the imaginary facts, the whole fabric is based on logical deduction; the minutest details must be mutually self-supporting; and the demonstration of some insignificant flaw involves the collapse of the entire structure ["Crime in Fiction," *Blackwood's*, August 1890].

And it hardly needs saying that Conan Doyle made deduction a constant theme in the Sherlock Holmes stories:

> "It is simplicity itself," he remarked, chuckling at my surprise,—"so absurdly simple that an explanation is superfluous; and yet it may serve to define the limits of observation and of deduction. Observation tells me that you have a little reddish mould adhering to your instep. Just opposite the Seymour Street Office they have taken up the pavement and thrown up some earth which lies in such a way that it is difficult to avoid treading in it in entering. The earth is of this peculiar reddish tint which is found, as far as I know, nowhere else in the neighborhood. So much is observation. The rest is deduction" [*The Sign of the Four*, 1890].

Indeed, deduction was one of the things that separated the new detectives from the old—as well as the private detective from the police:

> I have to-day been called in to investigate one of the most singular cases that has fallen in my way. It is one in which the usual detective methods would be utterly valueless. The facts were presented to me, and the solution of the mystery could only be reached by analytical deduction [Rodriguez Ottolengui, "The Azteck Opal," *The Idler*, April 1895].

But writing about problems and logic and solutions was hardly enough to create the immense success of the detective story at the turn of the twentieth century. There was the whole puzzle business. Instead of the reviewer's querulous take on puzzles and games in the review of *The Moonstone* cited above ("The word 'novel,' as applied to them, is an absurd misnomer, however that word is understood"), a more genial view of puzzles or games as an important defining feature of the detective story began to emerge. Not coincidentally, an increased appetite for puzzles had become pronounced near the end of the nineteenth century. Different kinds of puzzles caught the public's fancy, from the mathematical puzzles showcased in Lewis Carroll's *The Game of Logic* (1887), to a fad for Chinese tangrams in the 1890s. Professor Hoffman's *Puzzles Old and New* (1893) listed four hundred mechanical puzzles, and at the turn of the century jigsaw puzzles, formerly only made for children, were made for adults and quickly became popular. Conan Doyle's publisher, George Newnes, in fact, was what amounts to being the puzzle king of the era. In *Tit-Bits* he ran a story contest for which the prize was a seven room house and later ran a treasure hunt for five hundred sovereigns, buried in the country by Arthur Morrison, to be found following clues found in a story published in his magazine. It is worth noting, also, that, like other magazines of the time *Good Housekeeping* ran a section titled "Quiet Hours for the Quick Witted"; *Household Words* had "Puzzles for Prizes"; *Peterson's Magazine, The Hawaiian Monthly, Arthur's Home Magazine*, and *The Idler* had "Puzzle Departments"; *The Literary Digest* carried "Dr. Dalton's Prize Problems"; and *Ballou's Monthly* had a "Puzzle Page." Indeed at the close of the century the popularity of puzzles in contemporary periodicals elicited this comment in *The Strand*:

PUZZLES, in some form or other, have always been popular, and have provided amusement for all sorts of people from time immemorial, though perhaps they have never been so popular as at the present time, when almost every periodical and paper of any note whatever has its puzzle page [December 1899].

Starting in the 1880s detective stories began to be linked to puzzles. It happened originally in newspapers and magazines which were caught up in the contemporary fascination for games and puzzles and then began to include detective stories with other contests, puzzles, and games they ran. A minor manifestation of this was the prize contest for readers who wanted to write detective stories: in 1895, for example, *The Saint Paul Daily Globe* offered $10,000 in prizes for writers who submitted stories aspiring to be the best "Stories of Mystery." The preceding year *Cassell's Family Magazine* in Britain offered more modest rewards for detective story copy:

DETECTIVE STORY COMPETITION.—Three Prizes, of Five Guineas, Four Guineas, and Three Guineas respectively, are offered for the best, second-, and third-best DETECTIVE STORIES, suitable for publication in this Magazine. Each MS. must be legibly written, on one side of the paper only, must be not less than 3,000 or more than 5,000 words in length, and must comply in every respect with the requirements of the General Regulations, published in our December number. Attached to each MS. must be, in addition to the declaration required by the General Regulations, a short outline of the plot of the story, not to exceed 400 words in length. May 1st, 1894, is the latest date for receiving MSS. The words, "Detective Story Competition," must be inscribed on the wrapper enclosing each MS.

Indeed one of the most controversial publishing ventures of the eighteen nineties produced a wail of criticism concerning the means by which the Bacheller syndicate awarded the prizes in its detective story contest, a contest which produced the first real anthology of detective stories, *The Long Arm and Other Detective Stories*, in 1895.

Newspapers, however, were looking for readers more than they were looking for writers. And to that end they invented the puzzle (or guessing game) detective serial. Thus, for instance, there was the contest run by *The Boston Globe* in 1888 offering a prize to the reader who could accurately predict the solution to its serial *Written in Red* before the publication of its last chapter. This kind of newspaper-sponsored find-the-solution detective contest continued in Britain and America for three decades. In 1895, for example, Miss M.M. Elder won $150 for "the most correct account of the mystery" in *The Bride of a Day* published in *The Pittsburgh Times*, and the next year *The Chicago Record* ran syndicated ads offering $10,000 in prizes in a contest involving the solution to the mystery in *Fathers and Sons*. So popular were these newspaper contests, in fact, that in his first inverted detective story, "The Case of Oscar Broadski" (1912), R. Austin Freeman characterizes Dr. Thorndyke by having an officious provincial police detective tell him that "you must understand, sir, that this is a judicial inquiry, not a prize competition in a penny paper." The next year Melville Davisson Post's Monsieur Jonquelle characterizes the English by their love of puzzles: "Every Man in these Islands is fundamentally a solver of mysteries. Observe the puzzles on sale, and the device of journals to increase their circulation by exhibiting a jar full of beans to be guessed at, or by hiding a hundred guineas on the Epsom Downs" ("Found in the Fog"). Adding new twists to involve readers in a detective story contest became a sought after achievement in the first decades of the twentieth century. One such novelty was *The Million Dollar Mystery* contest in 1914 which brought the cinema into the arena: "The prize of $10,000 will be won by the man, woman or child who writes the most acceptable solution of the mystery, from which the last two reels of motion picture drama will be made and the last two chapters of the story written by Harold McGrath." But the biggest contest splash of the period involved Edgar Wallace's fiasco with the serial publication of his *The Four Just Men* in the *Daily Mail* in 1905. The paper, and £2,000 worth of ads plastered all over London, advertised £500 worth of prizes for guessing the method of the murder in Wallace's serial novel before it was revealed in the final installment in the paper. Wallace, however, neglected to specify that there would be only one prize each for first, second, and third place, and with correct answers pouring in, he reaped financial disaster.

The association of detective stories with games was not just limited to promotions in magazines and newspapers. On both sides of the century divide reviewers, critics, and writers increasingly came to identify (and justify) the detective story itself as a variety of game. G.K. Chesterton, for example, took up the theme of detective stories as puzzles and defended readers' interest in them:

> Now a whole department of popular fiction exists simply to give people riddles rather than romances; I mean the things commonly called detective stories. If the question is complex and the answer clever, the ordinary reader does not care whether the style is slipshod or the characters crude; and the ordinary reader is quite right. There is nothing in the least unintelligent in wanting the mere fun of seeing a puzzle pulled to pieces. Nor is there anything unintelligent in paying for what you want. He has as much right to prefer a puzzle in criminology to a study in human nature as I have to prefer a study in human nature to a problem in algebra. The point is that a love of puzzles exists and men are justified in gratifying it either in mathematics or in murders ["Why Books Become Popular," *The Bibliophile*, September 1908].

Not very surprisingly detective stories of the period repeatedly mention puzzles and riddles (which are a kind of puzzle). Indeed, the idea of the game or puzzle ("Something devised or made for the purpose of testing one's ingenuity, knowledge, patience, etc.," OED) came to be used to define detective stories—or a certain class of detective stories. They came to be seen as fictions in which readers' satisfaction came in part from seeing justice done, but, more importantly, from watching the hero successfully solve a problem—i.e., play a game. In Dick Donovan's *The Records of Vincent Trill of the Detective Service* (1899), for instance, readers are invited to watch the hero: "It was very much like trying to fit together the pieces of a complicated Chinese puzzle, and it was only with a vague hope that something might result from his labours that Trill worked." And in Louis Tracy's *A Mysterious Disappearance* (1905) a multiplicity of puzzles is at the center of the dilemma faced by the characters:

> "Surely not! The more pieces of the puzzle we have to handle the less difficult should be the final task of putting them together."
> "Not when every piece is a fresh puzzle in itself."

But more than just places to watch a detective solve a puzzle, detective stories also came to be and be seen as fictions that invited the readers themselves to play a game—to compete with the hero in solving the puzzle and to predict the ending. Thus Julian Hawthorne described this other application of games to contemporary detective stories—i.e., the game played between the writer and the reader:

> Reader and writer sit down to a game, as it were, with the odds, of course, altogether on the latter's side,—apart from the fact that a writer sometimes permits himself a little cheating. It more often happens that the detective appears to be in the writer's pay, and aids the deception by leading the reader off on false scents. Be that as it may, the professional sleuth is in nine cases out of ten a dummy by malice prepense; and it might be plausibly argued that, in the interests of pure art, that is what he ought to be. But genius always finds a way that is better than the rules, and I think it will be found that the very best riddle stories contrive to drive character and riddle side by side, and to make each somehow enhance the effect of the other [*Mystery and Detective Stories*, 1907].

Indeed, at Yale D. Carroll McEuen made the readers' response to the text the defining feature of the detective story:

> All this while we have left our reader without an answer to the question suggested at the beginning,—what is a detective story? Briefly we would define it as a story which gives us an opportunity to use our analytical faculty, which we sometimes forget we possess; in most books the analysis of character or situation is done for the reader; it is the characteristic of a detective story that it is left for him to unfathom himself. Thus a detective story is nothing more than an elaborate puzzle. Most detective stories present pros and cons and hold the solution to the last minute. Some detective stories do relate the process of reasoning; where this is powerful enough there is the same stimulus to the analytic faculty ["The Romance of Detective Stories," *The Yale Courant*, February 1907].

Viewing detective stories as games didn't change everything, but it changed things a lot. From the beginning of the form, writers, publishers and reviewers used the term "clever" to describe one of the defining characteristics of a successful detective hero. The OED has it that "clever" means two different things—(1) "possessing skill or talent," and (2) being "able to use hand or brain readily and effectively; dexterous, skilful; adroit." In the 1860s and 1870s readers found descriptions of detectives which tended to emphasize the former, possessing a distinct, unique, special skill or talent: "I wish I had a clever detective here! They find their way to everything" (Helen Wood, *Lady Adelaide's Oath*, 1867); "a glance in which the clever detective can read the inmost secrets of a man's soul" (*The Black Band*, 1877); and "heaven forbid that you should ever be very clever in such a line as this. There must be detective officers; they are the polished bloodhounds of our civilised age" (Mary E. Braddon, *Eleanor's Victory*, 1863). Approaching the turn of the century, however, the second meaning of the term "clever" (clever as describing an act or process) gained currency and it came to be used to describe the hero detective's expertise in action in addition to his or her native or acquired skill or talent. More important than that, "clever" came to mean "surprisingly novel." And significantly it was not just attached to the hero. It was applied to the creation of the narrative, to the writer, or to both. The satisfaction of a detective story, then, came both from observing the hero's skill and success as well as from the way the writer told the story. Thus

> GEORGE AFTEREM is the appropriate name or *nom de plume* of an author who has written a very clever, original and entertaining detective story, called 'Silken Threads' [Cupples, Upham & Co. ad frontispiece of novel, 1885].
>
> UNTIL Katherine Green wrote this book, it was feared that she had exhausted herself. 'The Mill Mystery' and '7 to 12' did not compare favorably with 'The Leavenworth Case' and 'Sword and Ring.' But this work reinstates her in her position as a writer of clever detective stories, even if it does not indicate increased literary ability [*The Critic*, January 19, 1889].
>
> The author of "The diamond button," "Jack Gordon, knight-errant," etc., etc., has again written a clever detective story [*The Man with a Thumb*], the scene of operation being New York city [*The Publishers Weekly*, January 14, 1891].

It is no surprise to find that critics and advertisers applied the same term to the Sherlock Holmes stories: thus publishers repeatedly quoted a piece from *The Chicago Times* that identified *A Study in Scarlet* as a "cleverly-constructed detective story, told in a terse, compact, and fascinating manner" (publisher's ad 1891), and another publisher announced that "All of the books in the Eureka Series [including *The Sign of the Four*] are clever detective stories, and each one of those mentioned below has received the heartiest recommendation" (ad 1894). And the review of *The Memoirs of Sherlock Holmes* in *The Literary World* uses the term as well:

> First we had the *Adventures of Sherlock Holmes* and now we have his memoirs. A good detective story is sure to find plenty of readers, and here are a dozen of them.

A. Conan Doyle has that rare gift in a story-teller—he knows when and where to stop. He never allows his reader to weary of any one story, although there is a certain sameness to this collection taken as a whole. Dr. Doyle is clever in his short stories [*The Literary World*, April 7, 1894].

In the 1880s, a kindred term partnered with "clever" in describing detectives and detective stories—ingenuity or "showing cleverness, talent, or genius." Occasionally it is used to describe the hero in the story, as in this piece of Gallic hyperbole: "The functionary understood that the interview was ended. So, after shaking hands, he hastened to the Palais de Justice, to try the plan which had been recommended to him by the most ingenious detective of the past, present, or future" (Fortuné Du Boisgobey, *The Old Age of LeCoq the Detective*, 1885). More often the term ingenious refers to writers and to narrative technique. And telling a story without telegraphing the ending became the *sine qua non* of the detective story writer's cleverness or ingenuity. Thus

> Mr. Vandam, in *The Mystery of the Patrician Club,* has produced a detective story of such ingenuity that it is impossible for the reader to solve the mystery until the last pages have been reached [*The Yale Literary Magazine*, October 1894].
>
> Yet it cannot be said that M. Lerminais [is] more than a passable member of the great school of detective romance-writers. He lacks the marvellous ingenuity and fecundity of invention of Gaboriau, and he has nothing of Mr. Conan Doyle's straightforward skill in solving his problems [*The Speaker*, July 21, 1894].
>
> Circumstantial evidence, of course, points to Durrant as the criminal, especially when the ring is found in his possession. How the matter ends let the reader discover by getting the book [*The Mystery of Landy Court*]. The plot is worked out with very considerable ingenuity, and holds the attention right up to the last two chapters, with their unexpected *denouement* [*The Publishers' Circular*, March 31, 1894].

Skill, cleverness and ingenuity on the part of the writer quickly became associated with the surprise ending of the detective story. It was seen as having been inspired by Poe and, here, by Collins:

> We doubt if there are stories in English in which the plots are more perfect than in the four we have named, in which the situations are more dramatic, or in which the mystery is more perfectly preserved to the very end. The surprise is usually complete, so complete that it excites a kind of involuntary laughter, and usually, in "The Moonstone" in particular, it is led up to with a high degree of artistic skill ["Wilkie Collins," *The Eclectic Magazine,* December 1889].

Surprise became one of the most important criteria for judging the successful detective story:

> Miss Braddon throws into the story [*Wyllard's Weird*] of a mysterious murder and the detective business of the search for the murderer more than usual interest. The scenes and characters are both French and English, and taken from refined circles. The plot is ingeniously planned, ending in a genuine surprise [*Publishers' Weekly*, March 28, 1885].

The story [*The Black Carnation*] is told by Major Granby, who sees the murder, and who, being bitten with detective fever, spends several weeks in trying to find the murderer, and in the end, with the help of a detective, he succeeds. As the story progresses, Major Granby finds himself, as he imagines, on the brink of discovery no less than six times, and each time his theory of the crime is almost convincing to the reader, and in the end, when the true murderer is disclosed, the reader is bound to be surprised, for the author has led up to his *denouement* very cleverly [*The Publishers' Circular*, October 22, 1892].

This is a collection of eleven short stories related by a lawyer [*My Mysterious Clients*], purporting to embody his actual experience. They are all told in charming style, and their mystery is carefully concealed until the denouement, when it is disclosed, in most cases, to the absolute surprise of the reader [*Albany Law Journal*, June 23, 1900].

Increasingly by the late 1880s surprise became so integral to the detective story that reviewers routinely refrained from mentioning the endings of detective stories in their reviews:

A VERY good detective story is "Silken Threads," by "George Afterem." The strong point of the novel is its ingenious plot; and beside being ingenious, it is entirely original, we believe, and certainly no higher praise can be bestowed upon a story involving a well-developed mystery. The smallest hint as to what the "Silken Threads" were would reveal the whole *motif* of the book, and we will not spoil the pleasure of any prospective reader [*The Book Buyer*, September 1885].

Reviewers did, however, occasionally compare the technique of the detective story writer with that of the magician or confidence artist:

One reads Stockton in the same mental attitude that he would devote to a sleight-of-hand performance—always expecting a surprise, and often being disappointed. There remains enough of the unusual to make the exhibition a success [*Life*, October 25, 1885].

To the reader, starting at the beginning, there is an appearance of mystery; but to the writer who starts with his conclusion the whole is no more than a clever piece of literary legerdemain. Poe discovered and showed how this legerdemain might be practised, but in his stories he had quite different objects [*The Best Tales of Edgar Allan Poe*, 1903].

But the writer of a detective story is more nearly in the position of a man working the three-card trick. The spectators prefer that the operator should not produce a fourth card from his sleeve. We are not charging moral obliquity against an author who prefers to adopt this method; but the best detective stories let the reader exercise his ingenuity [*Saturday Review*, August 24, 1907].

While new applications of the concepts of cleverness and ingenuity emerged in descriptions of detectives and detective fiction at the turn of the century, something different happened with the description of another aspect of what detectives do. Older and unsophisticated detective fiction metaphorically connected detectives with animals with innate abilities that lead them to prey, especially ferrets and bloodhounds: "Go to Scotland Yard; spend your money freely, and the detectives will ferret out the truth, if there be such a thing at the bottom of the bag ("Lady Flavia," *Chambers' Journal*, March 25, 1865), and

> But now comes in le perè Tabaret—generally called Tirauclair, from a favourite phrase of his—a secret detective for love of the sport, with a scent as keen as a bloodhound's, to whom the tracking of a criminal is an art, a science, and who builds up his hypothesis on the most precise and mathematical laws of human action. He has the eyes of a hawk, and a brain as sharp as his sight. When he enters the cottage, he goes about like a dog searching for the scent; soon he for paper and a pencil, then for plaster, water, and a bottle of oil. In a short time he returns, discoveries and hypothesis complete [*L'affaire LeRouge*, 1866].

In addition to following trails or scents, finding a "clew" or "clews" almost universally described the path to the detective's success. "Clew" originally meant a ball of string or thread, or the thread itself—as in the thread Theseus unspooled as he went into the labyrinth. A clew, then, was something to be found and then followed to an inevitable end. Thus

> As a clever detective, by a single, seemingly unimportant fact—the impress of a foot, the wadding out of a pistol—first gets hold of a clue that shall enable him to follow the tortuous windings of crime, and ultimately discover its guilty author, so did Bettina, on the spot, evolve a whole labyrinth of mystery and of crime from the condition of those nine yards of torn and blackened muslin [*Archie Lovell, The Galaxy*, September 15, 1866].

Indeed Matthew Hale Smith includes the same concept of the clew as in his description of the "Qualifications of a Detective":

> A detective must be quick, talented, and possess a good memory; cool, unmoved, able to suppress all emotion; have great endurance, untiring industry, and keen relish for his work; put on all characters, and assume all disguises; pursue a trail for weeks, or months, or years; go anywhere at a moment's notice, on the land or sea; go without food or sleep; follow the slightest clew till he reaches the criminal; from the simplest fragment bring crime to light;...The modern detective system is based on the theory that purity and intelligence has a controlling power over crime [*Bulls and Bears of New York*, 1874].

As the nineteenth century progressed, however, not only did the spelling of the word change from "clew" to "clue," the concept of what the detective did began to change. In its original sense, following a clew suggested the concept of "murder will out," that evil was obvious and inherently self destructive and following the thread would inevitably lead to the villain and to justice. This concept also embodied the same surety of providential justice as did the concept of physiognomy—that evil people looked evil and acted guilty. In the providential universe, then, the detective needed commitment, industry, patience, and experience—virtues available to everyone if properly cultivated and trained.

As it developed, in the last quarter of the century the fictional detective's job became significantly more challenging than the old detective's. The guilty no longer stood out because of their appearance or mien, because of their class or stature, or complexion or because they slouched or behaved furtively: thus the narrator's dismay in Mary Wilkins Freeman's "The Long Arm" (1895) when she discovers that the crime was committed by "that woman with the good face, whom I had heard praying like a saint in meeting." Justice was not infallible but capable of startling miscarriages based on faulty direct or, more commonly, circumstantial evidence: indeed, myriad period stories are entitled "Circumstantial Evidence." Individual pieces of evidence became minute, subtle, esoteric, confusing, enigmatic, and sometimes bizarre. And they multiplied: there was no longer one thread to follow but many clues to discover and understand. Thus clues became not simply something that illuminated the identity of a wrong-doer, they became parts of riddles or puzzles: no longer threads to be followed but individual pieces to be understood and related to one another. And they played a role not only in the fictional detective's solution to the crime but also in the ways in which readers approached and appreciated the detective story itself—by looking for and interpreting the clues provided for them by the author.

Along with this change in the meaning of clues, turn of the century writers often depended upon the term "theory." It was, first of all, another way of demonstrating the hero's cerebral talents. Thus

> the work of a detective can only be systematic and logical when it is based upon some sort of a theory. Between the meagre facts which he finds waiting for him at the place where secret crime has done its evil work, and the just punishment which he helps bring home to the guilty, there is always found a series of observations, examinations, comparisons, tests, etc., which demand time and hard labor on the part of the patient detective. All this work must be done with definite reasons in his mind for every step—or the results will be unsatisfactory [Clarence Boutelle, *The Man Outside, Frank Leslie's Popular Monthly*, April 1887].

And

> in other words, a detective, after carefully studying the details of any crime, must form a theory concerning it, and must work along that theory. As soon as he discovers any fact that fails to fit with his theory, he must modify it or form another; and he must keep on doing this until he finds the theory which agrees with all the facts—not all but one or two, but with every one. A good many detectives fall into the mistake of being satisfied with the theory which fits most of the facts—a serious error, for the right theory must, of course, inevitably fit them all. That's the scientific method and the only safe one. When a detective hits upon a theory which fits all the known facts, he's got as much right to assume it's true as an astronomer has or a physicist, who builds up the universe in just the same way [Burton Stevenson, *The Marathon Mystery*, 1904].

But since a theory is not proof, the term and concept were also used to build detective story plots. The notion provided a structure that justified going over and rearranging a set of facts again and again. In Lawrence Lynch's *No Proof* (1895), for example, the narrator presents readers with a laundry list of theories:

> This page was headed "Theories," and beneath was written:
> The Captain's Theory.—Suicide perhaps, or else that D. M., while trying on her bridal dress, had discovered an attempt at burglary, at her window, perhaps, and in a frantic attempt at self-defense had somehow shot herself. Or, possibly, while standing near the bed, and about to place the weapon beneath the pillow, it had discharged itself, perhaps through careless handling, and the victim may have fallen back upon the bed, dying, as found.
> On the opposite page was written:
> Theory First.—Impossible. No one could reach windows without a ladder from the ground, or a rope let down from roof. No ladder had been used, as condition of ground plainly shows.
> Theory Second.—Ditto. No entrance has been made through window, as proved by dust upon ledges, and by condition of screens and fastenings.
> Going back to the first page, the next entry read:
> Mrs. W.'s Theory. Suicide. Cause unknown.
> Then came:
> Miss W.'s Theory.—Suicide.
> Doctor R.'s Theory.—Murder or suicide. If suicide, caused by sudden shock and loss of reason. E. M.'s Theory.—Murder.

But more than simply being ways of explaining the detective's unique intellectual gifts or building a plot, the use of the concept of theory came to play a role in the reader-writer game that was beginning to be acknowledged in the fiction of the period. Thus the reviewer founds that Fergus Hume's use of the detective's theories in *The Red-Headed Man* was a way of "bamboozling the reader":

> He joins Mr. Torry, a detective, in trying to solve the mystery of a double murder in which a red-headed man is one victim, a woman the other. They have no clue worth speaking of; but then their theories are most convincing, and in turn we suspect every character in the book, except, of course, the right one. But, it is some consolation to find we fail in good company, for both novelist and detective are equally astounded when they discover the murderer who has so completely befooled them. This speaks volumes for the author's ingenuity in working out his plot and bamboozling his reader. But it is with the worthy detective we sympathise. He is badgered and baited all round; one theory after another is demolished; ladies of 'regal bearing' treat him with contempt, even the novelist turns on him. Poor Mr. Torry! Fate was indeed unkind; but after all he caught his man [Review, Fergus Hume's *The Red Headed-Man*, *The Literary World*, December 1899].

There was a growing consensus, moreover, that it wasn't quite right or fair to just "bamboozle" the reader. If writing and reading a detective story was a game, it ought to at least involve "sportsmanship," or "fair play." In *The Technique of the Mystery Story* (1913), along with a history of the genre and comment on contemporary authors, librarian turned writer Carolyn Wells quoted Burton Stevenson on how to play the reader-writer game:

> First, to play fair with the reader, the cards must all lie on the table. It isn't honest to keep any up your sleeve; and the problem is to surprise the reader by the unexpected way in which you combine them. The reader must have before him the facts which the solver of mystery has, and then the 'Solver' must get there first.

Beginning with responses to the Sherlock Holmes stories, by the time of the First World War literary criticism had established a number of things about the detective story: first, that the detective story existed as a separate genre; that at least a significant portion of detective stories were "riddle" or "puzzle" stories; that a special relationship between the writer and the readers defined them; and that a code of conduct, perhaps even a set of rules, governed that relationship. Thus, in a review of Arthur Morrison's *The Red Triangle*, the idea of fair play appears:

> One is inclined to protest against the introduction of hypnotism; to some readers at least the use of hypnotism in detective stories seems not to be quite fair play, as anything and everything can be explained on that basis. Mr. Arthur Morrison has done work in fiction of so much higher character than is found in this book that perhaps it is hard, to appreciate these stories at their real value [*The Outlook*, September 12, 1903].

In an essay in *The Reader*, Carolyn Wells makes a verb out of Conan Doyle's name as she plays with the concept of "rules of the game":

> But "The Gilded Lady" is a detective story that doesn't detect. Whoever wrote it doesn't know the rules of the game. It's a very old counterfeiting plot, and it's built from the end backward. Oh, well, of course detective stories often are, but they don't always show it so plainly. This book has its most self-evident facts announced as clever deductions. Now wouldn't that Doyle you? [Carolyn Wells, "Over the Book Counter," *The Reader*, October 1903].

In 1916 Joyce Kilmer discussed the writer's obligations to the reader of detective stories and, once more, insisted on the idea of fair play:

> And it seems to me that Dr. Watson —that the foil—should be the narrator. You see, the story should be told in the first person. If it is told in the third person it is evident that the omniscient narrator has information which he is concealing from the reader; therefore, he is not playing fair with the reader, as the writer of this sort of work should do. If the great detective himself tells the story there can be no surprise. He must reveal his deductions and conclusions as he goes along; he will not be surprised, and the reader will not be surprised—that is, unless he holds back a part of his information, thereby not playing fair with the reader [*The Editor*, January 29, 1916].

As in the world of play and games, at the turn of the century the notion of fair play in detective fiction generated an occasionally felt need to set down the rules to play by. But what they prescribed, how much of the writer's prerogative needed to be governed by those rules, and whether fiction written to adhere to rules could ever be more than divertissements were occasionally controversial subjects, subjects exemplified in the review of *The Mauleverer Murders* in 1907:

> Mr. A. C. Fox DAVIES is extraordinarily nimble at twisting and knotting the threads of a narrative until they are apparently an inextricable tangle, but he has not, to my mind, written an ideal detective story in *The Mauleverer Murders* (LANE). I think for a detective story to be really satisfactory the reader should be supplied with every clue, so that if he is ingenious enough he may solve the mystery for himself. The author should not take the mean advantage of concealing to the end, as Mr. Fox DAVIES does, the facts upon which everything hinges. He should—or so I think —boldly display his ingredients, and having given them all a fair show so manipulate them that he can defy the reader to say before the thing is complete which is the important one [*Punch*, July 24, 1907].

But Fox-Davies didn't agree:

> Is there an inexorable law governing the construction of a good detective story? If there is one, A. C. Fox-Davies, author of "The Mauleverer Murders," which we favorably reviewed the other day, would like to know all about it. One of his commentators has told him in the *Saturday Review*, that he hardly plays the game in making it impossible to guess who is the real murderer, for the most skilful type of detective story puts all the pieces on the board at the outset. Of course, Mr. Fox-Davies is moved to reply, and though he promises to play the game in framing the plot of the novel on which he is now working, he cannot forbear asking these questions: "Who made the rules of that game? Where are they to be found? What authority have they? ... Why on earth one should be required to 'table' all one's cards at the outset, or why one should be under the necessity of giving the reader the opportunity of guessing correctly, I fail to see." There is something to be said on both sides of the question. The masters of the detective story generally observe the rules of the game, in the sense understood by Mr. Fox-Davies's critic. But, on the other hand, the matter is hardly one to take with a great seriousness. To treat a book like "The Mauleverer Murders" in the light of a kind of classic standard is to break a butterfly upon a wheel. The main point, where these ephemeral novels of mystery are concerned, is that they should be amusing.—*New York Tribune* [quoted in *The Writer,* October 1907].

The whole issue of the role of rules in writing, reading or judging a detective story became a preoccupation for some for the next twenty years. Among the first formal set of rules was the seven axioms promulgated in *The Writer's Book* (1918) which included "Axiom III. *The working out of the theme should not be too legal, technical or involved.*" A decade later Willard Huntington Wright writing as Philo Vance published "Twenty Rules for Writing Detective Stories" in the September 1928 issue of *The American Magazine*. These began with "The reader must have equal opportunity with the detective for solving the mystery. All clues must be plainly stated and described," and the third of these ruled love interests as out of bounds: "There must be no love interest. The business in hand is to bring a criminal to the bar of justice, not to bring a lovelorn couple to the hymeneal altar." The next year Ronald Knox published a partly tongue-in-cheek Decalogue setting forth rules—rules that included "The detective must not light on any clues which are not instantly produced for the inspection of the reader," and another that specified that "no Chinamen must appear in the story."

Those sets of rules promulgated in the late teens and twenties were to some degree anticipated at the turn of the century by the attention critics and reviewers paid to the plot of the detective story, attention that focused on problem solving and the importance of surprise—witness the following:

> In *Detective Stories*, however, the plot is all-important, for the interest depends entirely upon the unraveling of some tangle; but even here it must contain but a single idea, though that may be rather involved. Such stories are really much simpler than they appear, for their seeming complexity consists in telling the story backwards, and so reasoning from effect to cause, rather than vice versa as in the ordinary tale [*Short Story Writing*, 1900].
>
> Its weakness arises from the fact that the plot, which is sufficient for a short-story (the hyphen is authorized by Brander Matthews) of good length, is totally inadequate for the needs of a 400-page novel. Haply, the assertion which recently appeared in the public prints is true: that the publishers require a certain length for a novel, and will accept nothing far short of that. Be that as it may, the story is too long by half. A detective story must be a detective story and nothing else. The infusion of any other element is sure to be resented by the reader, and The Reader, in mass, is the Court of Last Appeals [Review of *In the Shadow of the Rope*, *Pacific Monthly*, November 1902].
>
> *The Detective Story.* This division is the only one that makes the plot paramount. To the uninitiated the *detective story*, with its mystery following upon mystery, seems the most difficult to attempt. But, in reality, it is one of the easiest and simplest. It is like a piece of knitting. It must be unravelled backwards [Emelyn Partridge, "The Short Story," *The Suburban*, October 27, 1906].
>
> The *Detective Story* requires the most complex plot of any type of short story, for its interest depends solely upon the solution of the mystery presented in that plot. It arouses in the human mind much the same interest as an algebraic problem, which it greatly resembles [Charles R. Barrett, "Short Stories Classified," *The Editor*, August 1908].

These judgments, to some extent extensions of all of the contemporary discussion of the detective story as a game, suggested that other literary elements—style, character, tone, setting, theme, etc.—were of negligible importance. Thus Chesterton pronounced that "the ordinary reader does not care whether the style is slipshod or the characters crude" and in *Writing the*

Short Story (1909) Joseph Esenwein noted that "as a character, the detective cannot be much more than a dummy." Esenwein, however, went on to say the detective's "individuality cannot be brought out in a single short-story, except by a few bold strokes of delineation; but when he figures in a series of stories, as does Sherlock Holmes, the reader at length comes to know him quite well." Even a brief look at the stacks of short story collections published in the 1890s demonstrates that this is hardly something that writers and publishers had to be told about: fictional detectives, especially in magazines, rarely came as single spies.

While the evolution of puzzle-game plotting in detective stories at the turn of the century was one of the principal ways that changed fiction about crime from pseudo biography or sensation or moral tract into entertainment accepted as wholesome and even as useful (Baden-Powell recommended Sherlock Holmes as instructive reading in *Scouting for Boys*), it is easy to overestimate the importance of intellectual (or pseudo intellectual) machinery to contemporary readers and writers. Indeed the growing popularity of narration by the detective's admiring friend possessed not simply the advantage of keeping readers in the dark about the story's puzzle but it also allowed the author to expand on the hero's character traits not directly linked to problem solving. Here it is certainly worth noting that the best known detective stories of any age, the Sherlock Holmes stories, were not written as puzzle stories, that Conan Doyle's story telling was the gift most highly praised by contemporary reviewers, and that from the beginning it was Holmes' character that most fascinated reviewers and readers. In 1917 in *The Bellman* the writer finally articulated the conundrum that had been present with readers since 1887—that the most popular detective story writer of an age when the form was being defined by some as the use of clues and fair play to confront readers with a puzzle did not furnish his readers with clues, that Conan Doyle treated the readers as observers versus participants, and that he did not play fair:

> Dr. Watson, as he grows older, sometimes fails adequately to explain the grounds on which Holmes bases his reasoning. At the denouement of several of the tales there are statements indicating that, in his effort to reach an effective climax, he relies too much on intellectual legerdemain. This is scarcely fair play, for the conventions of the detective story demand that the process should, in the end, be quite clear, even though the reader be as obtuse as was Dr. Watson himself [*The Bellman*, December 22, 1917].

But failure to play fair was nothing new about the later Sherlock Holmes stories. Conan Doyle, in fact, was hardly coy about the fact that his stories were more than demonstrations of intellectual problem solving. Thus he began "The Adventure of Abbey Grange" by highlighting the blurred focus of Watson's story telling:

> Your fatal habit of looking at everything from the point of view of a story instead of as a scientific exercise has ruined what might have been an instructive and even

classical series of demonstrations. You slur over work of the utmost finesse and delicacy, in order to dwell upon sensational details which may excite, but cannot possibly instruct the reader.

And Conan Doyle was hardly alone in this: as will be seen in the following chapters, the majority of the writers who took up the detective story at the turn of the twentieth century sought to entertain by making their detective stories more than puzzle games.

The popularity of cheap American fiction may have had a small something to do with this. The purveyors of low-brow dime novel fiction in the U.S. hardly depended on the intellectual challenges of their fare to make a buck. They reckoned that their readers wanted excitement, and that detective stories could and should serve that up. And it showed in the advertising. In 1881, for example, Ogilvie advertised *Gipsy Blair the Western Detective* as "one of the most thrilling detective stories ever written ... [which] relates deeds of daring adventure, and consummate detective skill in tracing the violators of law. Every one should read it, because it is a story of intense interest and dramatic power." Munro's ads in 1880s for his Old Sleuth Library boasted that it was "A Series of the Most Thrilling Detective Stories Ever Published." In the last quarter of the century the words "Adventure" (an exciting or unusual experience) and "Thrilling" (a feeling of excitement) became the standard way a certain class of American publishers advertised their detective stories. Estes and Lauriat in Boston in 1881 even converted their ho-hum reprints of old notebook fiction (including *Recollections of a Policeman*) into their "Legal Adventure Library." By the mid 1880s British publishers had begun to market American dime novels and they used the same lures. Thus by 1886 Cameron and Ferguson's Detective Library (or, "Tales of Startling Mystery") advertised that in their reprints of American dime novels (including the aforementioned *Gipsy Blair*) "Modern Civilisation is developing Romance in its City Life more startling than those of the age of Chivalry or of Backwood Adventure." And in the early 1890s Aldine's reprinted dime novels in their Celebrated Detective Tales series which promised, "These thrilling 'SHADOW REVELATIONS' of the deep and cunning meshes of concealment, woven by astute and criminal men and women, often in high positions and spotless before the world, and the deadly dangers ever besetting the daring professional 'MAN-HUNTER,' are vividly depicted in these absorbing narratives" (ad, 1892). With this in mind, it's not much of a surprise that the terms "Thrilling" and "Adventure" turn up in ads, titles, and reviews of new detective stories of the period. Thus Dick Donovan's *The Adventure of Tyler Tatlock, Private Detective* (1896), Meade and Halifax's *Adventures of a Man of Science* (1897), and, of course, most of Conan Doyle's stories: *The Strand* labeled six of the first run of Sherlock Holmes stories "Adventures," the first published collection of Conan Doyle's detective stories was entitled *The Adventures of Sherlock Holmes,* and when they appeared in *The Strand* the stories that would comprise *The Memoirs of Sherlock Holmes* were labeled as "adventures," as in "The Adventure of Silver Blaze." Indeed the use of the term "adventure" became almost indiscriminate when applied to detective stories as witnessed by the Minerva Library of Indispensable Books uses the term in advertising their 1895 volume *Poe's Tales of Adventure, Mystery and Imagination.*

But writers hardly abandoned the puzzle part of the detective story, that had become the favorite topic of highbrow critics, in order to write like American dime novel writers. Part, perhaps even most, of the success of short detective fiction at the turn of the twentieth century came from the fact that most successful (and even most unsuccessful) writers combined puzzles with something else. This hardly went unnoticed; it's there in Holmes' comment to Watson cited above and a piece in *The Writer* in 1905 made the connection:

> Detective stories of the new school are in great demand. I do not mean the Old Sleuth or Captain Carter, or any of that class, where the chief element in the story is bluster, blood, and thunder, and killing of the characters in rapid succession, till none are left to tell the story. It is the detective story where the chief element is the mental side, which carries out the well organized development of an intricate and exciting plot, a story of situations, and thrilling and reasonable, not made gruesome and uncanny by constant catastrophe, giving a touch of romance mingled with comedy. Detective stories of that class are to-day welcomed by the reader, and hence are wanted by the publishers. They are on a much higher plane than the old school detective stories and such are not objectionable for children [*The Writer*, December 1905].

It took more, however, than abandoning the pseudo-biographical notebook fiction of the mid-nineteenth century or ignoring the action-adventure fantasies of American dime novels to make the detective story the literary juggernaut it became at the turn of the twentieth century. And it took more than the puzzles—the presentation of knotty problems and clever solutions—that displaced the old school detective stories. Most importantly it took the creation of interesting, idiosyncratic detective characters. And, inspired by Conan Doyle, the new generation of writers drew detective characters they defined not simply by their intellects but by intellects enriched or supplemented by gender, nationality, class, profession, or even personal idiosyncrasies. And it is worth noting that very few of them are orthodox police detectives. In addition to the embellishment of the character of the genius detective, moreover, the new generation of detective story writers also evolved methods of providing readers with excitement and adventure that differed from those provided by sensation novels, dime novels and other kinds of publications. The new, overwhelming popularity of the short story in the 1890s had much to do with downsizing (but certainly not eliminating) action and adventure. The new mandated puzzle element in the story, however, inevitably went beyond the simple narrative of discovering facts and became a contest, an event that in itself stimulates interest and excitement. Additionally the opposition in the contest opened myriad opportunities for writers to create interest and excitement—something clearly seen, for instance, both in Conan Doyle's use of gothic elements even before *The Hound of the Baskervilles,* as well as in the plots of most of his contemporaries. Then, too, mutant forms of the detective story which depended too much on action and adventure and too little on reason and logic quickly broke off and developed into sub-genres and audiences of their own—sub-genres like the master criminal story and the gentleman crook story to be encountered in later chapters.

3

From "A Scandal in Bohemia" to *The Hound of the Baskervilles*

In many ways the last ten years of the nineteenth century became the decade of the short detective story in Britain—even if it took another ten years for the form to fully take hold in the United States. Beginning in the late 1880s and early 1890s, writers interested in telling stories about detectives began to create fictional detectives whose exploits could be chronicled and whose characters could be depicted—not as functionaries to bring about the denouement in sensation novels or as thief takers' notebooks, but as heroes of short stories intended for the new audience of middle class readers. The introduction of Sherlock Holmes in "A Scandal in Bohemia" in 1891 had a lot to do with this. Much of this also corresponded with the birth and burgeoning of illustrated magazines with publishers eager to exploit the combination of copious illustrations of just about anything with the newly popular form of the short story. And because of Sherlock Holmes, the most popular form of the short story was the detective story: in the 1890s it is difficult to find an issue of *The Strand*, or *Pearson's*, or the *Royal*, or the *Windsor*, or the *Idler* that does not contain at least one detective story. Not only did popular writers accomplished in other genres like Cutcliff Hyne and Richard Marsh now occasionally try their hands at writing detective stories, in the late 1880s and early 1890s a sizable group of writers began to emerge who dedicated themselves to exclusively writing detective fiction. Before, during, and after the appearance of Holmes in *The Strand*, competing magazines, as well as boys' papers and newspapers, featured their stories about detectives. But these writers were not condemned to the inevitable obscurity of those ephemeral media. In the 1890s book publishers began to seek out magazine detective fiction and publish it between hard covers—granting it a new kind of status and guaranteeing it a larger degree of permanence. Ranging from collections of short stories about a single hero, to anthologies like *The Long Arm*, to semi-random collections of stories by one author like Headon Hill's *The Divinations of Kala Persad, and Other Stories,* books of short stories about detectives appeared on a number of publishers' lists in both London and New York. And detective stories published in book form, in turn, sometimes brought with them another kind of status: notice by and from reviewers. None of this, however, guaranteed a golden age for short detective fiction. A significant number of the new writers simply produced updated notebook fiction, and, for all of the criticism written about it, they largely ignored the technical potential of the puzzle story in favor of trying out heroes who did the same things Sherlock Holmes did.

While Conan Doyle's character presented in the new format of the short story demonstrably caused a lot of publishers and writers to think about the detective story as the next new thing, it was not immediately apparent to anyone in the early 1890s what exactly that new thing was supposed to be. To be sure, many of the new fictional detectives were simply reiterations of Sherlock Holmes' characteristics and a few of the new writers of the 1890s took up Conan Doyle's (or Poe's) narrative technique. But a fair number, perhaps even a narrow majority, of the detective stories to appear early in the decade simply continued trends going back to the crime fiction of the first part of the century. The allure of narratives about real criminals to both readers and writers begun by the original *Newgate Calendar* in the eighteenth century continued into the 1890s and beyond. Thus it's not too unusual to find stories about true crime mixed in with collections of short stories following the exploits of a fictional detective. And then there was the influence of Bulwer-Lytton and Dickens with the so-called Newgate novel, the novel of social comment centered on sentimental portraits of criminals plus incidental interest in the novelty of criminal sub-culture and patois, folded in with praise for suffering and patience as virtues and reliance on Providence to solve problems. There was also the continued magnetic pull of the emotion-wrought relationships of the sensation novel—which lasted well into the twentieth century. Finally, there was the influence of notebook literature begun by *Chambers' Edinburgh Journal* at mid-century and continued by book publishers in both Britain and the United States for several decades. Fiction passed off as autobiography, notebook stories, exploited the public's interest in the activities of detectives and detection: thus Dick Donovan's stories told readers about how detectives find evil doers and, reflecting the heightened interest in forensic science, L.T. Meade and her physician friends told readers what physicians could do about crime. But detectives and doctors were not the only new things that could be explored and exploited in new detective fiction. Writers in the 1890s invented or discovered the unique capacity of detective fiction to absorb or reflect almost anything with which it comes in contact. And, gradually loosened from the constraints and demands of older crime fiction, writers found that in the frenetic world of turn of the century Britain and America there was a great deal of interesting, even inspirational, material to stir in with the inherited problem-solution plot of the detective story. Thus, for example, there was the new world of forensic science: as soon as news hit about fingerprinting, or blood typing, or ballistics, detective stories appeared centered on it. From the world of social controversy, detective stories quickly factored popular causes involving women, ethnic minorities (especially Indians) and even other country's anarchists into their narratives. Literary fads from orientalism to late Victorian gothic didn't take long to appear in detective stories. Finally, there was the technology explosion at the turn of the century which led to detective stories built around trains, motor cars, telephones, x-rays, cameras, bicycles, and even hot air balloons. In short, the new detective story reflected and responded to the same glittering miscellany of current events made interesting and fashionable by the new illustrated magazines.

The Survey

DICK DONOVAN

Even before Conan Doyle began to write about detectives, James Edward Preston Muddock (also known as Joyce Emmerson Preston Muddock) was busy writing short detective stories for English magazines using the name of their narrator, Dick Donovan, as his pseudonym. The first collection of these was published as *The Man-Hunter: Stories from the Note-Book of a Detective* (1888) and four more collections followed before the first Holmes story appeared in *The Strand*: *Caught at Last! Leaves from the Notebook of a Detective* (1889); *Tracked and Taken: Detective Sketches* (1890); *Who Poisoned Hetty Duncan? and other detective stories* (1890); and *A Detective's Triumphs* (1891). At least in the beginning, *The Strand* quite literally attached the Sherlock Holmes stories to Dick Donovan's coat-tails. In July 1892 *The Strand* chose the conclusion of Dick Donovan's "The Jeweled Skull: A Romance from a Detective's Case-Book" as the place to make the announcement that the first run of Sherlock Holmes stories was over and that Conan Doyle had yet to complete the next set of stories:

> [It will be observed that this month there is no detective story by Mr. Conan Doyle relating to the adventures of the celebrated Mr. Sherlock Holmes. We are glad to be able to announce that there is to be only a temporary interval in the publication of these stories. Mr. Conan Doyle is now engaged in writing a second series, which will be commenced in an early number. During this short interval powerful detective stories by other eminent writers will be published. Next month will appear an interview with Mr. Conan Doyle, containing amongst other interesting matter some particulars concerning Mr. Sherlock Holmes.]

Later that same year, at the end of Donovan's "A Romance from a Detective's Case-Book: The Chamber of Shadows," readers of *The Strand* (November 1892) found this announcement:

> [Next month will appear the first of the new series of "The Adventures of Sherlock Holmes." Admirers of that eminent detective are also informed that "The Sign of

Four," the story of the wonderful adventure by which he gained his reputation, can now be obtained at this office. Price 3s. 6d.]

It's not hard to understand why the Sherlock Holmes stories eclipsed Dick Donovan's efforts. For one thing the Dick Donovan stories, or the run of them before Sherlock Holmes, are decidedly products of the last generation of detective stories. The Donovan stories are first person narratives supposedly taken, somewhat randomly, from the experiences of a successful police detective, and, as noted above, they use the same kind of sub-titles as those used a generation ago highlighting them as excerpts from a real detective's notebook. They pay scant attention to delineating the character of the narrator, revealing only that (in most of the stories) he is middle aged. Information about the hero's employment is inconsistent: although Donovan is supposed to be a Glasgow detective, the stories also make him a detective in other cities in Britain, and at times he seems to be sought out as a private detective. Typical of the notebook police detective hero, occasionally the narrator mentions superiors giving him orders, the failure of others to solve crimes, and his own ambition to succeed as a detective. While the stories demonstrate successful individual action, they also sometimes praise corporate law enforcement:

> We thus cleared the city of two very dangerous characters, and for a time at least had stopped the wolf in sheep's clothing from preying on the flocks of human baa-lambs ["Wolf in Sheep's Clothing"].

Like older notebook literature about crime, the Donovan stories seek to inform readers both about what detectives do and about the ways of criminals. Largely readers find that what detectives do is hunt and chase criminals—thus collections of Donovan's stories and the individual stories themselves feature terms such as Caught, Hunted, Tracked, and Found in their titles. Background about criminals, however, is more diverse. "Doing a Fence," for instance, focuses on the operations of receivers of stolen goods and "Checkmated" discusses how criminals case potential jobs:

> It may or may not be known to the public that professional cracksmen almost invariably spend some time in investigating premises they intend to rob, and where possible they make plans and obtain impressions of locks. Of course I am referring to 'big jobs,' as they are termed in the slang of the burglar's profession. These big jobs are seldom or ever undertaken without preparation, and if the industrious gentlemen could only be observed at the time they are reconnoitering many large robberies might be prevented. By a mere accident of chance I had that night been present at the preliminary operations of zealous cracksmen, and I was resolved to spoil their little game.

While the stories do sometimes deal with crimes caused by passion or occasion, professional criminals play a significant role in many of them—and these portray the detective's role as protecting society from a variety of criminal classes.

Some of those criminals are cunning as are those in "Robbing of the London Mail," and "A Wolf in Sheep's Clothing," but some are innately vicious:

> He was, in fact, one of those born criminals who, like the fierce and untamable hyenas, should either be caged or killed ["A Hunt for a Murderer"].

Reflecting the continuing allure of true crime (or Newgate) stories, Donovan had a predilection for including accounts of historic crimes in his volumes of collected short stories: thus in *Caught at Last* "A Tragedy in London and the Part Charles Peace Played in It" tells the story of Charles Joseph Peace a notorious burglar and murderer from Sheffield, and "Pritchard the Poisoner" recounts the crimes of Edward William Pritchard who poisoned his wife and mother-in-law. The collection *Suspicion Aroused* contains an account of the crimes of Percy Lefroy Mapleton, the "railway murderer," and "Reminiscences of the West Aukland Poisoner" in *Who Poisoned Hetty Duncan* is about Mary Ann Cotton who may have poisoned up to twenty-one people. Footnotes in Donovan's stories supply the same function of familiarizing readers with the exotic world of crime and criminals—as well as adding to the illusion of reality he strives to create—as those found in Bullwer-Lytton and Ainsworth's Newgate novels. The other side of Newgate fiction, the emotional/sentimental side, comes out as well in a lot of Donovan's stories. "The Missing Heiress," for instance, in *Caught at Last* opens with comments about its "sensational" contents—and indeed the story is much like the stolen marriage, abandoned child, discovered heiress plots of both Newgate and sensation novels. On the topic of emotion, in 1894 Donovan published *Only a Woman's Heart: The Story of a Woman's Love: A Woman's Sorrow.* His November 1892 story "A Romance from a Detective's Case-Book: The Chamber of Shadows" in *The Strand* ends with

> Altogether it was a pathetic tale of a man's love, a woman's fickleness, and full of a great moral lesson which we who are not without some vein of sentiment may take to hear.

Sir Gilbert Campbell

Along with Donovan and Thomas MacNaught's difficult to find books *Recollections of a Glasgow Detective Officer* (1887) and *Thrilling Detective Stories* (1891), Sir Gilbert Campbell's *New Detective Stories* (1891) is another backward-looking sign of the times. To start, in the front matter of the first (and only) edition of the book Ward and Lock printed an ad for their list of "Popular Detective Stories." It's a list that (1) includes only novels, and (2) headlines books by three foreign authors (Emile Gaboriau, and two Americans, A.K. Green, and Lawrence Lynch), along with a miscellany of British books (*A Detective in Italy, A Mysterious Case, On A Winter's Night, Bazi Bazoum; or a Strange Detective, B Confidential*, and *Mystery of Mandeville Square*). More than that, of the dozen very short stories in Campbell's slight book only one of them has an actual detective as its hero: in "The Mark on the Mat" Edgar Bramsleigh consults "a private detective, one Matthew Wenlock." Wenlock hunts for clues as avidly as any of his contemporary brethren and sisters:

> The detective opened, this door, and scrutinized first the walls and then the carpet. All at once he fell upon his hands and knees upon a rug composed of some dark skin, bending so closely over it that his nose almost touched the fur. "Take care where you tread," said he earnestly to Edgar; "if I am not mistaken I have found the clue to the murderer's identity."

And also like his contemporaries he withholds that clue from readers until the final paragraph of the story. While several other pieces like "The Mystery of Essex Stairs" contain police characters, the only one of them in which a police officer plays an active role in solving a mysterious crime is "An Enthusiastic Official" in which a disgraced French police agent disguises himself as an old woman and exposes his boss, the Prefect: "When a medical examination was made, the doctors certified that he [the Prefect] must have been insane for some time, and that the idea of a well-traced murder case and the price he would receive turned his brain." Rather than concern with what detectives do, Campbell's real interest in *New Detective Stories* resides with passions connected with crime, including those to be felt by his readers. Thus his stories are not simply accounts of crimes, often they are out of the ordinary crimes. They take place in exotic places: there's France in "An Enthusiastic Official," Belgium in "A Dagger of Glass," Spain in "Extradition Extraordinary," Germany in "An American Duel," India in "The Star of Oranipore," and Australia in "An Australian Ghost." It is, moreover, not simply the exotic setting that matters in the stories, but that they center on crimes of passion committed by foreigners—just as do many of the contemporary Sherlock Holmes stories. Along with the antipodean spirit in "An Australian Ghost," Campbell plays with ghost story motifs in "The Miser's Hoard," "An American Duel," and "Hanged by the Neck." Perhaps partly because a lot of the appeal of Campbell's stories comes from focus on sensations, justice in the stories depends upon Providence rather than upon reason and patient scrutiny. Thus several of the stories ("The Dagger of Glass," "Hanged by the Neck" and "The Star of Oranipore") end with voluntary confessions, and in one, "The Mystery of Essex Stairs," a poodle reveals the murderer.

LUKE SHARP

Making fun of detectives was nothing new—Mark Twain did it with "The Stolen White Elephant" in 1882. A piece by Twain, "The American Claimant," was also the lead story in the first number of Robert Barr and Jerome K. Jerome's new magazine *The Idler* in May 1892. Later in the same issue "Detective Stories Gone Wrong" by Luke Sharp (i.e., "look sharp") appeared, suggesting that it might be the first installment of a series of spoofs of the detective story. The subtitle of the May story was "The Adventures of Sherlaw Kombs." There were, however, no further installments of "Detective Stories Gone Wrong." The next year, however, *Punch* did run a series of eight Sherlock Holmes parodies with the collective title "The Adventures of Picklock Holes." The story that inspired the Picklock Holes stories, "The Adventures of Sherlaw Kombs" in *The Idler*, was actually written by Conan Doyle's friend Robert Barr and it begins with the fond parenthetical announcement that it was written and published "with apologies to Dr. Conan Doyle, and his excellent book, 'A Study in Scarlet.'" In the story itself Barr included several good humored jibes at Conan Doyle himself: an allusion to physicians' ignorance of science ("These facts are unknown to you because you are a doctor") and the reference to Scotsmen:

> So great was Sherlaw Kombs's contempt for Scotland Yard that he never would visit Scotland during his vacations nor would he ever admit that a Scotchman was as fit for anything but export.

There is also the name of the victim Barrie Kipson which connects with Conan Doyle's friend J. M. Barrie—indeed, in 1892 Doyle went to Scotland to help Barrie with the libretto of an opera. And the next year Barrie himself wrote a Sherlock Holmes send up "The Adventures of the Two Collaborators" written originally on the flyleaf of the copy of his new book *A Window in Thrums* which he gave to Conan Doyle. Barr's story possesses ingredients that would become standards in what is now over a century of Sherlock Holmes satires. First come the names—Kombs and Whatson—prefiguring myriad variations on the theme of Holmes and Watson. Then come the idiosyncrasies from violin playing ("I found him playing the violin with a look of sweet peace and serenity on his face, which I never noticed on the countenances of those within hearing distance") to the scope of knowledge ("Kombs was curiously ignorant on some subjects, and abnormally learned on others"). Barr puts in several preliminary deduction demonstrations before the detective's detailed unravelling of the case of the dead man in the railroad car. And at the end Barr provides an equally detailed explanation of the same facts provided by Scotland Yard that proves Sherlaw Kombs' solution to be entirely wrong.

GREENHOUGH SMITH

The first hiatus in the Sherlock Holmes stories began after *The Strand* published "*The Adventure of the Copper Beeches*" in June 1892. In the July issue at the conclusion of Dick Donovan's "The Jeweled Skull: A Romance from a Detective's Case-Book" Greenhough Smith added the notice promising additional Holmes stories in the future. But before that, as the second article in the magazine (following a photo article on Queen Victoria's dolls), Smith published his own detective story "The Case of Roger Carboyne." In six pages (atypically short for *Strand* fiction), "The Case of Roger Carboyne" recounts the inquest into the death of the title character which focuses on seemingly inexplicable, enigmatic circumstances and evidence surrounding the discovery of Carboyne's corpse: (1) his riderless horse is found in the middle of a broad, snow covered area near the edge of a cliff with no footprints surrounding it to account for Carboyne's absence, (2) his body is later discovered on a ledge under the cliff from which he threw his field glasses to attract attention to himself, and (3) he had not been robbed but his knapsack is missing. After these facts are elicited from witnesses, a stranger enters with Carboyne's knapsack and offers a wildly unexpected explanation of the circumstances recently established. Before any of this, however, Smith opens the story with a summary which explains his view of the purpose of the following story and, by extension, Smith's understanding of the purpose of detective stories like Conan Doyle's which he had been publishing in *The Strand*:

> The mysterious and extraordinary circumstances surrounding the death of Mr. Roger Carboyne have excited so much interest, that it is not surprising that the room in the "Three Crows" Inn, which had been set apart for the inquest, was crowded at an early hour. The evidence was expected to be sensational—and most sensational, indeed, it proved to be. But for the even more remarkable denouement of the case it is impossible that any person present could have been prepared.

In other words, it was the ingenuity and surprise that mattered to Smith.

ISRAEL ZANGWILL

The Big Bow Mystery concerns the investigation into the murder of philanthropist Arthur Constant who was found in an apparently locked room located in the Bow district (Chaucer's Stratford at Bow) of East London. Since the author, Israel Zangwill, knew his Poe, he went to the trouble of cataloging all the means of entry and exit from Constant's rooms for his readers. Indeed, he also alluded to Poe's story in the narrative with the wry comment that "a professional paradox-monger pointed triumphantly to the somewhat similar situation in 'the murder in the Rue Morgue,' and said that nature had been plagiarizing again." The plot proceeds very much in the manner of Poe sourced detective stories: first the discovery of the body followed by inquest, exploration of clues, arrest of the wrong party, and finally the surprise ending. Along the way Zangwill finds means of visiting and revisiting the questions of how and by whom the murder was committed. Thus the story includes a coroner's jury, the introduction of two detectives—one retired and one a member of the force—the on-going debate between outsiders, and the introduction of letters to the editor to give readers repeated views of the celebrated Bow mystery. Each element provides Zangwill the opportunity not only to articulate the essential problem-solution essence of the detective story but the opportunity of developing characters that have been called "Dickensian." These go from landlady Mrs. Drabdump ("Mrs. Drabdump was a widow. Widows are not born, but made, else you might have fancied Mrs. Drabdump had always been a widow"); to detective Edward Wimp ("Wimp was at his greatest collecting circumstantial evidence; in putting two and two together to make five"); to free thinking cobbler Peter Crowl and his debates with poet Denzil Candercot about truth and beauty. Zangwill in fact adds a bit of comedy both to the tone of the narration and to his descriptions of most of his characters, down to the juryman who finds the reading of "Shoppinhour" (i.e., Schopenhauer) an incriminating pastime.

The Big Bow Mystery was published in book form in 1892, and is the first novel of the period to appear in Ellery Queen's list of the 125 Most Important Detective-Crime Fiction Books. It was not, however, originally a book; like most detective novels of the day it was originally a newspaper serial—in fact, it was the first serial published by *The Star* (a paper that owed its original popularity to its sensational coverage of the Jack the Ripper crimes in 1888), running in August and September 1891. But Ripperish anxiety and fear were hardly what Zangwill was after in his narrative. Like other detective serials of the period, *The Big Bow Mystery* was intended to pique readers' curiosity and engage them in a contest to solve the crime before the last installment appeared in print. In his preface to the bound edition of the novel Zangwill made his intent in writing *The Big Bow Mystery* pretty clear. First of all there is "fair play":

> And not only must the solution [to the puzzle] be adequate, but all its data must be given in the body of the story. The author must not suddenly spring a new person or a new circumstance upon his reader at the end. Thus, if a friend were to ask me to guess who dined with him yesterday, it would be fatuous if he had in mind somebody of whom he knew I had never heard.

But for Zangwill, playing fair does not entirely mean letting the readers solve the puzzle:

> The indispensable condition of a good mystery is that it should be *able and unable to be solved by the reader*, and that the writer's solution should satisfy [my italics].

The "able and unable" paradox lies at the heart of the detective story as designed by Poe—that is, the detective story is a narrative that gives readers the means and the motive to solve a puzzle which is ingenious enough to surprise them in spite of their efforts.

RODRIGUES OTTOLENGUI

Because the short detective story had not yet become popular in the United States, when Rodrigues Ottolengui, one of the founders of modern dentistry, started out writing detective stories, he started with novels; he wrote four of them (*An Artist in Crime* [1892], *A Conflict of Evidence* [1893], *A*

Modern Wizard [*1894*], and *The Crime of the Century* [1896]) before turning to short stories in 1898. There are signs in *An Artist in Crime* that Ottolengui was beginning to think of the detective story in a new way. One of those signs is the author's knowledge of Poe: thus Mr. Mitchell asks Mr. Barnes, the detective, "Have you never read Edgar Poe's story in which a letter is stolen and hidden?" A light-hearted wager that one of the principal characters can commit a perfect crime provides one of the structures of the novel. And, as in "The Purloined Letter," the detective knows of the plan and the perpetrator knows that the detective knows. Indeed *An Artist in Crime* is partly built upon solving a jewel burglary, a jewel theft, and a murder which become contests linked to the perfect crime wager that frames the novel. While he does not directly involve readers as other than spectators, Ottolingui does provide a chapter of entries from the detective's diary for his readers to consider, and at junctures in the dialog he has his characters decline to answer questions in an enigmatic manner. None of these, however, make *An Artist in Crime* anything particularly new in the detective novel line. Just as Conan Doyle turned to Gaboriau for his model when he started out to write detective novels, Ottolengui started out depending on the inserted narrative that revealed hitherto unknown facts to explain the mysteries encountered by the characters in the narrative. Thus near the end of the novel, Ottolengui includes trips to both New Orleans and Paris in order to explain the crimes and enigmas readers encountered earlier. Indeed, Ottolengui alludes to M. Lecoq in *An Artist in Crime* and as in Gaboriau lost love, betrayal, revenge, bigamy, and an orphan take over at the end of a novel that began with a glimmer of something new in it

HARRY BLYTH

Taking an altogether different direction, Harry Blyth introduced detective Sexton Blake in "The Missing Millionaire" in the boys' publication *The Halfpenny Marvel* on December 20, 1893. While directed at a different audience than that of *The Strand*, Blyth's character, like Donovan's and Campbell's, belonged to the last generation of fictional detectives, influenced by the sensation novel and Gaboriau rather than by Poe and Conan Doyle. Thus, in the beginning, the character who would become the hero to generations of British boys played second fiddle to a Frenchman, modeled on Gaboriau's detective: Sexton Blake's partner and mentor was Jules Gervaise, "the most astute of cosmopolitan detectives, the expertest unraveller of mysteries, and the most profound of observers...[and] terror to evil-doers" ("The Accusing Shadow"). While Blyth's stories included conventional detective story crimes like theft and murder, they quickly moved from glib examination of evidence and capsule deduction demonstrations to bringing in master criminals, gangs and conspiracies. Thus there's a criminal known as "The Slaughterer" in "Sexton Blake's Triumph" and the manipulative Julia Barretti in "The Accusing Shadow," while in "The Missing Millionaire" there are the "Red Lights of London," in "Sexton Blake's Peril" the "Terrible Three," in "The Golden Ghost" the "Zeefri," and in "The Lamp of Death" the "Sea Wolves." Blyth's Sexton Blake pieces in the mid 1890s also usually include a distressed damsel beginning with Rose in "The Missing Millionaire," and then Myra Finch in "A Christmas Crime," Daisy in "The Accusing Shadow," and Muriel Lane in "The Lamp of Death," thereby converting the motif of the suffering woman from the sensation novel into popular melodrama. The surfeit of action in the Blake stories has and perhaps ought to be connected with the importation of American dime novels reprinted in the 1890s by firms like Aldine Publishing Company. In 1894 Alfred Harmsworth began publishing *Union Jack* as well as his *Halfpenny Marvel*. The publisher wrote that *Union Jack* would become "a library of high class fiction," and, perhaps to that end, "Sexton Blake—Detective: The Story of a Great Mystery" appeared in the second issue. But this was Harmsworth's detective not Blyth's and the publisher turned Sexton Blake over to what would eventually become a congregation of writers whose first move was to shape Blyth's old fashioned hero into Sherlock Holmes for boys.

HEADON HILL

While most detective stories in the early 1890s maintained the old approaches to crime and detectives, new writers began to hop on the Sherlock Holmes bandwagon. One of the first of these was Francis Edward Grainger who wrote as Headon Hill. Just about everyone knew what Granger/Hill was doing. Thus, on March 10, 1894, *The Publisher* ran the following review of his second collection of detective stories, *Zambra, the Detective: Some Clues from his NoteBook* (1894):

> The public appetite for detective stories seems to 'grow by what it feeds on,' and each week sees fresh mysteries unravelled, fresh clues followed up by writers all anxious to partake of the large measure of success which has fallen to the share of the creator of Sherlock Holmes. Mr. Headon Hill has produced one or two earlier volumes of detective stories, so that readers know something of what to expect in a new book bearing his name. In the present book there are a dozen stories—some of them rather farfetched but on the whole entertaining and likely to please a large circle. Most of them, it must be confessed, strike one rather as sketches for stories than as completed wholes.

There's more than a bit of misdirection about Hill. As un–English as the name Zambra sounds, rather than being an exotic foreigner (a type of detective hero that would emerge before the end of the century) Sebastian Zambra was as English as Sherlock Holmes. Additionally, rather than being a feature of the first set of stories, *Clues from a Detective's Camera* (1893), the camera turns out to be an incidental adjunct to them; thus this offhanded statement from "The Case of the Sapient Monkey" in the collection:

Photography is of the greatest use to me in my work. I generally arrange it myself, but if you have chanced to take the right picture for me in this case so much the better.

Hill's Zambra stories originally appeared in the penny paper titled *The Million*. Presented in the traditional notebook format, they are almost all first person accounts of the "great detective's" cases: in the first collection the titles of all the stories begin with "The Episode of..." In the second book they all begin with "The Clue of...." Hill clearly presents Zambra as a private detective: he has an office, he has office routines, and he has assistants. And mostly, as did his literary forbearers, he treats the police with contempt. During the stories, often at the start of the narrative, Zambra makes observations about the story he is telling:

> Let me say here, in reviewing past cases, to recall the moment when the first scent of the trail broke upon me, and I know now that the thrill which I experienced at the sight of Otto Chetwynd's music rack was prescient of coming discovery ["The Clue of the Painted Missal"].
>
> The occasions are rare when, on starting on an expedition, I go to the bureau in the corner of my office and transfer from a drawer to my pocket a compact, but hard-hitting Smith and Wesson bulldog revolver ["The Clue of the Poppy-Head Pillow"].
>
> It is not an uncommon experience for cases introduced to my notice in a shape verging on the ridiculous to develop by sharp and sudden turns into phases of grimmest tragedy ["The Clue of the Haunted Houseboat"].
>
> The crime which they were relating to me ... did not, as will be seen, baffle me for long; but it was of a nature so entirely unique in the annals of criminal biology that I cannot omit it from these records ["The Clue of the Severed Hand"].

As with the Sherlock Holmes stories, however, these are not reader-writer games but narratives showing the hero arriving at a surprising, sometimes shocking, conclusion, the result of an ingenious interpretation of a clue based on a combination of the hero's acute powers of observation and encyclopedic knowledge ("Like lightening from a cloud, there flashed across my memory the old chemical formula the 'invisible words written in a weak solution of guaiacum and alcohol turn green when subjected to violent rays'" ["The Clue of the Painted Missal"]) or on patient research—which in some cases, like "The Episode of the Sapient Monkey," is done by his assistants, one of whom has a "thorough knowledge of the slums and the folk who dwell there" ("The Episode of the Sapient Monkey"). Often atypically short short stories, one of the remarked about features of Hill's detective stories at the time was their occasional sensationalism. Along with complaints regarding Hill's inaccuracies in details of post office routines in "The Postmaster General's Story," in January 1893 *St. Martin's Le-Grand; the Post Office Magazine* complained that "instead of logic and perceptivity Headon Hill gives us strainings after effect and elephantine gambollings painful in their grotesqueness." Perhaps the most absurdly grotesque of all of the Zambra stories is "The Clue of the Severed Hand" in which the severed hand grasping the dagger in the victim's chest was that of a woman wrongfully accused of romantic intrigue, amputated by her physician husband while she was in a hypnotic trance during which he made her commit the murder.

CATHERINE LOUISA PIRKIS

Women heroes were not entirely new to the detective story—there were certainly stories about women detectives before 1893—but in the changed marketplace in the early 1890s Loveday Brooke was new enough. And people took notice:

> We have recently been treated by many writers to lives, experiences, and reminiscences of various detectives, but something of a novelty attaches to a book dealing with the doings of a lady detective; certainly there is no lack of interest in "The Experiences of Loveday Brooke," although we may in reading them fancy that her powers of fixing upon a clue and following it up seem at times nothing short of inspiration. Some decidedly dramatic and tragic stories are among the seven different cases which Miss Loveday Brooke was called upon to investigate, and they are all recounted in a decidedly interesting and exciting fashion. The volume should be a popular one [*The Publishers' Circular*, March 31, 1894].

Catherine Louisa Pirkis wrote six of the seven of the Loveday Brooke stories for *The Ludgate Monthly* between February and July 1893. With the addition of "Missing" they appeared in book form as *The Experiences of Loveday Brooke, Lady Detective* the following year. As noted in *The Publishers' Circular*, part of the attraction of the Loveday Brooke stories lay in the introduction of a woman detective. Pirkis provides a brief biography of her hero in the first story:

> Some five or six years previously, by a jerk of Fortune's wheel, Loveday had been thrown upon the world penniless and all but friendless. Marketable accomplishments she had found she had none, so she had forthwith defied convention, and had chosen for herself a career that had cut her off sharply from her former associates and her position in society. For five or six years she drudged away patiently in the lower walks of her profession; then chance, or, to speak more precisely, an intricate criminal case, threw her in the way of the experienced head of the flourishing detective agency in Lynch Court. He quickly enough found out the stuff she was made of, and threw her in the way of better-class work—a work, indeed, that brought increase of pay and of reputation alike to him and to Loveday ["*The Black Bag Left on a Door-Step*"].

The head of that detective agency, Ebenezer Dyer, appears in each of the stories. In the first story Dyer makes clear his appreciation of Loveday Brooke as one of his detectives:

I don't care twopence-halfpenny whether she is or is not a lady. I only know she is the most sensible and practical woman I ever met. In the first place, she has the faculty–so rare among women–of carrying out orders to the very letter: in the second place, she has a clear, shrewd brain, unhampered by any hard-and-fast theories; thirdly, and most important item of all, she has so much common sense that it amounts to genius—positively to genius, sir [*"The Black Bag Left on a Door-Step"*].

The stories, however, show very little of "the first place" (carrying out orders), and a lot of the second and third place virtues—a shrewd brain and common sense. Indeed Brooke is not so much an employee of Dyer's private detective agency as the director's equal, and many of the stories begin with Dyer and Brooke disagreeing about crime-related facts. As the third-person narrator notes in "Drawn Daggers":

On the various topics that had chanced to come up for discussion that morning between Mr. Dyer and his colleague, they had each taken up, as if by design, diametrically opposite points of view.

In some respects Loveday Brooke plays roles circumscribed by the times and her gender. Thus Dyer explains:

But they want someone within the walls to hob-nob with the maids generally, and to find out if she has taken any of them into her confidence respecting her lovers. So they sent to me to know if I would send down for this purpose one of the shrewdest and most clear-headed of my female detectives [*"The Black Bag Left on a Door-Step"*].

While several of the stories ("The Redhill Sisterhood," in particular) emphasize the unique gifts and talents of women as detectives, the crimes Loveday solves in the stories are hardly limited to domestic kafuffles that need to be cleaned up and then hushed up. There's robbery, theft, house-breaking, and murder. "Missing," "Drawn Daggers," and *"A Princess's Vengeance"* may turn on runaway marriages and marital mysteries, but these subjects were also the staple of the detective stories of virtually all of Pirkis' male contemporaries. Likewise, although she sometimes assumes the disguise of a superior servant to gather information, in "A Princess's Vengeance" Loveday Brooke simply asks to be introduced as a detective. From her introduction in *"The Black Bag Left on a Door-Step"* Pirkis made her detective stand out by establishing her superior intelligence. First of all, she is focused and fast: Loveday's cases take only a day or two and Pirkis gives her readers the impression that her detective knows the solution as soon as the exposition begins. More importantly, Pirkis establishes her hero's prescience by the repeated pattern of Loveday, Holmes-like, mentioning two seemingly irrelevant and disparate items at the beginning of the action and bringing them together in the solution of the problem at the end. Pirkis makes the point at the end of "The Black Bag Left on a Door-Step":

It was not until close upon midnight that Mr. Dyer found himself seated in the train, facing Miss Brooke, and had leisure to ask for the links in the chain of reasoning that had led her in so remarkable a manner to connect the finding of a black bag, with insignificant contents, with an extensive robbery of valuable jewelry.

Equally apparent in a number of the stories is the point that Loveday could have revealed the solutions presented at the end without creating her own mysteries, but she chooses not to do so. To be sure Pirkis does this to embellish the surprise ending, but she does justify it by making it Loveday's response to the prejudice and arrogance she encounters:

> To be quite frank with you, I would have admitted you long ago into my confidence, and told you, step by step, how things were working themselves out, if you had not offended me by criticizing my method of doing my work ["The Black Bag Left on a Doorstep"].

L. T. Meade and
Clifford Halifax, M.D.

Eighteen ninety-three was a big year for detective stories. Starting in that year *The Strand* began a series entitled *Stories from the Diary of a Doctor* running in tandem with the last set of *The Memoirs of Sherlock Holmes*. A second series of *Diary of a Doctor* stories appeared in *The Strand* in 1895. Stories from the *Diary of a Doctor* were written by L. T. (Elizabeth Thomasina) Meade and Clifford Halifax, M.D. Meade became a name to be reckoned with in detective circles, for later in the decade she would team up with Robert Eustace to write *A Master of Mysteries* (1897–1898), *The Oracle of Maddox Street* (1898–1904), five stories about Florence Cusack in *Harmsworth Magazine* (1899–1900), and in the new century *The Sorceress of the Strand* (1904). The *Diary of a Doctor* stories are accounts of the real or imagined Dr. Halifax's involvement in a variety of unusual consultations. *The Strand* made a point of emphasizing their scientific accuracy when announcing the beginning of the stories in the second series:

> These stories are written in collaboration with a medical man of large experience. Many are founded on fact, and all are within the region of practical medical science. Those stories which may convey an idea of the impossible are only a forecast of early realization.

Indeed, Meade and Halifax began by starting the first story of the series with an allusion to the biggest name in real world forensic science, Alfred Swaine Taylor:

> By a strange coincidence I was busily engaged studying a chapter on neurotic poisons in Taylor's "Practice of Medical Jurisprudence," when a knock came to my door, and my landlady's daughter entered and handed me a note ["My First Patient"].

The *Diary of a Doctor* stories superficially follow the pattern of notebook literature found in the authors' contemporaries providing the allure of a behind-the-scenes look at the way members of a profession perform said profession. The *Diary of a Doctor* stories also follow the pattern of problem and unexpected solution associated with the new, post–Sherlock Holmes detective story—patients, their family members, or Halifax's friends seek him out and present him with what seem to be intractable medical problems which he solves. The stories, however, don't follow up on the promise of centering on technical, scientific evidence, knowledge, or specialized skill—the kind of thing seemingly promised by the mention of Taylor's *Medical Jurisprudence.* Only a few of the stories in the collection turn on medical-scientific evidence and pretty mundane scientific evidence at that—"My First Patient" has opium poisoning and "The Wrong Prescription" has morphine addiction. Indeed most of the *Diary of a Doctor* stories depend more on what might loosely be called psychiatry than on facts associated with medical science. The issue in "My Hypnotic Patient" is mesmerism, it's blind obsession in "A Death Certificate," kleptomania in "The Ponsonby Diamonds," amnesia in "Ten Year Oblivion," and suicide pacts in "My First Patient" and "The Horror of Studley Grange." "The Heir of Chartelpool," in fact, departs altogether from the world of objective reality and recounts Dr. Halifax trepanning a patient in a dream state. More than stories based on demonstrating science as fact or science as method, the *Diary of a Doctor* stories exploit the suffering of innocents. While a child is the sufferer in "The Heir of Chartelpool," the majority of the stories center on women—often specifically and literally beautiful women—who are threatened or persecuted. In "My First Patient," for example, an innocent wife is being poisoned by her husband in a plot echoing *Lady Audley's Secret*; a woman is made to commit a murder while under hypnosis in "My Hypnotic Patient"; and a wife is prematurely pronounced dead in "A Death Certificate." The stories in *Diary of a Doctor*, in fact, miniaturize the basics of the sensation novel—the suffering of innocents and the figure of the detective problem solver—and package them as entertainment to a new generation of readers.

ARTHUR MORRISON

Stories from the Diary of a Doctor took up some of the slack left by Conan Doyle's sabbatical from writing about Sherlock Holmes in 1893, but just to be sure, *The Strand* added Arthur Morrison's stories about detective Martin Hewitt as backup. Morrison wrote seven Martin Hewitt stories for *The Strand* between March and September 1894. The next year he wrote a second series of them which ran for a year in *The Windsor Magazine.* After the turn of the century a third series came out in *The Harmsworthy London Magazine.* From the start, the Martin Hewitt stories were clearly a response to and replacement for the Sherlock Holmes stories which ended (apparently forever) in December

1893. That *The Strand* assigned Sidney Padget to illustrate both the Sherlock Holmes and the Martin Hewitt stories is one indication of their kinship. Indeed Morrison's stories aim to be both the same thing as Conan Doyle's stories and to be something different. They have their Watson—Brett, a journalist, acts as narrator in most of the Hewitt tales. As in Conan Doyle, Brett plays the part of the Great Detective's student who is even subject to the occasional pop quiz:

> You often speak of your interest in my work, and the attention with which you follow it. This shall be a simple exercise for you. You saw every thing in the room as plainly as I myself. Bring the scene back to your memory, and think over the various small objects littering about, and how they would affect the case. Quick observation is the first essential for my work. Did you see a newspaper, for instance? ["The Case of Mr. Foggatt"].

But unlike Conan Doyle's roommates, there is rank condescension rather than friendship in the relationship between Hewitt and Brett:

> "I consider you, Brett," he said, addressing me, "the most remarkable journalist alive. Not because you're particularly clever, you know; because, between ourselves, I hope you'll admit you're not; but because you have known something of me and my doings for some years, and have never yet been guilty of giving away any of my little business secrets you may have become acquainted with" ["The Lenton Croft Robberies"].

Morrison, however, did take some pains to make his detective hero superficially different from Conan Doyle's flamboyant hero:

> Indeed, the man had always as little of the aspect of the conventional detective as may be imagined. Nobody could appear more cordial or less observant in manner, although there was to be seen a certain sharpness of the eye—which might, after all, only be the twinkle of good-humour ["The Lenton Croft Robberies"].

Unlike Holmes, who rarely speaks of money, Hewitt frequently makes it clear to Brett that he investigates things because he is paid to do so—in the first story Morrison repeats the term "business" in connection with his hero and notes as well that Hewitt's success enables him to increase his fees. In several stories, in fact, Hewitt states that he does not take cases out of humanitarian impulses or to vindicate innocence unless he is hired to do so. While the stories often center on the usual upper crust crimes—jewel robbery, missing papers, etc.—Morrison occasionally exposes his detective to other strata of society, as in "The Loss of Sammy Crockett" which revolves around the kidnapping of a popular race runner. Thus, "it was, of course, always a part of Martin Hewitt's business to be thoroughly at home among any and every class of people, and to be able to interest himself intelligently, or to appear to do so, in their various pursuits" ("The Loss of Sammy Crockett"). While not making him a polymath, Morrison does make his detective possess varieties of arcane lore—like the knowledge of Romany speech in "The Quinton Jewels Affair." As in the Sherlock Holmes tales, Morrison devotes conspicuous attention to the subject of thinking. Somewhat disingenuously he has Brett bring up Hewitt's lack of system in the first story—"Some curiosity has been expressed as to Mr. Martin Hewitt's system, and as he himself always consistently maintains that he has no system beyond a judicious use of ordinary faculties" ("The Lenton Croft Robberies"). Then, however, he goes on to devote seven of the story's thirty five pages to explaining how the detective arrived at his solution to the jewel robberies. Several months later, in "The Case of Mr. Foggatt," Morison in effect recognized that the stories were really about thinking and offered a name and explanation to Hewitt's methods: "Almost the only dogmatism that Martin Hewitt permitted himself in regard to his professional methods was one on the matter of accumulative probabilities." Morrison is arguably more knowledgeable than Conan Doyle about current developments in forensic science—in "The Case of Mr. Foggatt," for instance, he bases Hewitt's conclusions on bite mark evidence, reflecting contemporary developments related to the admissibility of evidence. Morrison also sometimes introduces crime-scene illustrations for his readers: torn pieces of a letter appear in "The Loss of Sammy Crocket," and there is a room drawing in "The Case of the Dixon Torpedo." These, however, hardly make the Martin Hewitt stories into reader-writer puzzles. Hewitt keeps observers in the stories in the dark partly because he has his own, proprietary "little business secrets," and he also uses tricks to achieve the necessary surprises in the stories: "Hewitt smiled, and patted his host's shoulder. 'I'll explain all my little tricks when the job's done,' he said, and went out" ("The Loss of Sammy Crocket").

M.P. SHIEL

Unlike the approach undertaken by Morrison and other writers for the popular press, in 1895 M.P. Shiel contributed a different, more radical variation on the theme of Sherlock Holmes, one based on a kind of looking backward. His slim volume *Prince Zaleski* (1895) contains three stories: "The Race of Orven," "The Stone of Edmunsbury Monks," and "The S.S." Technically they are detective stories—they all concern the solution to crime problems that Shiel, the eponymous narrator, brings to Prince Zaleski. And Shiel the author hangs them on the narrative patterns developed by Poe and made fashionable by Conan Doyle. Prince Zaleski, however, is a lot more like Poe's LeGrand, Roderick Usher, or maybe even Dupin than he is like Holmes. Just as with Poe's heroes, Zaleski is a ruined aristocrat living in exile who demonstrates his genius both by his seemingly limitless store of knowledge, arcane and otherwise, as well as his intellectual prowess. He participates with the world, however, only when asked by his friend Shiel, and in fact solves two of the "cases" without leaving his mansion. Shiel the writer divides the Prince's genius into two categories. First, solving most mysteries and enigmas is child's play to him. Thus in "The Race of Orven," for example, he knows the solution as soon as Shiel the narrator manages to lay the puzzling facts of the locked room before him. And in "The Stone of Edmunsbury Monks" it's just a matter of timing: "I may say at once that this meaning is entirely transparent to me. Pity only that you did not read the diary to me before." But there is another side to the Prince's character. As with Dupin, deep thought affects Zaleski physiologically:

> His small features distorted themselves into an expression of what I can only describe as an abnormal inquisitiveness—an inquisitiveness most impatient, arrogant in its intensity. His pupils contracted each to a dot, became the central *puncta* of two rings of fiery light; his little sharp teeth seemed to gnash ["The Race of Orven"].

These changes are but one sign that the Prince's powers go beyond the mundane:

> He seemed to me—I say it deliberately and with forethought—to possess the unparalleled power not merely of disentangling in retrospect, but of unraveling in prospect, and I have know him to relate *coming* events with unimaginable minuteness of precision ["The Stone of Edmunsbury Monks"].

Like Poe's heroes, Shiel's Zaleski is magnificently eccentric. He lives in a mansion as spooky and desolate as Dupin's shuttered mansion or Roderick Usher's house, furnished with weird bric-a-brac including a half unwrapped mummy. The gothic atmosphere of the mansion carries over to the mysteries the stories center upon. Of course there is a fascination with facts surrounding violence and death:

> There are, I assure you, to my positive knowledge forty-three—and in one island in the South Seas, forty-four—different methods of doing murder, any one of which would be entirely beyond the scope of the introspective agencies at the ordinary disposal of society ["The Stone of Edmunsbury Monks"].

Immersed in gothic technique, Shiel adds auras of age by linking violence and mystery with spooky bygone times: "The Race of Orven" and "The Stone of Edmunsbury Monks," for example, both bring in dark deeds from the dark ages. And as in Poe, madness is a central issue in all of the Prince Zaleski stories: congenital insanity in "The Race of Orven," a variety of monomania and mass suicide in "The S.S." and "The Stone of Edmunsbury Monks." Shiel put the patterns of the detective story to uses unlike those intended by other writers of the time. Just as the problems in the stories are not simply problems but exercises in gothic imagination, argument, becoming a basic element of detective fiction in the 1890s, is not entirely a means of arriving at or demonstrating truth, but a framework, an excuse even, for Shiel to unloose his luxuriant, allusive, self-indulgent decadent prose on his readers. Here is a sample:

Long, I tell you, long and often, have I pondered that history, and sought to trace with what ghastly secret has been pregnant the destiny, gloomful as Erebus and the murk of black-peplosed Nux, which for centuries has hung its pall over the men of this ill-fated house. Dark, dark, and red with gore and horror is that history; down the silent corridors of the ages have these blood-soaked sons of Atreus fled shrieking before the pursuing talons of the dread Eumenides ["The Race of Orven"].

It's just the way Prince Zaleski talks. And it's an early indication of the writers using the framework of the detective story to achieve their own artistic ends.

DAVID CHRISTIE MURRAY

Back in the mainstream, in 1895 a well-connected and popular journalist, David Christie Murray's collection of detective stories, *The Investigations of John Pym* (1895), got passable notices when it came out:

Mr. John Pym is a detective, who probes the most difficult cases with delightful ease and illuminates the most fuliginous mysteries with his lightning-like intelligence. He is, it needs scarcely be said, no professional hand, though he has relations with Scotland Yard. Like M. Dupin, or M. Parent, or Mr. Sherlock Holmes ... he pursues his own method and is in a sense "unattached." There is no lack of invention or of novel circumstance in these stories of Mr. Christie Murray [*The Saturday Review*, February 2, 1895].

Mr. Christie Murray is the author of several successful novels, and if this new collection of 'detective stories' does not take rank with the best of its kind, it is nevertheless eminently readable from first to last. There are half-a-dozen stories in the collection, all of which will be found decidedly exciting and interesting [*The Publishers' Circular*, February 16, 1895].

The Pym stories adhere to the established pattern of the Sherlock Holmes oeuvre—obtuse admiring narrator, eccentric genius detective, efficiently plotted crime problems with surprise solutions. Here's the introduction of John Pym in "The Case of Muelvos Y Sagra":

At the time of which I, Ned Venables, write, my friend John Pym gave little promise of becoming known to the world at large. I used to think him the most irritating man of my acquaintance, though he was for years my dearest friend. There was hardly a walk of life in which he might not have achieved success, and he did practically nothing. He has the largest and most varied intellectual armory of any man I know, but he has spent his life in furbishing his weapons and adding new ones with no apparent object. He studied by turns anatomy, medicine, chemistry, natural history, geology, botany, languages, and literatures; amassing learning at a frightful rate, and doing nothing at all. I am a man of action, and it has been the business of my life to lay before the public, piping hot, every new thing that I have learned and seen. To a man of my habits and way of thinking, there was something scarcely tolerable in the spectacle of this astonishing savant grubbing and grinding among his books for ever, and leaving all the wide fields of his learning sterile and unused.

This story, which opens *Investigations of John Pym*, also demonstrates the ability of competent, even affable literary style to blind the eyes of readers and reviewers: it is a relatively transparent retelling of Conan Doyle's "The Speckled Band" which replaces the trained snake with a South American Hairy Spider.

R.T. CASSON

In 1895 R.T. Casson followed up his boys' book *Will Evans Collier Hero* with two books about detectives—*Sam Smart, A Detective's Reminiscences: From the Diary of Sam Smart* and *Strange Cases from a Detective's Diary*—written for a slightly different audience—perhaps for newspaper readers, since Tillotson syndicated some of Casson's work. As the titles suggest, these are both collections of notebook stories, fiction written under the guise of autobiography. Each book contains eight stories which take place in and around Liverpool and Manchester and highlight the successes of Sam Smart. In several of the pieces Casson has his hero talk to his readers about the vicissitudes of his profession. First there is a backward-looking reflection on the difference between the status of a professional detective and that of the eighteenth century bounty hunter thief taker:

> The case would be a godsend to me, and bring business. But above all other considerations, it would release my old friend from prison and restore him to his birthright. I should be the hero of the hour. So far I had had little pride in my profession, for my father had not scrupled to call me a thief-catcher. What would he think of me now? ["The Deepdale Tragedy"].

Smart also talks about the difference between police and private detectives: "Some years previous to leaving the force, and whilst I was only an ordinary detective" ("A Fatal Piece of Paper"). He inserts a dig at do-nothing London detectives in "A Crime-Gotten Inheritance." And in a later story he reflects on the problems of working in a police department:

> Thirteen years passed away. I had left Manchester, the prospect of promotion being too remote, for I had somehow managed to get in bad odor with the "chief." I went to Liverpool, where my friend Dunn was head of the detective department, and was gladly welcomed by him ["A Fatal Piece of Paper"].

In spite of his name, Sam Smart is not quite the boys' story hero, and his are not exactly stories for boys. For one thing, practically all of them feature Smart's energetic and opinionated wife, Maria. Moreover, the narratives also present in miniature many of the elements of the sensation novel. Thus the problems they present principally center on illicit and abusive relationships between men and women. Some of the stories (e.g., "A Wife's Devotion" and "A Dastardly Husband") turn on mentally ill or vile and detestable men, a lot more (e.g., "The Deepdale Tragedy," "Big Blue Eyes," "A Cunning Woman," "A Reckless Woman," and "The Widow's Trick") deal with conniving, wicked women. The detection, likewise, turns on the same kind of thing as it does in sensation novels; thus the discovery of missing or forged documents—wills, certificates of birth, marriage, and death—loom large in the Sam Smart stories.

THE LONG ARM AND
OTHER DETECTIVE STORIES

Prize contests run by newspapers and then by magazines were part of the literary landscape since the mid–1880s. While some of these contests focused on different kinds of popular fiction (love stories, sea stories, etc.), contests having to do with detective fiction were the most popular. These fell into two classes—the guess the solution contest (which would eventually bankrupt Edgar Wallace) and the contest for writers challenged to submit the best detective story. In 1894 in the United States the Bacheller syndicate offered the mammoth prize of $2,000 in a detective story writing contest, the winner to be chosen from anonymous entries—entrants were to submit their names in sealed envelopes along with their stories. Bacheller, however, actively solicited stories from Mary Wilkins (Freeman), then at the height of her popularity, and Brander Matthews, Professor of Literature at Columbia University. The winners of the contest then turned out to be Wilkins in first place (with "The Long Arm") and Matthews (with "The Twinkling of an Eye") in second—followed by Englishmen George Ira Brett (who wrote "The Murder at Jex Farm") and Rev. Albert Eubule Evans writing as Roy Tellet (who wrote "The Secret of the Treaty"). While the authors' agreed only to have their stories appear in newspaper syndication as part of the contest, Bacheller went on to publish Wilkins' story in his magazine, *The Pocket Magazine*, and then resold the stories to Chapman and Hall in Britain who published them as *The Long Arm and Other Detective Stories* (1895). This is the book that Ellery Queen identified as the first anthology of detective stories.

The collection reflects a number of threads in the contemporary development of the detective story. First, it is notably transatlantic, containing both American and English writers, underlining the fact that by the 1890s the detective story had become an Anglo-American genre. The collection also contains a story that would later be classed as a spy story—the kind that was making E. Phillips Oppenheim famous: "The Secret of the Treaty" concerns international consternation regarding the theft and publication of a treaty, but can be construed as a detective story because the narrator ("I was at one time myself in the diplomatic service, as unpaid attaché") solves the knotty problem of how the treaty was stolen. "The Murder at Jex Farm" fulfills most of the criteria of the puzzle-based story. In it Inspector Battle presents readers with a variety of materials: his own narrative ("I like to put down my impressions on paper, pretty fully and quite freely, as I go on. I am doing so now, not as a report for my chief, nor for any sort of publication, but just as a help to myself"), an excerpt from a county newspaper, records of interrogations, pages from a suspect's diary, reports of a forensic expert ("*Sergeant Edwardes' Report on the footprints near the spot where the body of Miss Judson was found*") and ballistic facts. These materials lead him to arrest one suspect, and then an alternate explanation leads to a verifiable confession from another suspect. The fascination with scientific technology, specifically cameras, provides the central focus of Matthews' "The Twinkling of an Eye." Wilkins' story (co-authored by Joseph Chamberlin) likewise introduces machines (a microscope) and scientific method (the use of grids for searching), and together with the portrait of an enterprising woman protagonist "The Long Arm" touches on serious issues of appearance and reality and good and evil.

MAX PEMBERTON

Max Pemberton's 1895 collection of ten stories *Jewel Mysteries I Have Known: From a Dealer's Note Book* again looks backward toward the category of notebook fiction begun in *Chambers Edinburgh Journal* and more recently popularized by Dick Donovan's detective titles. Because most notebook fiction had to do with lawyers, police officers, or physicians, a lot of it centered on narratives about detection. The original purpose of the notebook form, however, was to provide readers with a glimpse into the routines of particular professions that captured the public's attention. That was why Pemberton took up the form, jewelry having gained increased public attention especially after the opening of South African diamond mines in the last quarter of the century, but it was an added bonus that crime was an occupational hazard of those concerned with the world of valuable jewels. Pemberton makes jeweler Bernard Sutton of Bond Street the narrator of the stories. Sutton's profession connects him with a number of detective story motifs—discerning the quality and provenance of gems, guarding valuable items, and protecting them from false claimants and thieves, etc. And while he is not a detective, it's a role sometimes thrust upon him:

> I have said often, in jotting down from my book a few of the most interesting cases which have come to my notice, that I am no detective, nor do I pretend to the smallest gift of foresight above my fellow man. Whenever I have busied myself about some trouble it has been from a personal motive which drove me on, or in the hope of serving some one who henceforth should serve me. And never have I brought to my aid other weapon than a certain measure of common sense. In many instances the purest good chance has given to me my only clue; the merest accident has set me straight when a hundred roads lay before me ["The Ripening Rubies"].

Sutton, moreover, is not conspicuously successful when called upon to act as a detective—he's robbed of the jewel in "Treasure of White Creek," he neither prevents the murder nor catches the murderer in "The Pursuit of the Topaz," and he is duped in "My Lady of the Sapphires." In "The Necklace of Green Diamonds" and "The Ripening Rubies" Sutton does manage success as a detective. In many of the other stories his role is more that of an observer. But what he observes often moves him away from the detective story and connects him with people who buy gems and jewelry and the passions that drive them—chiefly covetousness, pride, and love: "the heartburnings, the jealousies, and the crimes which hover over the possession of precious stones" ("The Pursuit of the Topaz"). The aim of a number of the stories ("The Opal Of Carmalovitch," "The Comedy Of The Jeweled Links," "My Lady Of The Sapphires," and "The Accursed Gems"), therefore, is to display the pathos that often attends the possession of precious gems.

HEADON HILL (AGAIN)

1895 was the year for detective anthologies, or miscellanies. Ward, Lock, and Bowen came out with *The Divinations of Kala Persad, and Other Stories* containing ten new stories by Headon Hill—four featuring Mark Poignard and Indian seer Kala Persad, two stories reusing Hill's old hero, Sebastian Zambra, and four others each featuring a new detective. Nothing binds the collection except its covers, the fact that all of the stories involve the solution of a crime, and the publicity stir caused by the publication of *The Long Arm and Other Detective Stories*. The principal draw of *The Divinations* is its exotic aspect—i.e., the introduction of Indian snake-charmer-seer Kala Persad:

> "Sahib," he said, "Kala Persad can read darker riddles than a man's face. In my own *gaum* in the hills below Mahabuleshwar my words were much sought by those who wish to learn secrets. When any person killed, or bullock stolen "—he pronounced itishtolen—"*patel* come to me and I give him *khabar*—news—of the bad man. Plenty people hanged in Tanna jail through Kala Persad's talk " "[The Divination of the Afghan"].

The first story takes place in India, but the rest of the Kala Persad pieces move to Britain where Mark Poignard sets up a private detective agency essentially founded on Kala Persad's divinations: the seer eavesdrops on interviews and divines the truth without seeing any of those involved or leaving his room. Readers learn little of Kala Persad's gift—how or why it works, particularly in a culture alien to the seer. What it does is give Poignard, the nominal detective, a supernatural leg up before he visits crime scenes and comes up with a rational, materialistic explanation of the crimes. The first story, "The Divination of the Afghan," reprises the trained animal killer of "The Speckled Band." Poignard's other cases, based on Persad's "divinations," rest on forensic facts: Tanghin poison, the Vagus nerve, and photography. Hill's mixture of the exotic with science and technology, however, hardly covers up his often cavalier approach to motive:

The point as to motive will never be quite cleared, but there is little doubt that Ames, who, it transpired, had pressed unwelcome attentions upon Mrs. Merwood to the verge of insult, desired to remove the husband in the hope of succeeding him. By the Merwoods' wish the real facts that led up to the Collector's mysterious suicide were confined to the four who knew them, and as two of these—Mark Poignand and Kala Persad—shortly left for England, there is little fear that the true story will ever filter into the *gup* of the cantonments ["The Divination of the Afghan"].

The four stories in the middle of the collection which serve as filler between the Kala Persad and Zambra stories wander all over the detective map. "How the Baby Found the Clue" is a retelling of an old story from France; "The Face On the Spoiled Negative" takes up Hill's interest in cameras reflected in his first collection of Zambra stories; "The Blind Clue" tells of a detective who is distracted from seeing the real clue; and "The Revelation of the Dark Slide" features a Scotland Yard detective and a gang of house robbers. The same lack of focus characterizes the two Zambra stories at the end of the collection—"The Secret of the Envelope," and "The Red Lamp in Hoblyn's Alley." The first, which Hill bills as "A Reminiscence of Zambra the Detective," is a hum drum plot where Zambra saves an innocent woman from false accusation by observing minutiae. "The Red Lamp" returns to interest in science. The narrator, Zambra's Watson-friend, is the maker of scientific instruments and he and the detective have been tinkering with "a new photographic thief-detector for use in banks, which we were trying to perfect." Scotland Yard calls on Zambra, their consultant for "those nicer minutiae which demand scientific knowledge," to examine fingerprints on the neck of a murder victim, and the story consequently becomes an early example both of fingerprint evidence and of strategies used to avoid identification.

Fergus Hume

A decade after his first novel, *The Mystery of the Hansom Cab,* wowed audiences in Australia, Great Britain and America, Fergus Hume published *The Dwarf's Chamber and Other Stories* (1896). Tucked away in this collection of nine stories are four about detectives—and those stories possess some of the features that would begin to redefine detective fiction two decades later in the Golden Age. The four are "The Green-Stone God and the Stockbroker," "The Jesuit and the Mexican Coin," "The Rainbow Camilla," and "The Ivory Leg and the Diamonds." First of all, these pieces all center on cleverness. To start, there is the cleverness of the wrong-doer. "The Rainbow Camilla" turns on a housemaid who contrives to be falsely accused in order to gain the money she needs to get married, and the title of "The Ivory Leg and the Diamonds" pretty much telegraphs the method of hiding stolen diamonds. Then there is cleverness of the problem solver. Thus the detective-narrator of "The Green-Stone God and the Stockbroker" says:

I think myself clever, but after that interview at Alfred Place I declare I am but a fool compared to this woman. She put two and two together, ferreted out unguessed-of evidence, and finally produced the most wonderful result.

But more than anything else, the tone of these four stories sets them apart from most contemporary detective fiction and anticipates that of Golden Age writers. First of all Hume sets about to define his stories by contrasting his heroes with detectives in detective stories. Thus

as a rule, the average detective gets twice the credit he deserves. I am not talking of the novelist's miraclemonger, but of the flesh and blood reality who is liable to err, and who frequently proves such liability. You can take it as certain that a detective who sets down a clean run and no hitch as entirely due to his astucity, is young in years, and still younger in experience. Older men, who have been bamboozled a hundred times by the craft of criminality, recognize the influence of Chance to make or mar. There you have it! Nine times out of ten, Chance does more in clinching a case than all the dexterity and mother-wit of the man in charge. The exception must be engineered by an infallible apostle. Such a one is unknown to me—out of print ["The Green-God and the Stockbroker"].

Then, Hume's stories have a light, sometimes even comic tone. More important than either of these, however, is the relationship Hume creates between his narrators and their readers. It is particularly apparent in "The Green-Stone God and the Stockbroker." Thus

had it not been for the Maori fetish—but such rather ends than begins the story, therefore it is wise to dismiss it for the moment. Yet that piece of green stone hanged a person—a person mentioned hereafter.

   The chain of thought is somewhat complicated, but it began with curiosity about the idol, and ended in my looking up the list of steamers going to the Antipodes. Then I carried out a little design which need not be mentioned at this moment. In due time it will fit in with the hanging of Mrs. Vincent's assassin.

What he does, then, is to use expectations about narrative structure to tease his readers, thereby creating a different relationship between reader and writer than in those detective stories that assume readers to be principally observers, awestruck and otherwise.

HERBERT KEEN

Beginning in February 1896 *The Idler* ran a series of six stories by Herbert Keen collectively entitled "Chronicles of Elvira House." Narrated by one Mr. Perkins, a credulous, middle-aged clerk at an insurance company, the stories take place in the Elvira House, the boarding house of the bird-brained Mrs. Nix and her ne'er do well husband, Major Nix. In the first story a detective, Mr. Booth, takes a room in the house disguised as a deaf clergyman in order to arrest an American con man boarding at Elvira House. Ostensibly retired, Booth is actually a working detective:

> He and I soon became very good friends, as he had predicted; but he always maintained the most absolute reserve respecting his former avocation. He let it be understood that he had retired from business, but I noticed that he usually absented himself for some hours daily, as though he still had some kind of occupation; and, occasionally, he went out of town for a day or two ostensibly to attend race meetings. This hobby, of which he made no secret, might have created a prejudice against most men, but in the case of Mr. Booth it was merely regarded as an amiable idiosyncrasy....
>
> Sometimes, as he sat in his accustomed arm-chair in the smoking-room, enjoying his after-dinner cigar, and listening with quiet attention to the conversation around him, I used to wonder whether this innocent-looking little gold-spectacled bald-headed gentleman, with the scrupulously neat and spotless attire and benevolent aspect, could ever by any possibility have been engaged in the stirring career of a detective or enquiry agent ["The Deaf Clergyman"].

Keen based his plots on Perkins' Watson-like innocence and Booth's knowledge of people—from psychological insights about personality types to the identities of criminals. And Keen based what happened in the stories on that contrast of naïve and worldly characters. Thus the tables are consistently turned when Booth demonstrates that he knows what is really going on and then explains the convoluted events to Perkins—and (the writer assumes) surprises the reader. Knowing the truth from the onset, Booth often treats the events in the stories as games. In "Herr Dolle's Diamonds" and "The Missing Heir," therefore, in addition to the guessing games he plays with the narrator, Booth also plays cat and mouse games with the criminals. That divertissement, moreover, takes away some of the danger implicit in the superior/inferior (or Holmes/Watson) relationship—the same motive seen in "The Missing Heir" when Booth saves Perkins' inheritance, and in "The Young Lady in Blue" where Booth and Perkins become temporary guardians of a fugitive's daughter.

GEORGE R. SIMS

George R. Sims began *Dorcas Dene, Detective, Her Life and Adventures* (1897) with a first chapter in which he created a kind of cozy domestic Baker Street headquarters-retreat in St. John's Wood peopled by Dorcas Dene, the second woman detective of the decade, Paul Dene, her husband, Dorcas' mother, Mrs. Lester, their bulldog, Toddlekins, and Mr. Saxon, the narrator who drops in so often he becomes an adjunct member of the family. In "The Council of Four," the first chapter, after Saxon gives a brief account of how and why she became a detective, Dorcas Dene tells him that the group at St. John's Wood acts as a sounding board and brain trust to help her unwind the mysteries she encounters as a detective. And in this role, her husband's blindness plays a significant role: as he puts it,

> Seeing nothing physically, my mental vision is intensified. I can think a problem out undisturbed by the surroundings which distract people who have their eyesight.

The history Sims created for Dorcas was hardly the product of enlightened times. It argues that aspects of detective work are unsuitable for women:

> If I found that being a lady detective was repugnant to me—if I found that it involved any sacrifice of my womanly instincts—I should resign.

And he grounds Dorcas' character on self-sacrifice from her early days working as a bit part actress to support her profligate father, to her work as a private detective to support her husband who was blinded by illness. Once the stories begin, however, all of this becomes framework. Dorcas clearly is in charge of both thinking and acting with Saxon trailing behind. In "The Mysterious Millionaire" she comes up with the idea of nocturnal breaking and entering and both procures the burglar tools for the job and has to drag the reluctant Saxon along. As in Conan Doyle, the stories depend upon and highlight the detective hero's intelligence, with the obtuse narrator occasionally serving to magnify the detective's brilliance. Indeed Dorcas Dene herself compares what she does to the exploits of genius detectives of fiction as if they were real:

> There is a mystery and a romance behind it—a tangled skein which a Lecoq or a Sherlock Holmes would have been proud to unravel—and I think I have a clue ["The Helsham Myster"].

While in several of the cases his detective appears in disguise, employing her talents as a gifted actress, and interpretation of material evidence plays roles in several stories, Sims mostly takes the problem-solving of the narratives off stage and, Holmes-like, Dorcas figures things out by herself and then tells Saxon. The introductory chapter, "The Council of Four," is followed by chapters about five of Dorcas' adventures narrated in groups of several chapters each: "The Helsham Mystery," "The Man with the Wild Eyes," "The Diamond Lizard," "The Mysterious Millionaire," and "The Haverstock Hill Murder." Unlike the idyllic frame of Dorcas' circle at St. John's Wood (and perhaps in contrast to it) and in spite of her protestations about the things repugnant to her "womanly instincts," the five narratives center on sordid, often sex-related crimes: "The Helsham Mystery" involves child switching and suicide, "The Man with the Wild Eyes" involves spousal abuse and suicide, "The Diamond Lizard" centers on a promiscuous husband, "The Mysterious Millionaire" has to do with bigamy, kidnapping, and attempted murder, and "The Haverstock Hill Murder" turns, once more, on a dead spouse. After all of these episodes centering on crimes reminiscent of those in sensation novels, Sims ends his brief collection of Dorcas Dene stories with several perfunctory paragraphs in which Dorcas reads a letter expressing a mother's gratitude for saving her son and then says, "These are the rewards of my profession, ... They compensate for everything."

ARTHUR GRIFFITHS

Arthur Griffiths knew his crime and criminals: he was Inspector of Prisons from 1878 to 1896 and penned such titles as *Mysteries of Police and Crime: A General Survey of Wrongdoing* and *Secrets of the Prison House or Gaol Studies and Sketches*. Beginning in 1897 he also wrote a series of stories for *The English Illustrated Magazine* which were collected and published in book form in 1900 as *In Tight Places: Adventures of an Amateur Detective*. These feature one Lionel Macnaghten Innes who, while stationed in India, was seconded to the local police and served as a remarkably successful detective until poor health forced him out of the Army. Rather than describing escapes from danger, the "in tight places" of the title refers to the fact that Innes has only a measly pension and foresees that he will have trouble making ends meet—in the first story at least. That's the first misleading element of the title, the second is the "amateur detective" part, for Innes both has had experience as a professional detective and once back in England becomes a paid consultant of the law firm of Black and Brightsmith. One could also quibble about the term "adventure" as well. Narrated by the detective, there is little in the way of danger or suspense in the stories, many of which deal with white collar crime (forgery, extortion, absconded financiers), and which Innes solves by knowing things, knowing whom to talk to, and knowing the local culture:

> My only superiority was a deeper insight into Oriental ways and perhaps a broader method of analysis, with more imagination in dealing with such signs and symptoms as might show themselves ["Yussef the Dragoman"].

Other than "Gasparone," a rare example of the contrasting treatment of socialists by police detectives in France and Britain, in spite of the author's experience with real criminals, Griffiths stories reveal little about the criminals. Indeed they are as much about exotic local color as they are about solving crime problems—thus the locales in Spain, France, and Egypt.

DICK DONOVAN (AGAIN)

In 1897 the latest of Dick Donovan's collections of detective stories was another of the expeditions into the exotic that happened in detective fiction in the mid-eighteen nineties. It is also a sign of how undiscriminating readers (and publishers) were about detective stories—the contents of *The Chronicles of Michael Danevitch* (1897)—are not, in fact, all about the Russian detective; a novella entitled "The Clue of the Dead Hand," featuring Edinburgh detective Peter Brodie, fills the last five chapters of the volume.

Donovan's Russian detective is another of the Great Detectives who inhabit the fiction of the 1890s:

> I knew then from the name that I had formed the acquaintance of one of the foremost detectives in the world—a man who had had more to do with unravelling political crimes than any living being; and there was hardly a civilized Government that had not, at some time or other, availed itself of his services. He was endowed with wonderful gifts, and having once got on to the track of a criminal the criminal was to a certainty doomed ["Introduction"].

The stories demonstrate his preternatural skill at disguise:

> It was known almost throughout Russia that this remarkable man had a protean-like faculty for changing his appearance. He could so alter his voice and features that, in combination with change of dress, he could defy detection even by those who were well acquainted with him ["The Mysterious Disappearance of a Million Rubles"].

But more importantly Donovan seeks to invest each of the nine Danevitch stories with an aura of logical thinking:

> In taking up a case of this kind, one must ever feel in the initial stage that he is groping in the dark; but the trained mind at once begins to reason the matter out, and the very first thing sought for is a feasible and probable motive. Motive is the very keynote in all detective work, and when the motive has been more or less accurately guessed, the next stage is to try and determine who was likely to have been actuated by that motive.
>
> No Chinese puzzle, complicated and ingenious as most of them are, was ever harder to do. But human ingenuity, coupled with exemplary patience, will accomplish much, and Danevitch at last succeeded in getting all the scraps together ["The Merchant of Riga"].

Consistently, however, the mention of logical steps and patient examination has very little of do with the solution of the crimes in the stories. More than being demonstrations of solving problems, the allure of the Danevitch stories lay in the exotic setting. In each of the stories Donovan doles out a portion of local color, from descriptions of Russian diet (iced fish soup in "A Modern Borgia"), to geography, to judgments on Russian law and politics:

> This arbitrary and high-handed proceeding is common to all parts of Europe outside of Great Britain. But though the liberty of the subject and of the foreigner is ever menaced on the Continent, and a simple indiscreet act may serve to bring the might of the law down on the luckless offender, this state of things is nothing as compared with that which prevails in Russia. It is a plain statement of fact to say that, of all the countries which boast of their civilization, Russia is the least civilized. The Russians themselves are a most hospitable people, they are clever, they make good friends and good neighbours; but their laws are antiquated, the method of government is barbarous, while the system of espionage which is in force all over the country would irritate a Briton into madness ["The Fate of Vassilo Ivanoff"].

The Danevitch stories all touch on politics in one way or another, but most of them (with the exception of "The Great Conspiracy" which is about an attempt to assassinate the Czar) center on the kinds of things common to fiction of the period—concern about circumstantial evidence, seemingly impossible crimes, and dysfunctional familial or marital relationships.

MATTHIAS McDONNELL BODKIN

The extended life of Matthias McDonnell Bodkin's Paul Beck and his family began in *Pearson's Magazine* with stories that were collected as *Paul Beck the Rule of Thumb Detective*, published in 1898. The "rule of thumb" phrase in the title, stressing common sense and routine versus genius, telegraphs a minor theme of Sherlock Holmes parody that runs throughout the stories. This appears in a number of places where characters (and Paul Beck himself) insist that Beck has no plan, no system, no method other than blundering about:

> No system, no nothing. He just blunders through somehow like a blind man in a fog, when those who use their eyes get run over. The proofs drop into his mouth of their own accord. He keeps it open on purpose ["A Miniature Halter"].

In two of the stories ("The Vanishing Diamonds" and "By a Hair's Breadth") Bodkin focuses the parody by contrasting his hero's proletarian lack of method with a thinly disguised caricature of Sherlock Holmes:

> "Of course you knew the face of the famous detective, Mr. Murdoch Rose. He doesn't object to be called 'famous.' I had hoped that you and he might work this case together. But he has gone off in a temper, and left me in a worse one."
>
> "It wouldn't have worked out any way, Duke," said Mr. Beck quietly. "He don't like me. He says—so I'm told—that I am the last of the slow coaches, that my brains are waterproofed against the teaching of science" ["By a Hair's Breadth"].

All of this is amusingly disingenuous. Other than being somewhat on the portly side, Bodkin makes his hero every bit the genius detective. He is a master of disguise (a plot device linked to magic that Bodkin uses in a number of stories), a master of minutiae possessed of encyclopedic knowledge and exhaustive scientific background (he uses x-rays, for example, in "By a Hair's Breadth"), and constantly capable of quick-witted cunning. The purpose of the twelve stories of course is to demonstrate Beck's genius and to try to differentiate him from the other great detectives peopling contemporary fiction. Rather than demonstrating the success of ploddingly mundane reasoning, Bodkin's method of making Beck and the Beck stories stand out is to center on puzzles and legerdemain. Mirroring a lot of talk in contemporary magazines about detective stories, Bodkin lets his readers know from the start that he intends the Paul Beck stories to present physical puzzles in which disparate pieces need to be fitted together, as well as intellectual puzzles. Coupled with his detective's disclaimers about possessing no systematic approach to problem solving, Bodkin introduces "puzzle" as a verb to describe Beck's methods. Thus

> but I'm a detective by trade. I've puzzled and muddled a few things in my time, but never anything queerer than this ["The Dog and the Doctor"].
>
> a man who had puzzled out the mysteries where even the famous Mr. Murdoch Rose had failed ["The Vanishing Diamonds"].

In "A Miniature Halter" Beck attaches his skills to one variety of puzzle: "I was always a first-class hand at conundrums." And in "The Vanishing Diamonds" Bodkin shows Beck playing with Pigs in Clover, a rolling-ball dexterity puzzle invented in 1889:

> Anyone with an eye to the key-hole ... might have seen Mr. Beck drop onto an easy-chair with one of the two cases in his hand, turning it slowly round and round with that look, puzzled yet confident, which so many people wore when that delightful problem "Pigs in Clover" was the rage.

Along with puzzles and games, Bodkin makes magic a major component of the Paul Beck stories. Indeed, the first story in *The Rule of Thumb Detective* largely rests upon legerdemain. In it Bodkin introduces M. Grabeau, whom he makes Beck's dishonest double. "The Vanishing Diamonds," in fact, begins with Grabeau disguised as Beck, and in the narrative Beck outlines his skills:

> He was a marvelous mimic and ventriloquist, a quick change artist, but above all and beyond all, a conjuror. He could maneuver a pack of cards as a captain his company.

And in addition to physical skills and the use of crowd psychology, magicians' tricks often rely upon clever, hidden mechanical contrivances. Thus Bodkin tells readers that among his other skills, Grabeau constructs mechanical devices: "In the construction and manufacture of mechanical tricks and toys he was possessed of a skill and ingenuity almost beyond belief." Indeed, with jewels apparently disappearing from a sealed box, the whole effect of "The Vanishing Diamonds" depends on the same principles as the magician's trick of pulling a rabbit from a hat. In the Beck stories aspects of the magician's craft inform Bodkin's plots centered upon cunning devices like the burning glass in "Murder By Proxy," or misdirection like the altered coins in "The Slump in Silver." That same craft also becomes a defining aspect of both good and bad characters—with Paul Beck being the most accomplished conjurer.

In 1900 Bodkin published *Dora Myrl, Lady Detective*, adding twelve more stories to the current fashion of depicting the exploits of a woman detective. *The Spectator* (February 24, 1900) greeted the book this way:

> Mr. Bodkin has followed up the lively adventures of his "rule of thumb detective," Paul Beck, with a companion collection entitled *Dora Myrl: The Lady Detective*.

Dora Myrl, we have no hesitation in saying it, was one of the most remarkable specimens of new womanhood ever evolved in modern and ancient fiction. At the age of eighteen she was already a Cambridge Wrangler; by twenty she had completed her medical education, given up medical practice, and successively occupied the posts of telegraph girl, telephone girl, and lady journalist. Fortunately for the reading public, she found her true vocation while acting as a companion to a weak-minded matron, who was being blackmailed by an unscrupulous nurse, and thenceforth leapt into a large and lucrative practice. Her methods, as illustrated by a dozen of the cases on which she was professionally employed, might be described as intuitive. She was an adept at disguises, and could pose with equal success as a lady palmist, a messenger boy, or a dapper little Frenchman. The society in which Dora moves is highly aristocratic; in particular, we meet with a Lord Millicent who is presumably the same as the Lord Mellecent who appears in a previous episode. But then spelling never was a strong point with the aristocracy. The book is full of absurdities and solecisms, but its simplicity and vivacity are irresistible. We may be forgiven for doubting, however, whether children of twelve are now sent to prison for theft.

As a sign of the times—as well as a sign of how the detective story was evolving—in 1909 Bodkin switched from short story to novel and in *The Capture of Paul Beck* (1909) brought Beck together with Dora Myrl in a plot that ended with their marriage. Three years later with *Paul Beck, a Chip Off the Old Block* (1911) Bodkin introduced their son.

Fergus Hume (Again)

Also moving from novels to short stories, Australian Fergus Hume's collection, *Hagar of the Pawn Shop* (1897), focuses more on the matter of the sensation novel than that of the detective story. Built on a frame story concerning Hagar Stanley's self-imposed task of running her deceased uncle's pawn shop until his heir is found, *Hagar of the Pawn Shop* contains ten stories organized by articles brought in to be pawned. In each case the pawned article yields a story, stories in which the exotic and sentimental outweigh the interest, presentation, or analysis of problem solving:

> Out of a giant tooth, an unburied bone, a mighty footprint, Cuvier could construct a marvelous and prehistoric world. In like manner, from some trifle upon which she lent money, Hagar would deduce tales as fantastic as the Arabian Nights, as adventurous as the story of Gil Bias ["The Fifth Customer"].

Thus enter murderous Chinese, Italians, and Persians, and accounts of tyranny, betrayal, and marital infidelity, all of which principally demonstrate Hagar's sympathy with the persecuted and her upright nature. Only four of the stories center on problems solved in the manner of orthodox detective stories. In two of them ("The First Customer" and "The Fifth Customer") Hagar, although minimally educated, solves ciphers connected with the discovery of treasure.

In two others she helps the police solve murder cases confused by misleading circumstantial evidence ("The Second Customer" and "The Eighth Customer"). Even in the detective pieces, Hume places more emphasis on the sentimental than on problem solving. Granted, he does occasionally mention Hagar's talents and these he usually connects with gender. Thus

> Hagar had almost a genius for reading people's characters in their faces. The curve of the mouth, the glance of the eyes—she could interpret these truly; for to her feminine instinct she added a logical judgment masculine in its discretion. She was rarely wrong when she exercised this faculty; and in the many customers who entered the Lambeth pawn-shop she had ample opportunities to use her talent ["The Ninth Customer"]

and

> Julf saw that the girl was shrewd and clever from the remarks she had made anent the pawning of the boots; so he was quite willing to discuss the affair freely with her. In contrast to many self-sufficient detectives, Julf always believed that two heads were better than one, especially when the second head was that of a woman. He had a great respect for the instinct of the weaker sex ["The Eighth Customer"].

Be all of this as it may, the Hagar stories are decidedly 1899ish:

> Hagar questioned her closely concerning the events which had taken place on the night of the murder in the house at Bedford Gardens, and elicited certain information which gave her great satisfaction. This she communicated to Horval when he one day paid her a hurried visit. When in possession of the facts, Horval looked at her with admiration, and on taking his leave he paid her a compliment.
>
> "You ought to be a man, with that head of yours," he said; "you're too good to be a woman!" ["The Third Customer"].

L.T. MEADE AND ROBERT EUSTACE

In 1898 L.T. Meade teamed up with a second physician, Robert Eustace [Barton], for a new series of stories, *The Master of Mysteries*. Their hero, John Bell, introduces himself not as a detective but as a ghost buster:

> It so happened that the circumstances of fate allowed me to follow my own bent in the choice of a profession. From my earliest youth the weird, the mysterious had an irresistible fascination for me. Having private means, I resolved to follow my unique inclinations, and I am now well known to all my friends as a professional exposer of ghosts, and one who can clear away the mysteries of most haunted houses.... To explain, by the application of science, phenomena attributed to spiritual agencies has been the work of my life. I have, naturally, gone through strange difficulties in accomplishing my mission. I propose in these pages to relate the histories of certain queer events, enveloped at first in mystery, and apparently dark with portent, but, nevertheless, when grappled with in the true spirit of science.

Meade and Eustace, however, hardly deliver much in the way of exposing ghosts or exorcizing haunted houses. While they do occasionally provide a brief nod to erroneous beliefs in the supernatural—"How Siva Spoke" is about a supposedly speaking idol, and "The Warder of the Door" is about a family curse— the core of all of the stories lies in solving problems, mostly problems associated with crimes. Thus the six tales in the collection focus on mysteries which the hero solves by discovering overlooked material causes which explain enigmas— material causes such as a coffin filled with magnetic ore which pulls an iron door closed, and "carbonic acid gas—the deadliest gas imaginable"—which accumulates when not dissipated by the air rush of passing trains. Indeed, part of the draw of the stories lies in the writers' introduction of machines. In "The Mystery of the Felwyn Tunnel," in fact, the writers portray their hero as more scientist/inventor than debunker of spirit scares: the story begins with "I was making experiments of some interest at South Kensington, and hoped that I had perfected a small but not unimportant discovery." While this hint lies fallow and the hero lacks any individualizing traits, most of the stories center on Bell's discovery of a machine used or intended to be used to commit a crime. This begins with the patently absurd reiteration of the dated bedroom murder machine plot in "The Mystery of the Circular Chamber" and continues through the midget submarine and diving suit in "The Eight Mile Lock," and the "wonderfully skilful imitation of a human larynx, which, by a cunning mechanism of clockwork, could be made exactly to simulate the breathing and low moaning of a human being" in "To Prove an Alibi."

The year after creating John Bell, Meade and Eustace began a series of stories about Florence Cusack for the *Harmsworth Magazine* ("Mr. Bovey's Unexpected Will" [April 1899], "The Arrest of Captain Vandaleur" [July 1899], "Mrs. Reid's Terror" [March 1900], "A Terrible Railway Ride: The Story of the Man with the False Nose [July 1900], and "The Outside Ledge: a Cablegram Mystery" [October 1900]). These replay patterns of the stories contained in *A Master of Mystery*. Although the Florence Cusack stories follow the trend of the nineties of creating women detectives ("As one glanced at this handsome girl with her slender figure, her eyes of the darkest blue, her raven black hair and clear complexion, it was almost impossible to believe that she was a power in the police courts, and highly respected by every detective in Scotland Yard" ["Mr. Bovey's Unexpected Will"]), Meade and Eustace's female detective is as underdeveloped as the male hero of *A Master of Mysteries*. She does possess a tragic secret that binds her to detective work ("I have no choice; I am under a promise, which I must fulfill" ["Mr. Bovey's Unexpected Will"]), but Meade and Eustace in effect make Florence Cusack into a secondary character in her own stories—the narrator, one Dr. Lonsdale, does most of the work. As in the stories about John Bell, the use of a scientific/mechanical device to commit crimes (such as the use of dry ice in "A Terrible Ride") is the driving force of the Florence Cusack stories.

RODRIGUES OTTOLENGUI (AGAIN)

After four detective novels, Rodrigues Ottolengui turned to short stories with *Final Proof, or, The Value of Evidence* (1898). By the time of the twelve short stories in the collection Ottolengui had redefined his Robert Leroy Mitchell, the wealthy socialite from his novels, as an amateur detective to compete with his private detective Jack Barnes. It is hardly surprising that now Ottolengui connects them with Conan Doyle's detective instead of Gaboriau's Lecoq; thus in the first story in the collection:

> Why, thank you, I will take some, but how do you know that I came off in a hurry and had no coffee at home? It seems to me that if you can tell that, you are becoming as clever as the famous Sherlock Holmes ["The Phoenix of Crime"].

Nor is it unusual that Ottolengui centers the stories on thinking:

> Mr. Barnes was wondering whether he would soon have a case which would require special mental effort in its solution. "Something that will make me think," was the way he phrased it to himself. The same idea had occupied him for some time. Not that he had been idle, but his "cases" had all been of such a nature that with a little supervision it had been safe to intrust them entirely to his subordinates ["A Novel Forgery"].

As in his novels, however, Ottolengui uses his detectives as more than characters and uses evidence as more than an avenue to proof. First, he uses both his characters and their discoveries as a means of providing structure for the stories in *Final Proof.* In one way or another, each of the stories is based both on the competition between facts and mystery as well as the competition between Barnes and Mitchell, one which Mitchell almost always wins. This provides Ottolengui with a way to present evidence, a defining feature of his fiction—and one of his contributions to the modern detective story. It is not simply that he presents novel kinds of evidence (there is real forensic dentistry with a facsimile dental chart in "The Phoenix of Crime" and x-ray evidence in "A Shadow of Proof") but also the ways in which he uses the competition between his detectives to reprise the evidence, an approach that defines his version of the detective story. Thus his stories typically begin with the development of a reasonable solution to the problem at hand based on the gathering of facts and building of logical assumptions only to have it overturned by another set of equally logical facts and assumptions. In the most complicated of the stories, such as "The Phoenix of Crime," Ottolengui's narratives present the readers with multiple, seemingly intractable problems and then put forth more than one answer which explains them. Ottolengui takes a pass at justifying his approach to presenting evidence by using the traditional scheme of amateur versus professional:

> I am merely a tyro, but not being professionally engaged on this case I was perhaps freer to see things with eyes unblinded by traditional methods of work ["The Phoenix of Crime"].

But the approach to evidence is about more than just bringing in new points of view: Ottolengui briefly alludes to the epidemic corruption of American police forces in the 1890s and the fact that one cannot trust the evidence the police come up with:

> But as for myself, I felt that I could not place this matter in the hands of men whom my husband always distrusted. Perhaps his prejudice was due to his politics, but he frequently declared that our police force was corrupt ["The Phoenix of Crime"].

More significantly, he brings in the courts as precedent with cases turning on competing experts:

> "But this identification was quite complete, being backed up by scientific reasons advanced by experts."
> "Yes, but did you ever see a trial where expert witnesses were called, that equally expert witnesses did not testify to the exact contrary?" ["The Phoenix of Crime"].

The real reasons for the treatment of evidence and the multiple solutions in the stories, however, lie in the world of play and games. Mitchell admits as much:

> Partly because I wanted all the glory, and partly because I saw a chance to make you admit that I am still the champion detective-baffler ["The Montezuma Emerald"].

Indeed, two of the stories in the collection, "The Missing Link" and "The Nameless Man," are pranks or jokes which Mitchell plays on Barnes—in the former to see if the body of an ape can be passed off as a human and in the latter to see if a supposed victim of amnesia can be identified. In Ottolengui's stories, then, evidence is ductile and characters take part in a game.

GRANT ALLEN

Canadian Grant Allen had busied himself on the fringes of the detective story for quite a while before the serial version of *Miss Cayley's Adventures* appeared in *The Strand* from March 1898 to February 1899. His "The Great Ruby Robbery: A Detective Story" in *The Strand* (September 1892) has detective figures and turns on a surprise ending. But confidence tricksters attracted more of Allen's attention resulting in the publication of his very popular *The African Millionaire* in 1897. Rather than being a detective story, *Miss Cayley's Adventures* is more about portraying a bright, independent young woman and is more picaresque than problem oriented—thus the plot follows Lois Cayley from England to Germany, Switzerland, Italy, and India as she serves as a lady's companion, a bicycle racer, a bicycle sales agent, a typist, and a journalist. In two of the episodes she does prevent a confidence man from duping others, an action based more on her honesty and forthrightness than any special detective qualities. In the final portion of the book, however, she saves her lover from prison (and penury) by foiling a plot using her knowledge of the pecu-liarities of type of individual typewriters.

After the Miss Cayley stories finished in *The Strand*, the magazine began running another series of Allen's stories which were collected in 1900 as *Hilda Wade: A Woman of Tenacity and Purpose*—for which Conan Doyle wrote the last chapter after Allen's death in 1899. The Hilda Wade stories repeated the essential elements of Grant's Miss Cayley stories showing an intelligent and resourceful woman confronting a series of obstacles, only Hilda Wade is a nurse, and her quest is to clear her father's name from false accusations of murder. Nar-rated by the love-struck Dr. Hubert Cumberledge, the stories bounce from England to Zimbabwe to India to Tibet and back to England following Hilda as she first keeps her eye on the malevolent Dr. Sebastian and then flees his attempts to kill her. Sebastian is an ineptly drawn Master Criminal with huge intellect and unlimited powers—he is behind stirring up the natives in Zimbabwe (echoing events of the Second Matabele War), and blood-thirsty Buddhists in Tibet in order to murder Hilda and the ineffectual Cumberledge. Several of the early episodes do center on problem solving—the second, for instance, involves exposing the true character of an adventuress and preventing an unwise marriage. Allen includes a Holmes-like deduction demonstration to highlight Hilda's intel-lect, and in the stories he also bandies about the term "psychologist" to charac-terize Hilda's insights into people and events. As in the Miss Cayley stories, Allen discusses gender-related differences regarding insight into said people and events:

> "Most women," he said to me once, "are quick at reading THE PASSING EMOTION. They can judge with astounding correctness from a shadow on one's face, a catch in one's breath, a movement of one's hands, how their words or deeds are affecting us. We cannot conceal our feelings from them. But underlying character they do not judge so well as fleeting expression. Not what Mrs. Jones IS in herself, but what Mrs. Jones is now thinking and feeling—there lies their great success as psychol-ogists. Most men, on the contrary, guide their life by definite FACTS—by signs, by symptoms, by observed data. Medicine itself is built upon a collection of such reasoned facts. But this woman, Nurse Wade, to a certain extent, stands interme-diate mentally between the two sexes. She recognises TEMPERAMENT—the fixed form of character, and what it is likely to do—in a degree which I have never seen equalled elsewhere. To that extent, and within proper limits of supervision, I acknowledge her faculty as a valuable adjunct to a scientific practitioner."

Allen, however, has Hilda Wade mouth one of the most misogynistic state-ments in an age of misogyny when she argues that a certain physical type of women are always assaulted:

> "THAT is what is central and essential to the type. They have THIS sort of profile. Women with faces like that ALWAYS get assaulted."

And the episode in which this statement occurs demonstrates the maxim and is followed by an episode expressing sympathy for the man who murdered his wife.

CHARLES E. CARRYL

Like Ottolengui's collection of short stories, American Charles E. Carryl's seven stories collected in *The River Syndicate and Other Stories* (1899) do not follow the Sherlock Holmes pattern witnessed in the majority of short detective fiction published in Britain. While Ottolengui takes a decisive turn toward the puzzle story, Carryl's stories take different directions. His third person narration inclines his stories more toward crime fiction than orthodox detective stories. Indeed he begins the first story of the collection with a realistic appraisal of police work:

> It being, as a rule, the appointed lot of the police force to find their experience in criminal matters somewhat narrowly confined to the sphere of the poor and ignorant, it is a natural impulse, peculiar to these functionaries, to greet, with something approximating relish, those exceptional cases where crime diverges from its customary channel and involves the clever and well-to-do ["The River Syndicate"].

In this case, however, the inspector finds only disappointment:

> The inspector, gathering the purport of this dialectical communication without much difficulty, at once recognized that instead of a highgrade criminal mystery, nothing lay ahead of him save a prosaic hunt for stolen money. This induced an immediate collapse of interest in Mr. Snedecor and his affairs ["The River Syndicate"].

Carryl's detectives, significantly, are all police officers versus the private operatives or amateurs featured in most other period detective fiction. They are competent but prosaic individuals—Mr. Moals featured in "The River Syndicate" simply shadows people around the city, and in "Mrs. Porter's Paragon" Mr. Stalker is introduced this way:

> Early the following morning the policeman reappeared, accompanied by a rat-featured gentleman whom he introduced, or, more properly speaking, identified, as "Mr. Stalker, from the Central Office," and whom Mrs. Porter, still in a condition of tremendous excitement, received with the liveliest anticipations as a person presumably gifted with almost superhuman powers of discernment .... Much to the disappointment of Mrs. Porter, who had confidently expected an immediate solution of the affair and a prompt identification of the criminal by name, Mr. Stalker listened to the story without any comment whatsoever, and then, escorted by Gerald and the policeman, made a careful examination of the looted quarter. The detective, a quiet mannered man, with eyes like a ferret, took in all the points with professional exactness.

Rather than turning on solving knotty enigmas, the stories in *The River Syndicate*, while occasionally (and atypically) paying lip service to criminal conspiracies (a criminal conspiracy lead by "The Baron" and "The Baroness" in "The River Syndicate" and a supposed band of anarchists in "The Pasha Club"), offer a variety of perspectives on crime. Thus "The River Syndicate" centers on shadowing, "The Pasha Club" is a practical joke, "Mrs. Porter's Paragon" is light satire, "The Asper Agency" is an almost naturalistic study of the consequences of crime, and "The House Over the Way," and "Captain Black" concern bystanders drawn into the investigation of mysteries. Failure of fiduciary responsibility lies at the center of four of the seven stories—which is not surprising as the author held a seat on the New York Stock Exchange.

RICHARD MARSH

In 1897 two smash hits of gothic fiction arrived at booksellers—Bram Stoker's *Dracula* and Richard Marsh's *The Beetle* (which was even more popular than *Dracula* at the time). In the last section of his phantasmagoria Marsh introduced a private detective, the Honorable Augustus Champnell. The next year he brought Champnell back in his novel *The House of Mystery* (1898), and as *divertissements* Marsh wrote four short stories featuring Champnell ("The Lost Letter," "Lady Majendie's Disappearance," "The Burglary at Azelea Villa," and "The Stolen Treaty") for several Midlands newspapers, *The Newcastle Weekly Courant, Leeds Mercury,* and *Manchester Times.* Along with ten miscellaneous pieces of fiction originally appearing in *Household Words* and other magazines, Marsh published his four Champnell detective stories in one volume entitled *The Aristocratic Detective.* The only one of Marsh's Champnell stories currently available is in the online newspaper archive of *The* [Christchurch, New Zealand] *Star* which reprinted "The Burglary at Azelea Villa" on June 17, 1899. In this piece Marsh left the lower-middle class detective of the Victorian sensation novel and introduced one who was a member of the upper class and who displayed the drawl and insouciance of the kind of characters who would later be drawn by P.G. Wodehouse:

> It may sound incredible to those who are acquainted with Lord George Carman, he actually betrayed symptoms of uneasiness! He looked at the ceiling, as if seeking for inspiration there, then looked back at Mr. Champnell.
>   "Fact is, I couldn't go to the beastly police, don't you know, really. So I've come to you. You're one of us. So it's different" ["The Burglary at Azelea Villa"].

"Azelea Villa" has a comic burglar, a petted and domineering show girl (Miss Tottie Darling), switched bags, and magic lantern slides—the kinds of things that would later characterize the exploits of Bertie Wooster. And since it (and the other Champnell pieces) was short newspaper fiction, the solution to the assorted bizarre events is short and snappy. That's why in their blurb about *The Aristocratic Detective* the *Eastern Morning News* wrote that "the whole of the sketches are vigorous and racy, being told in a lively, up-to-date manner."

C. CUTCLIFFE HYNE

Just as Richard Marsh's popularity rested on his immersion in the gothic, in the late 1890s the sea-faring adventures of the swashbuckling Captain Kettle were C. Cutcliffe Hyne's meal ticket. But Hyne, too, took time out to try his hand at writing detective stories. In 1898 his "The Tragedy of the Third Smoker" appeared in *Harmsworth's Magazine*, followed the next year by "The Banknote Forger." The first story begins with a mock protest about makers of detective stories:

> "I ABOMINATE detective stories," said the Q.C., laying down his cue along the corner of the billiard-table and going across to the shelf where the cigar-boxes stood. "You see, when a man makes a detective story to write down on paper, he begins at the butt-end and works backwards. He notes his points and manufactures his clues to suit 'em, so it's all bound to work out right. In real life it's very different,"—he chose a Partaga, looking at it through his glasses thoughtfully—"and I ought to know; I've been studying the criminal mind for half my working life."

Lawyer Grayson, however, proceeds to narrate two encounters with crime in which he begins at the butt end and works backward. In both stories he is confronted with defending a man indicted —in one case for murder and the other for other forgery—by seemingly irrefutable circumstantial evidence. In both he adopts the theory that another explanation is possible and then he (or in the case of "The Banknote Forger" his clerk) finds and interprets concrete evidence (the shape of a wound and a fingerprint) which exonerates his clients. Hyne's two brief stories, moreover, are as much about the joy of story telling as they are about problem solving. And they are also chances for the writer to revel in the casual, decorously insubordinate prose that was increasingly becoming the vogue among the smart set. Thus this snippet from "The Banknote Forger":

> "Now, savaging your own underlings may, as sheer dissipation and amusement, be very pleasant in its way; but it isn't solid satisfactory vengeance, and it has no connection with the *lex talionis*, both of which are far more businesslike and to the point."

HESKETH VERNON HESKETH-PRICHARD

In January 1898 *"The Story of the Spaniards, Hammersmith,"* the first of the Flaxman Low stories by Hesketh Vernon Hesketh-Prichard and his mother, Katerine Ryall Pritchard, appeared in *Pearson's Magazine*. In the next year all twelve of the Flaxman Low stories from *Pearson's* appeared as *Ghosts: Being the Experiences of Flaxman Low* (1899). Flaxman Low is "a noted psychologist." In the stories he evaluates evidence, forms theories, and explains phenomena no one else can—he acts like a detective. Except his solutions involve incursions of spirits into the real world:

> "To begin at the beginning," said Flaxman Low, "everybody who, in a rational and honest manner, investigates the phenomena of spiritism will, sooner or later, meet in them some perplexing element, which is not to be explained by any of the ordi-

nary theories. For reasons into which I need not now enter, this present case appears to me to be one of these. I am led to believe that the ghost which has for so many years given dim and vague manifestations of its existence in this house is a vampire" ["The Story of the Baelbrow"].

Earlier in the decade M.P. Sheil tiptoed along the line that separates detective stories from ghost stories, but in 1898 the Hesketh-Pritchards quite purposely stepped over it: *Pearson's* labeled the Flaxman Low pieces "Real Ghost Stories" instead of detective stories, and in "The Story of the Yard Manor House" the writers themselves tell their readers that

> "looking through the notes of Mr. Flaxman Low, one sometimes catches through the blue-steel hardness of facts, the pink flush of romance, or more often the black corner of a horror unnameable" ["The Story of the Yard Manor House"].

HARVEY SCRIBNER

Less conspicuous than Marsh's collection or Flaxman Low's encounters with unnamed horrors was Harvey Scribner's *My Mysterious Clients* (1900), eleven short stories, some of which were published in American magazines, and eight of which connect with contemporary developments in detective fiction. While the stories begin with "My First Client" and seem to adhere to some of the conventions of the notebook tradition (the use of legal documents, for instance, as the center of "The Romance of a Stolen Will" and "Was it Forgery?") the majority of them have to do with crimes committed and wrongs righted by characters acting as detectives. In them Scribner displays an acute interest in evidence: thus he presents an explanation of handwriting analysis in "Was it Forgery?" and a very early exploration of ballistics—along with test shots fired into a pail of water to retrieve spent bullets—in "The Grooved Bullet." At the same time, however, his lawyer-detective characters also depend upon the dynamics of judicial trials as a means of discovering truth. In "The Unexpected Witness," for example, Hoffman says:

> Down at the bottom the company is to blame. At present everything points to the conductor, but in the excitement of the trial facts will develop that you have not dreamed of that will show the liability of the company.

The use of the trial as a means of not exposing but of discovering truth was becoming one of the signs of the separation of lawyer fiction from detective fiction during the period. Most of Scribner's stories revolve on the actions of pairs of lawyers, pairs that inevitably consist of one who is young and energetic and one who is older, experienced, and universally knowledgeable. Thus in "My First Client" Fred Hoffman "seemed to possess almost universal knowledge. History, politics, philosophy, law and literature were on familiar and intimate terms with him." Although Scribner is hardly consistent about this, he also nods to the growing tendency toward developing the worthy opponent for the genius detective—"Such an expedient would have been brilliant, and would never occur to any one but a genius in crime" ("The Resurrected Witness").

Anna Katharine Green

When "Scandal in Bohemia" appeared in *The Strand*, Anna Katharine Green was the best known detective story writer in the world—in fact, on his first trip to America Conan Doyle journeyed to Buffalo to meet her. In 1891, however, her fame rested on her novels. At that point she had published only one collection of short stories, *The Old Stone House and Other Stories* (1891). Although all of the stories in that collection deal with crime and passion ("The awe of some tragic mystery" ["The Old Stone House"]), only one of them is a genuine detective story—plus an anti-detective story with "Shall He Wed Her" in which the detective fails to discover the truth. In "A Mysterious Case" a woman physician apprehends one of her patient's rivals after she witnesses her adding poison to prescribed medicine.

At the end of the decade Green assembled a second collection of her stories which was published as *A Difficult Problem, The Staircase at Heart's Delight and other stories* (1900). As in the first collection, *The Difficult Problem* contains a story about a political conspiracy—"The Bronze Hand" centers on a Civil War conspiracy while in the earlier collection "The Black Cross" concerned the Ku Klux Klan, and "A Memorable Night" involved German anarchists in New York. While Green continued to be committed to use her stories to explore passions, *The Difficult Problem* does contain two pieces (both significantly featured in the title of the collection) which correspond more closely with other traditions of detective fiction. Unlike the other stories in the collection, professional detectives narrate "A Difficult Problem" and "The Staircase at Heart's Delight"—indeed both stories are in effect the same kind of notebook fiction found in stories by Dick Donovan and other writers in the 1890s. "A Difficult Problem" and "The Staircase at Heart's Delight," however, offer two different kinds of pseudo-biographical notebook fiction. "A Difficult Problem," while possessing a sensation story background of emotional turmoil, focuses on the detective's description of the steps he takes in problem-solving: "I was confident that his death was not a natural one, and entered upon one of those secret and prolonged investigations which had constituted the pleasure of my life for so many years." In "The Staircase at Heart's Delight" Green brought back the detective she had used in the majority of her novels to date, Ebenezer Gryce, who begins the story with perspective in his career with the police force:

> "I was a young man in those days, and full of ambition. So, though I said nothing, I did not let this matter drop when the others did, but kept my mind persistently upon it and waited, with odd results as you will hear."

Like "A Difficult Problem," the crime in "The Staircase at Heart's Delight" turns on a mechanical contrivance. While "A Difficult Problem" depends upon the detective's use of reason to understand the crime, Gryce's story depends on the detective's encounters with suspense and danger.

Reprise

When Sherlock Holmes and his followers were created, the real world was a lot more dangerous and violent than theirs. From 1883 to 1885 Irish and Irish Americans carried out a protracted series of terrorist bombings in London, including exploding a bomb planted in a urinal at Scotland Yard. During her long reign there were multiple attempts to assassinate Queen Victoria, including one by Roderick MacLean who was incensed by the Queen's lack of interest in his poetry. Echoes of Jack the Ripper came in 1889 when the "Pinchin Street torso" was found in Whitechapel. During the same period, assassins killed two American Presidents. In 1886 someone threw a dynamite bomb when police tried to disburse the crowd at Chicago's Haymarket. And the murder of Police Chief David C. Hennessey and hysteria about the Mafia led to lynchings in New Orleans and a break of diplomatic relations between Italy and the United States in 1891. Additionally, during the decade of the 1890s there were financial panics in 1890 and 1893, and Britain and America were almost continuously at war with someone—from the Anglo-Burmese War to the First and Second Matabele Wars to the Fourth Ashanti War to the Second Boer War to the wars against Native Americans ending at Wounded Knee to the Spanish American War and the Boxer Rebellion. It's worth noting here that while newspapers and some magazines were intimately involved with publishing (and exploiting) sensational events like these, during the transitional years of the 1890s detective stories were decidedly not—they might center on crime and contain a bit of suspense, but no gruesome descriptions, no on-stage violence, no politics or social comment, nothing to disturb their readers. In large measure this anomaly—fiction centered on crime and violence that is not about crime and violence—was in part a response to what some publishers were looking for at the end of the nineteenth century. And *The Strand Magazine* played a seminal role in the rise of the new detective story. George Newnes, the publisher of *The Strand,* was quite clear about his editorial principles and stated them in *The Review of Reviews* the year before he published the first Sherlock Holmes story:

> There is another kind of journalism which has no such great ambitions. It is content to plod on, year after year, giving wholesome and harmless entertainment to crowds of hard-working people, craving for a little fun and amusement. It is quite humble and unpretentious. That is my journalism.

And so for readers "craving a little fun and amusement," in the first half of the 1890s Newnes not only gave them Sherlock Holmes, he also gave them most of the first wave of new detective story writers—from a retooled Dick Donovan to L.T. Meade and associates, Arthur Morrison, E.W. Hornung, and Grant Allen.

But it wasn't just publishers like Newnes who helped remake the detective story. It was the short story too. After less than a decade, because of its adoption by the illustrated magazines and popularity with the reading public, by 1900 the short story had become one of the accepted forms, maybe even the accepted form, of the detective story. Furthermore, it wasn't the same kind of short detective story readers found in the 1880s. Of course the popularity of Sherlock Holmes caused a lot of this: magazine editors and then book publishers were on the lookout for stories that appealed to the same audience and sold as well as Conan Doyle's did. But the form itself also had something to do with creating the new detective story—just as it did to Sherlock Holmes when Conan Doyle moved from novellas to short stories in 1891. As it evolved in the 1890s, the hallmarks of the new detective short story came to be problem solving, ingenuity, and innovation—all aimed at entertaining readers. Added to the space constraints of the short story, the new criteria also served to edge out or at least minimize both moral concerns about crime as a subject matter as well as many of the elements of the sensation novel that characterized a lot of detective fiction in general and short detective fiction in particular before 1891. Once preferred, by the turn of the century, pseudo biographical notebook stories were fewer and further between—mainly because of the emergence and popularity of a new kind of story-telling and a new kind of detective hero.

4

From *The Hound of the Baskervilles* to the Great War

After what seemed like an endless drought, it was what the world was waiting for: a new Sherlock Holmes serial in *The Strand Magazine* running from August 1901 to April 1902, and then, in 1903, "The Empty House," a new short story about the Great Detective—but this time published first in America, a month before it appeared in Britain. They both met with a far different reception than did Conan Doyle's first efforts to write detective novels and short stories a decade earlier. Moreover, they were not quite the same kind of fiction he wrote when he created *A Study in Scarlet* and "A Scandal in Bohemia." Although Conan Doyle has never had any real competitors when it came to detective stories, at the turn of the twentieth century he had more would-be rivals than he did when he began writing, a lot more. Then, too, on the new side of the century mark, in the world of the detective story, things had changed. This wasn't so much the case in Britain where writers continued with the Sherlock Holmes inspired conundrum/adventure story published in magazines like *The Strand* and *The Idler* whose principal purpose was to entertain middle class readers. It was in the United States where both media and readers were decidedly different from those in Britain—and they kept changing.

As in Britain, in the U.S. from the 1860s until the 1890s a number of different kinds of media and different kinds of audiences existed for the detective story. Thus, before Sherlock Holmes, genteel readers read sensation novels like *The Dead Letter* and *The Leavenworth Case*, adolescents consumed dime novels about Old Sleuth and other harum-scarum heroes, and the majority of readers followed detective stories in their daily or weekly newspapers. The latter were meant to be read quickly—along with news, human interest pieces, and advertising. In order to move to the kind of short detective story form developing (mainly) in England, the majority of readers attracted to detective stories had to become accustomed to longer short fiction. For Americans S.S. McClure and Sherlock Holmes did just that. S.S. McClure bought the American rights to the first set of Conan Doyle's stories and, beginning in July 1891, his syndicate sold rights to them to newspapers across the U.S. But, as McClure reflected in his autobiography, it took a while for readers in the U.S. to warm up to longer fiction:

> When I began to syndicate the Sherlock Holmes stories, they were not at all popular with editors. The usual syndicate story ran about five thousand words, and these ran up to eight and nine thousand. We got a good many complaints from editors about their length, and it was not until nearly all of the first twelve of the Sherlock Holmes stories had been published, that the editors of the papers I served began to comment favorably upon the series and that the public began to take a keen interest [*My Autobiography*, 1914].

While detective short stories and serials were published in newspapers in the U.S. relatively continuously from the 1830s until the 1940s, their history in "literary," middle class magazines was less continuous. *Harper's, Scribner's, Lippincott's, The Atlantic*, etc. all published detective stories until the 1860s when they stopped and, in effect, relinquished the form to story papers, dime novels, and newspapers. At the turn of the century, however, a new kind of magazine emerged in the United States—a kind of magazine devoted to exposing the manifold corporate and governmental corruption which had become routine in the country. These were the muckraking magazines: *McClure's, Collier's, Everybody's, The American, Hampton's*, and, reinvigorated, *Harper's Weekly*. At the turn of the century these journals ran exposés of Standard Oil, the meat packing industry, patent medicine manufacturers, politics, and other corrupt enterprises. They also took a close look at the police. On the positive side, S.S. McClure financed Ida Tarbell's articles about the wonders of Alphonse Bertillon and the Paris crime lab, and published a series of articles about the successes of both the Pinkertons and the "Great Cases of Detective [William J.] Burns." Although embarrassed by the 1894–1895 Lexow investigation which revealed wholesale corruption in the New York Police Department, Inspector Thomas Byrnes came back as a hero both in Hawthorne's notebook novels and in *Harper's* 1905 "Recollections of a Police Inspector." But a much darker view of the police supplanted the accounts of their successes. Lincoln Steffens discovered systemic graft in police departments across the country in his pieces in *McClure's* that would become *The Shame of the Cities* (1904). In 1900, anticipating the Wickersham Commission's scathing report by more than 30 years, Peter McArthur wrote about police use of the "third degree" in *Everybody's*. *Harper's* in 1907 published a piece entitled "New York's Secret Police," and, comparing the New York City police to the Mafia, *Collier's* came out with "The Police Camorra" in 1909. At the same time that these magazines campaigned against police corruption, brutality, wire-tapping, and widespread violations of *habeas corpus* and other civil rights, they became enthusiastic purchasers and publishers of contemporary British detective fiction. Thus in 1893 *Harper's* published all of the second series of Sherlock Holmes stories—with the exception of "The Final Problem" which *McClure's* somehow snagged. *McClure's* also became the American publisher of R. Austin Freeman and G.K. Chesterton. *Collier's* outbid rivals for the third set of Sherlock Holmes stories—indeed published them before they appeared in *The Strand*. *Everybody's* printed Hornung's Crime Doctor stories, and *Hampton's* published Edgar Jepson's detective fiction. And this made for very, very strange bedfellows indeed, bringing together journalistic crusades against epidemic police brutality and corruption with fiction founded upon genius detective and intellectual playfulness. But the muckraking journals didn't just publish imported detective fiction—their own writers, the same ones devoted to exposing the moral rot in American business and government, started to write their own detective stories. Thus *McClure's* carried detective stories by Cleveland Moffit, Flynt and Walton, Harvey O'Higgins, and Arthur B. Reeve; *Collier's* also published Harvey O'Higgins; *The American Magazine* published Arthur Train and one of the biggest names in muckraking, Lincoln Steffens; stories by Arthur Train crop up, along with those by Arthur Stringer, in *Everybody's*; *Hampton's* had Edwin Balmer and William B. McHarg; and, although somewhat off the muckraking reservation, *Success Magazine* published Samuel Hopkins Adams. Just as in the 1890s, in the first decade of the twentieth century it was difficult to pick up a middle class magazine that did not contain at least one detective story—only this time it wasn't just in Britain, it was in the United States too.

The Survey

L.T. MEADE AND ROBERT EUSTACE (AGAIN)

L.T. Meade and Robert Eustace may have played around a bit with the occult in *The Master of Mysteries* (1898), but in the new century they leaned upon it more heavily with their stories about their second woman detective, Diana Marburg, the "Oracle of Maddox Street," published in *Pearson's,* and the stories about her evil counterpart, Madame Sara, "The Sorceress of the Strand," published in *The Strand* beginning later in 1902 and collected in book form in 1904. In the former series they took a bit of the occult from their concept of detective John Bell in *The Master of Mysteries* and introduced their second woman detective, thought reader and palmist Diana Marburg, the "Oracle of Maddox Street":

> My name is Diana Marburg. I am a palmist by profession. Occult phenomena, spiritualism, clairvoyance, and many other strange mysteries of the unseen world, have, from my earliest years, excited my keen interest ["The Dead Hand"].

Marburg appeared in three stories in *Pearson's Magazine* ("The Dead Hand" [January 1902], "Finger Tips" [August 1902], and "Sir Penn Caryll's Engagement" [December 1902]). These were reprinted along with seven other miscellaneous stories (including "The Secret of Emu Plain" written for a story prize competition in *Cassell's Magazine*) as *The Oracle of Maddox Street* in 1904. While the writers include bits of palm reading and associated character analysis in each of the stories, the narratives rest most securely on the effect of the technical/scientific material introduced in the solution to crimes. Thus, one finds stories turning on an electric eel, Morse code transmitted by blinking, and an early example of the use of fingerprints:

> I felt myself turning pale as I noticed them, for I saw that, by leaving these marks of the finger-tips, poor Captain Cunnyngham had doubly convicted himself of the crime; as surely, in fact, as if he had confessed it fully. I remembered Professor Galton's well-known and exhaustive researches on finger-prints, the fact which he has abundantly proved being that no two persons in the world have the same skin ridges, and also that these ridges never alter in the most remote degree, except in growth, from babyhood to old age ["Fingertips"].

BARONESS ORCZY

Baroness Emmuska Magdalena Rosalia Maria Josefa Barbara Orczy wrote a lot of detective stories. Her first set of stories began in *The Royal Magazine* in 1901 and featured a cranky, obsessive-compulsive, anonymous old man—the Old Man in the Corner. The Old Man became so popular that *The Royal Magazine* carried a drawing of the character on the cover of its April 1902 number and included a photo and a brief biography of the author following her Old Man story "The Glasgow Mystery." The Old Man in the Corner appeared first in *The Royal* with "The Mysteries of London," a run of six stories set in the British capitol ("The Fenchurch Street Mystery," etc.), then in "The Mysteries of Great Britain," a run of seven stories set in major British cities ("The York Mystery," "The Glasgow Mystery," etc.), and then in miscellaneous stories published until 1908. A number of Orczy's earliest Old Man stories were published in book form in *The Old Man in the Corner* (1908), but the first collection of stories about him was *The Case of Miss Elliott* (1905) containing twelve stories published in *The Royal Magazine* from 1904 to 1905. On one hand there was not a lot of daring in the plots of Orczy's Old Man stories. Pretty much she either gathered together old chestnuts like the inheritance plot ("The Tragedy in Dartmoor Terrace"), or the self-sacrifice plot ("The Ayrsham Mystery"), or she brought in popular topics from jewel theft ("Who Stole the Black Diamonds?") to horse racing ("The Hocussing of Cigarette"). Orczy brings anarchists into "The Fate of the Artemis," reflecting the rippling tensions brought about by the events in Russia which led to the 1905 revolution. And, looking backward to the women detectives in the 1890s and forward to her Lady Molly stories, the Old Man stories contain some contemporary, tactful feminism (the series narrator is a woman newspaper reporter, and Miss Elliott of "The Case of Miss Elliott" is "a good-looking, youngish, lady-like woman, fully qualified in the medical profession and in charge of the Convalescent Home in Suffolk Avenue"). Often Orczy's plots rely upon impersonation, and the theater plays a significant role in a number of the Old Man stories. Her earliest stories present readers with formal lists of *dramatis personae* after their titles, and their division into four numbered parts is reminiscent of the structure of a four act play. Like many of her contemporaries, Orczy knew that some of the allure of the detective story lay in the narration and the narrator. It's what *The Royal* advertised in April 1902:

> LAST September the *Royal Magazine* published the finish of a series of thrilling and cleverly conceived detective stories entitled, "London Mysteries," told to a lady journalist by a remarkable personage who goes by the name of "The Man in the Corner," since he always sits in one particular corner in the A.B.C. shop, where he is interviewed. His chief peculiarity is the knotted string in his fingers and his glass of milk at his side.

Remarkable he may be, but he is more Coleridge's gray-beard loon than the avuncular-looking cover portrait in the *Royal*. Orczy makes the Old Man obsessed with newspaper accounts of crime and attending inquests, almost physically dependant on having string to knot as he speaks, and irascible and unpredictable ("I had no wish to make a remark, knowing of old that my one chance of getting the whole of his interesting argument was to offer neither comment nor contradiction ["The Case of Miss Elliott"]). He's sarcastic:

> "What do you mean?" I asked.
>
> "Do you mean to say you never thought of the real solution of this mystery?" he retorted sarcastically.
>
> "I confess—" I began a little irritably.
>
> "Confess that I have not yet taught you to think logically, and to look at the beginning of things" ["The Murder of Miss Pebmarsh"].

Both the Old Man and the journalist narrator emphasize the emotional, sensational impact of the narratives:

> I, of course, was at my usual place—well to the front—for I was already keenly interested in the tragedy, and knew that a palpitating mystery lurked behind the old lady's death ["The Tragedy at Dartmoor Terrace"].
>
> "There was yet another act in that palpitating drama of her life—one act—the dénouement as unexpected as it was thrilling" ["The Murder of Miss Pebmarsh"].

But they also tell readers that the stories are about the solutions to puzzles, solutions that, except for the readers, no one (especially the police) listens to and which will (publicly at least) remain unsolved.

Bertram Fletcher Robinson

Enormous, vicious dogs, it seems, were much on writers' minds at the turn of the century. There was Conan Doyle's "gigantic hound" from August 1901 to April 1902, and the next year *The Strand* published "The Teeth of the Wolf," the last of the Sorceress of the Strand stories. Antedating both, however, was the trip from South Africa during which Bertram Fletcher Robinson told Conan Doyle the stories about Dartmoor and legends of monstrous hounds which became *The Hound of the Baskerville*—and during which Robinson wrote up the legends himself as "The Terror in the Snow," a story eventually published in *The Ladies Home Magazine* in 1904. Indeed Robinson's "The Vanished Millionaire" (aka "The Vanished Billionaire") in *Pearson's* adds "Collaborator with A. Conan Doyle of 'The Hound of the Baskervilles'" after the author's name. "The Vanished Millionaire" with seven other pieces were published in book form as *The Chronicles of Addington Peace* (1905). It goes without saying, however, that in the world of the detective story Robinson owed more to Conan Doyle that Conan Doyle owed to him. First there are the characters and the story telling. An artist-turned enthusiastic amateur detective, Mr. Phillips, chronicles the cases of brilliant detective Addington Peace. Unlike Holmes, Peace is an official, Scotland Yard detective policeman, and he is hardly physically memorable—"He was a tiny slip of a fellow, of about five and thirty years of age. A stubble of brown hair, a hard, clean-shaven mouth, and a confident chin—such was my impression" ("The Story of Amaroff the Pole"). Other than the official title and unimpressive physique, however, Robinson does little to differentiate his detective from the assemblage of private and amateur detectives in the pages of contemporary magazines who prove their intellectual metal by means of inserted deduction demonstrations ("He had been called away in a hurry. There was modeling clay in his finger-nails, and a slash of plaster on his right trouser leg. It is really quite simple, you see" ["The Story of Amaroff the Pole"]); and who solve crime problems with surprises, like footsteps in the snow that stop ("The Vanished Millionaire"), a wolf and a naked man ("The Terror in the Snow"), and a locked room and a hobby horse ("Mr. Taubery's Diamond"). The one variation of a theme apparent in Robinson's chronicles of detective Peace is what he does with Phillips in the first few stories. From Poe to Conan Doyle both hero-worship and pedagogy define the relationship between detective and narrator. Although those elements certainly contribute to the detective-narrator relationship in Robinson's stories, he adds a Victorian lotus-eaters theme. Thus he draws Phillips as an aesthete disdainful of the sordid realities of life:

> He asked me to go into a part of London that I had always carefully avoided. It was sufficient to know that filth, immorality, and crime exist without personally inspecting the muck-heap ["The Story of Amaroff the Pole"].

The detective, however, offers him a new life of excitement—if not commit-ment—in the first story in the collection:

> You can do better things than remain a wealthy dilettante, Mr. Phillips. You are too broad in the shoulders, too clear in the head, for living in the world that is dead. Such little incidents as these—they drag you out of the shell you are building about you ["The Story of Amaroff the Pole"].

And in all of the following stories he has a case of detective fever as acute as Wilkie Collins Betteredge's.

BRET HARTE AND MARK TWAIN

In 1902 two well-known American writer spublished responses to Sher-lock Holmes: "The Stolen Cigar Case, by A. Co—n D—le," in *Condensed Novels* (second series) *New Burlesques* by Bret Harte, and *A Double Barrelled Detective Story* by Mark Twain. Both pieces are markedly different in tone from the parodies done by Conan Doyle's friends a decade earlier in Britain. Harte's short story, a purloined letter plot in which Hemlock Jones's apparently stolen cigar case is found where it is supposed to be, takes the usual satirical pot shots at Holmes' minute observations and deduction demonstrations, and then up-ends them and shows the Great Detective to be entirely wrong. The principal object in Harte's piece, however, lies in his development of the rela-tionship between Holmes and Watson. He makes the Watson character's servile obsequiousness one of the principal points of the story. Thus Watson's narrative begins with "With the freedom of an old friend I at once threw myself in my old familiar attitude at his feet, and gently caressed his boot." And later the Sherlock Holmes character validates this with

> You, who have for years rapturously accepted my confidences, passionately admired my inductions and inferences, placed yourself at my beck and call, become my slave, grovelled at my feet, given up your practice except those few unremunerative and rapidly-decreasing patients to whom, in moments of abstraction over *my* prob-lems, you have administered strychnine for quinine and arsenic for Epsom salts; you, who have sacrificed everything and everybody to me—*you* I make my confi-dant!

Just as he exaggerates Watson's side of the relationship, Harte radically alters Holmes' side and makes him surpass aloofness and become arrogant and abu-sive—indeed he threatens to shoot Watson. At the end of the story Holmes banishes Watson and the narrator's life becomes markedly better:

> I never saw him again. I am bound to say, however, that thereafter my business increased—I recovered much of my old practice—and a few of my patients recov-ered also. I became rich. I had a brougham and a house in the West End.

Nevertheless, the old, servile Watson remains:

> But I often wondered, pondering on that wonderful man's penetration and insight, if, in some lapse of consciousness, I had not really stolen his cigar-case!

Twain's *A Double Barrelled Detective Story* hardly reflects his reputation as America's premiere satirist. The two parts of the long short story (or short novella) combine the search of Archy Fuller for his brutal and absconding father and the death of Fetlock Jones' equally nasty employer. In the two parts Twain presents very different detectives: in part one Archy Fuller chases a man whom he suspects to be his father around the world without catching him, and in part two Sherlock Holmes and Archy both look into the death of Holmes' nephew Fetlock's brutal employer. The denizens of Hope Canyon quickly perceive the difference between the two detectives—in Sherlock Holmes they expect science and intellect:

> Then we'd have seen scientific work. Intellect—just pure intellect—away up on the upper levels, dontchuknow. Archy is all right, and it don't become anybody to belittle him, I can tell you. But his gift is only just eyesight, sharp as an owl's, as near as I can make it out just a grand natural animal talent, no more, no less, and prime as far as it goes, but no intellect in it, and for awfulness and marvelousness no more to be compared to what this man does.

The science, if not the intellect, they expect is borne out when Holmes goes to the crime scene:

> With a tape he took measurements of the cabin site; of the distance from the wall of chaparral to the road; of the height of the chaparral bushes; also various other measurements. He gathered a rag here, a splinter there, and a pinch of earth yonder, inspected them profoundly, and preserved them. He took the "lay" of the place with a pocket-compass, allowing two seconds for magnetic variation. He took the time (Pacific) by his watch, correcting it for local time. He paced off the distance from the cabin site to the corpse, and corrected that for tidal differentiation. He took the altitude with a pocket-aneroid, and the temperature with a pocket-thermometer.

This being burlesque, Holmes' investigation results in the wrong answer. The murderer understood this would happen: "But what's the use of being afraid of him? Anybody that knows him the way I do knows he can't detect a crime except where he plans it all out beforehand and arranges the clues and hires some fellow to commit it according to instructions." This idea would give rise to Lincoln Steffens's 1908 story "Mickey Sweeney, Detective of Detectives." In spite of the fact that Twain gives Conan Doyle several nudges about resurrecting his dead hero, *A Double Barrelled Detective Story* is hardly a landmark for either satire or the detective story.

ARTHUR TRAIN

Almost from their inception detective stories had much to do with the law and lawyers—usually they recounted attorney heroes correcting miscarriages in a fundamentally sound system of justice. In the 1890s Melville Davisson Post' pieces about Randolph Mason continued the tradition of stories about lawyers, but with a fundamental change of direction: they posited a corrupt system of justice which needed to be manipulated. Arthur Train continued that tradition, but added an inclination toward irony and comedy of manners. Train, an assistant in the office of the New York district attorney, started writing with "The Maximilian Diamond," a tale told by Dockridge, his first fictional lawyer. The story, which originally appeared in *Leslie's Monthly* in 1904, unfolds the travails of a well-intentioned bill poster innocently caught up with crooks, the police, and the law over stolen diamonds. Having been mistreated by fate (and everything else), in the end his only recourse is to become a detective:

> "Yes," he explained in answer to my surprised expression, "I've gone into the detective business. My unfortunate conviction is only a sort of advertisement, you know, and then I was the victim of an outrageous conspiracy!"

Train included a handful of lawyer tales in his first collection of short stories, *McAlister and His Double* (1905). These center on the vagaries of laws concerning extradition, the admissibility of confessions, and the competence of counsel. But the bulk of the stories in that collection concern a character and a world that anticipate P.G. Wodehouse's Drones Club, Bertie Wooster, and Jeeves. Six of those seven stories about "Chubby" McAlister have some connection, albeit sometimes tenuous, with crime and detectives. Train bases all of them on the confusion caused by the fact that McAlister's valet, Wilkins, is also the wily and notorious burglar "Fatty" Welch, and that the two men look very much alike. In the first story, "McAlister's Christmas," Train uses Detective Barney Conville's mistaken arrest of McAlister to walk readers through a realistic description of the arrest process. Hence this description of taking Bertilion measurements:

> Tom opened a door and pushed the clubman gently into a small, low-ceiled chamber. Charts and diagrams of the human cranium hung on one wall, while a score of painted eyes, each of a different color, and each bearing a technical appellation and a number, stared from the other. Upon a small square platform, about eight inches in height, stood a half-clad Italian congealed with terror and expecting momentarily to receive a shock of electricity. The slender young man was rapidly measuring his hands and feet and calling out the various dimensions to an assistant, who recorded them upon a card. This accomplished, he ordered his victim down from the block, seated him unceremoniously in a chair, and with a pair of shining instruments gauged the depth of his skull from front to rear, its width between the cheekbones, and the length of the ears, describing all the while the other features in brief terms to his associate.

As a Christmas story, however, all of this is in the service of McAlister understanding the suffering of others:

Now that he knew something of the real sufferings of men, his own life seemed contemptible. What mattered the laughter of his friends, or sarcastic paragraphs in the society columns of the papers? What did the fellows at the club know of the game of life and death going on around them? of the misery and vice to which they contributed? of the hopelessness of those wretched souls who had been crushed down by fate into the gutters of life?

In both "Baron de Ville" and "The Governor General's Trunk," however, McAlister acts as a detective and thwarts his double's jewel thefts; in the latter, in fact, he almost catches detective fever:

> "Jiminy, but this is great!" he exclaimed, slapping Barney upon the back. "And to think of your doin' it for a livin'! Why I'd sit here all day for nothin'! What happens next? And what becomes of the feller that's just gone out?"
>
> "Oh, you ain't seen half the show yet!" responded Conville, pleased. "It is pretty good fun at times. But, o' course, this is a star performance, and we're sure of our man. Oh, it beats the theayter, all right, all right! Truth's stranger than fiction every time, you bet. Now take this Oyster—why he's a regular cracker-jack! Got sense enough to be an alderman, or president, or anythin', but he keeps right at his own little job of liftin' trunks, an' he ain't never been caught yet. His pal'll be along now any minute."
>
> ...
>
> McAllister admitted delightedly that it was a great game. By George, it beat playin' the horses! ["The Governor General's Trunk"].

But while Train's handful of McAlister stories served as recreation for readers, he ultimately felt more secure concentrating on lawyers and the law and proceeded to tell stories featuring lawyers Artemas Quibble and then Ephraim Tutt.

Alfred Henry Lewis

Confessions of a Detective presents in microcosm a snapshot of the state of the detective story in the United States (but not Britain) in 1906. The collection of five stories begins with the title story, "Confessions of a Detective," a narrative which carries over the attitude of Alfred Henry Lewis' muckraking journalism (which produced, among other things, the series "Owners of America" in *Cosmopolitan Magazine*). The first person narrator of "Confessions" portrays the extent to which politics had polluted policing in New York City, and his revelations reproduce the detailed exposure of massive corruption by the Lexow Commission in 1895. Thus

> every once in a while an investigating committee comes butting in from Albany, to go nosing on the trail of police graft.... So far I've played in luck; for I've met three of these question-asking gangs, and succeeded in sidestepping them every time.... The best behaved copper on the force, one who having paid his three hundred dollars to become patrolman, his five hundred to be made roundsman, his

three thousand to become detective sergeant, and his fifteen thousand to call himself Captain of Detectives, should be forgiven for saying that he has fairly earned his promotions, might wake up some bright morning and find that he's been investigated once too often. There's always that chance out; and so, d'ye see, having gathered in my fortune, and rounded off my heap, I held it the part of wisdom, without waiting for any age-limit to reach me, to pack in and quit. I'll need full twenty years anyway to get my morals on an even keel, after playing thief taker for over thirty.

The other four stories in the collection, however, come from a different world, the world that had been reshaped by Sherlock Holmes. Appearing first in *Success Magazine* from July through October 1905, they feature Inspector Val of the New York City department—a character introduced in Lewis' novel *The President* in 1904—and his assistant Sergeant Sorg. The pair owes much to the Holmes-Watson combination, layered with Val's playful attitude:

> "Then you've changed your mind," observed Mr. Sorg, in dismay. "You don't think he's the murderer now?"
>
> "Now? I never thought so. We shall, since it is the obvious thing to do, lock him up until after the coroner makes his inquiry. But, take my word for it, he's not our man."
>
> "Who then?"
>
> "'Look for a cripple with a crutch. Also, look for the woman who was his companion."
>
> "The woman, and a cripple with a crutch!" repeated the astonished Mr. Sorg ["The Washington Square Mystery"].

Their roles as police officers, however, echo the new concepts of August Vollmer's police reform movement which advocated college educated officers and disciplined troops. Regardless, Inspector Val is the genius detective readers expected who solves intractable and knotty crime problems that leave others scratching their heads. While "The Murder at Santa Marie" deals with Val in disguise bantering in underworld cant with a group of thuggish home-invaders, the three remaining Inspector Val stories have plots reminiscent of those in most post–Holmes fiction: the wrong suspects plot in "The Washington Square Mystery," the impossible crime plot in "The Man who Flew," and the treasure hunt plot in "The Stolen Red Diamond." "The Man Who Flew," in fact, puts Lewis' Inspector Val stories securely in the Sherlock Holmes tradition, for it takes the central surprise from Greenhaugh Smith's 1892 story "The Case of Roger Carboyne" published in *The Strand* and converts it from a court room puzzle story into a fully articulated detective story.

CLIFFORD ASHDOWN

Between the Romney Pringle crook stories he wrote with John J. Pitcairn and his introduction of Dr. Thorndyke in the novel *The Red Thumb Mark*

(1907), R. Austin Freeman and Pitcairn, writing as Clifford Ashdown, published six stories in *Cassell's Magazine* beginning in December 1904 that came to be collected under the title *From A Surgeon's Diary*. They decidedly come from the note-book tradition in that the principal aim of these writers is to reflect the daily routines of a working professional (in this case a *locum tenens*, a physician who substitutes for the absent owners of medical practices) and to spice up those routines by including exceptions to the daily rounds. In this context, the stories deal with crime and add a medical twist—a fake death certificate in "The Adventure at Heath Crest," a bogus physician in "How I Met a Very Ignorant Practitioner," an apparent bank robbery and amnesia in "How I Helped to Lay a Ghost," paranoia and a Mafia revenge plot in "How I Attended a Nervous Patient," and paralysis and insurance fraud in "How I Cured a Helpless Paralytic." The one exception is "How I Acted for an Invalid Doctor" which centers on a physician who is also a secret house burglar. While the *Surgeon's Diary* stories may all deal with crime, they do not deal with detection—in each case the dirty work at the center of the plot reveals itself without the narrator's intervention—or even awareness. Thus, for example, in "An Invalid Doctor" the police discover the identity of the house burglar after he is involved in a bicycle crash with the narrator, and the real physician walks in to unmask the phony one in "Very Ignorant Practitioner." Dr. Wilkinson, the narrator of the stories, as a substitute should, does his job conscientiously and competently, and in one story, "How I Cured a Helpless Paralytic," he undertakes tests to discover how an entire village is being exposed to lead poisoning. But he hardly has the time to be a scientist. That aspect of the physician's world Freeman would explore several years later in the Dr. Thorndyke stories.

Robert Barr

Robert Barr had been around Sherlock Holmes almost from the start. He and Conan Doyle were part of a coterie of writers—which included J.M. Barrie and Jerome K. Jerome—associated with Barr and Jerome's somewhat eccentric magazine *The Idler* in the early 1890s. Barr traveled with Conan Doyle on his first trip to the United States and Canada and in November 1894 *McClure's Magazine* published the biographical "A Dialogue Between Conan Doyle and Robert Barr" —the accompanying photo quite literally showing Barr seated at Conan Doyle's feet. But there was another side to Barr's association with Sir Arthur and his Great Detective. In May 1892, under the name Luke Sharp, he published "Detective Stories Gone Wrong. The Adventures of Sherlaw Kombe" in *The Idler*. This was one of the earliest of the Sherlock Holmes spoofs and it set the stage for Barr's 1906 collection of short stories *The Triumphs of Eugene Valmont. The Triumphs* is a collection of eight untitled short stories narrated by the title character. Barr wrote it in the same double edged spirit that created "Detective Stories Gone Wrong." First of all *The Triumphs* possesses a consciousness about the history of the genre. One of the stories mentions "The Purloined Letter" and the background of the hero mirrors that of the first modern detective, Eugene Vidocq—like Vidocq, Eugene Valmont was head of the Sûreté who, after being ousted for political reasons, emigrated to London to set up as a private detective. And the stories in *The Triumphs* reflect the cleverness that had become central to the genre—gold, for example, hammered into sheets and glued to the walls under the wallpaper in one of the collection's treasure hunt pieces. Barr also uses the plot motifs favored by detective stories both ancient and modern: in *The Triumphs* these go from treasure hunts and secret marriages to stolen jewels, anarchists and kleptomaniacs. Barr's inclination to playfulness comes in with the hero. He's in large part a comic Frenchman—opinionated, arrogant, and garrulous. But he is also a comic French detective which means first that he is grossly outspoken about the differences between English and French law and law enforcement. Valmont mocks the principle of innocent until proven guilty, ignores rights with respect to search and seizure, and even has a secret cell built in his flat to imprison suspects. And his opinion of the minions of Scotland Yard is markedly condescending:

> Myself, I like the English detective very much, and if I were to be in a *melee* tomorrow, there is no man I would rather find beside me than Spenser Hale. In any situation where a fist that can fell an ox is desirable, my friend Hale is a useful companion, but for intellectuality, mental acumen, finesse—ah, well! I am the most modest of men, and will say nothing.

Rather than recording Valmont's triumphs, moreover, Barr lays out plots in which, in spite of his puffery and rationalizations, the hero is most often wrong. Thus, for instance, in one story he rescues the wrong man from an American prison, in another he not only fails to protect the priceless necklace but receives a mocking letter from its owner at the conclusion, and in another he needs to be told what clues to follow by his principal suspect. With all of these things, then, Barr anticipated the serio-comic tone that came into much detective fiction after the First World War.

JACQUES FUTRELLE

Long before the beginning of the twentieth century, newspapers—more than books or even magazines—had been the principal purveyor of detective stories, especially in the United States. And this was particularly the case in Boston where *The Boston Globe* had published short stories and serials about detectives from the 1880s. It was no great surprise, then, at the beginning of the new century when Jacques Futrelle took a job at Hearst's *Boston American* that he would take up writing detective stories for his paper. The stories about his detective, Augustus S.F.X. Van Dusen, began in 1905 and ended on Futrelle's return from England on the *Titanic*. In all Futrelle wrote close to fifty stories about Van Dusen, the Thinking Machine—"It was a newspaper catch-phrase applied to him at the time of a remarkable exhibition at chess; he had demonstrated then that a stranger to the game might, by the force of inevitable logic, defeat a champion who had devoted a lifetime to its study" ("The Problem of Cell 13"). A small collection of them appeared in book form in *The Thinking Machine* (*1907*) and *The Thinking Machine on the Case* (1908). Futrelle knew Conan Doyle's secret to success: a distinctive detective character and an ingenious plot. Thus there is Professor Van Dusen. Even before Futrelle's stories really begin readers know the hero is a genius. He has credentials:

> Practically all those letters remaining in the alphabet after Augustus S. F. X. Van Dusen was named were afterward acquired by that gentleman in the course of a brilliant scientific career, and, being honorably acquired, were tacked on to the other end. His name, therefore, taken with all that belonged to it, was a wonderfully imposing structure. He was a Ph.D., an LL.D., an F.R.S., an M.D., and an M.D.S. He was also some other things—just what he himself couldn't say—through recognition of his ability by various foreign educational and scientific institutions ["The Problem of Cell 13"].

On top of all of the degrees, Futrelle's detective has the physique of the evolved big brain:

> In appearance he was no less striking than in nomenclature. He was slender with the droop of the student in his thin shoulders and the pallor of a close, sedentary life on his clean-shaven face. His eyes wore a perpetual, forbidding squint—the squint of a man who studies little things—and when they could be seen at all through his thick spectacles, were mere slits of watery blue. But above his eyes was his most striking feature. This was a tall, broad brow, almost abnormal in height and width, crowned by a heavy shock of bushy, yellow hair. All these things conspired to give him a peculiar, almost grotesque, personality ["The Problem of Cell 13"].

Although Holmes may have Irene Adler, Futrelle's hero does not: "The Thinking Machine started in, saw a woman—Miss Clarke, who had returned from luncheon—and stopped. There was one thing on earth he was afraid of—a woman" ("The Ralston Bank Burglary"). From the first story, "The Problem of Cell 13," Futrelle's purpose was to focus on complex problems with which to confront readers—seemingly impenetrable brain-teaser puzzles or riddles (he used both terms)—and then have his big brain hero solve them. And he was able to come up with poser after poser. Indeed *The Bookman's* review of *The Thinking Machine on the Case* makes that precise point:

> But what, above all, marks Mr. Futrelle's work in this as well as the earlier book, is not the cleverness of any particular tale, but rather the consistent excellence and fertility of invention of them all [*The Bookman*, July 1908].

Unlike the Watson-Holmes combination where Holmes does almost everything and Watson watches and reports, Futrelle developed a division of labor
whereby the detective does all of the thinking and the companion-assistant
does all of the leg work, often without knowing why: thus, for instance, these
instructions to Van Dusen's associate Hutchinson Hatch: "I am leaving all this
to you because you know better how to do these things than I do. That's all,
I think. When these things are all learned come back to me" ("The Scarlet
Thread"). The division of labor also intends to place readers in Hatch's situation of having facts (or clues) but not conclusions and also confident that the
conclusion will be forthcoming:

> Hatch was over his head and knew it. He was finding out things and answering
> questions which, by the wildest stretch of his imagination, he could not bring to
> bear on the matter in hand—the mystery surrounding the murder of Marguerite
> Melrose, an actress ["The Great Auto Mystery"].

That Hatch is a newspaper reporter whose job is to report and not analyze
perhaps carries more significance in that the stories were written for a newspaper whose ostensible mission was the objective presentation of facts.

George F. Butler

In 1908 George F. Butler M.D. published a new edition of his *A Text-
Book of Materia Medica, Pharmacology and Therapeutics*. The same year he
also published *The Exploits of a Physician Detective*, a collection of twelve
short stories following in the tradition of L.T. Meade's her physician partners
and Clifford Ashdown which coupled the note-book tradition with the evolving techniques of the detective story. Like his British peers, psychiatric illness
lies at the center of several of Butler's physician stories—religious mania in
"The Hautover Case" and kleptomania in "The Kleptomaniac." Butler makes
his detective an advocate for science in general:

> Do you realize how many different branches of science I have used already in this
> search, branches which the police know only by name, and some of them not even
> that much? Ten! Telepathy, botany, criminology, medicine, surgery, history, reli-
> gion, mathematics, psychiatry, and logic ["The Hautover Case"].

Given his interest in medical literature, however, Butler's stories turn on esoteric medical facts more often than the recent clump of British doctor stories.
Thus in *The Exploits of a Physician Detective* the diagnosis of Meniere's disease
unravels "The Tragedy at the Colonial," the presence of "Bacteriologic culture
of trypanosomes" explains "The Strange Sickness of Mr. Whittaker Ransome,"
and discovery of cerebrovacuisitis, otherwise ophthavitreossitis, is the key to
what happens in "The Man with the Glass Eye." But the stories do more than
introduce surprising medical diagnoses to explain enigmatic circumstances.
In the first story in the collection, "The Hautover Case," Butler suggests that

there will be a kind of Lombroso tilt to the stories when he introduces Dr. Furnivall, his hero, as "resident physician in the state penitentiary ... whose name was famous in penology" ("The Hautover Case"), But Furnivall doesn't have anything to do with analyzing criminals. His real expertise rests in hypnosis, as broadcast in the headline in "The Man with the Glass Eye":

> 'DR. FURNIVALL'S MYSTERIOUS POWER AGAIN! ANOTHER CRIMINAL FOUND BY ITS AID! SCIENTISTS AND POLICE ALIKE PUZZLED BY THIS OCCULT FORCE WHICH COMPELS A MAN TO ALWAYS SPEAK THE TRUTH!'

And so in the stories when confronted with the doctor-detective, his power compels the guilty to confess. Furnivall's power over suspects added to the use of obscure medical facts hardly provides the variety of suspense and surprise for readers fast becoming requisite in contemporary detective stories. Butler, however, does understand the kind of excitement and exhilaration readers sought in their detectives and he put it into his initial description of his physician detective:

> On seeing body ...when you said at dinner that I should be a detective, I believe you hit it. It was what I was thinking about that very moment.... Why I never felt such interest in anything, so much life fluid sparkling and boiling in me, in my life as I do this instant. I'm a new man. I feel the pure, unmixed power of the cosmos itself moving me about as a champion moves chessmen on a board. If that doesn't mean a man has found his vocation, what does? It's what is called genius. I know now that I've got it, along this line, at any rate, and I'm devilish sure I never had it in medicine, as well as I succeeded. That was all work, hard, hard work, and no play. But this! Why, it's joy, it's exhilaration, intoxication! ["The Hautover Case"].

LINCOLN STEFFENS

At about the same time Butler wrote that, Lincoln Steffens was affected by a different kind of detective euphoria. His articles on American cities published in *McClure's Magazine* beginning in 1902 (which would become *The Shame of the Cities*) demonstrated a different kind of detective work—one based on revealing the graft, corruption, and downright humbug of police forces across America. A bit later, in "Mickey Sweeney, Detective of Detectives," published in the *American Magazine* in July 1908, Steffens gave readers a dose of his brand of detection combined with a wry look at Sherlock Holmes. Steffens based "Mickey Sweeney, Detective of Detectives" on the assumption that one of the principal purposes of police and detectives was self-promotion—thus their attitude toward newspapers:

> The police everywhere warn citizens not to let anybody but the police know of such troubles. They say that if the newspapers get hold of the news they will publish it; this will frighten away the thieves and prevent the police from recovering the stolen property. This is only a police trick to avoid criticism. They give to the press

all their successes; they suppress their failures, and thus keep up the appearance of efficient service. As a matter of fact, the first thing that the victim of a robbery should do is to telephone to the newspapers—all of them. That would soon show what a small proportion of the reported cases a detective bureau like that of New York "detects" and—it will make the police work on your case.

In the story Steffens made Inspector Foley, Chief of Detectives, one of the most artful practitioners of the art of self-promotion:

> He was very successful; and the whole city had faith in him. Leading citizens especially believed in Foley, and he served them especially well. Many of them could tell wonderful stories of his detective skill. For that matter, however, Foley himself could tell wonderful stories of his triumphs, and he did, often. That was one reason why he was a favorite among the newspaper men, excepting only Mickey Sweeney.

Foley, as Sweeney learns, is a devotee of Sherlock Holmes:

> "Sherlock Holmes is a character in fiction," he said, "fiction which seems to have the approval of our highest class of literary publications. It is indeed fiction, but that don't mean that it ain't onto the biz all right all right."

Indeed Foley tries to dispel Sweeney's skepticism about his competence by using a Holmesian gambit—a startling statement which unravels the crime at hand: he hails a seemingly random wagon in the street and solves the "silver robbery up Madison Avenue." Only Sweeney does not fall for it, does his own detective work—"You're no Dr. Watson; you're a pretty good Sherlock Holmes yourself"—and discovers that Foley engineered the whole Sherlock Holmes trick solely as a mean of impressing the reporter.

MARY ROBERTS RINEHART

In a decade when writers increasingly turned to forensic evidence as the basis of their detective stories, Mary Roberts Rinehart did not. While she does compare what is going on in her novel *The Circular Staircase* (1908) to "a Chinese Puzzle," the narrator tells her readers that

> I looked for footprints, which is, I believe, the conventional thing to do, although my experience has been that as clues both footprints and thumb-marks are more useful in fiction than in fact.

Instead of forensics (with which her middle class characters would have had no experience) Rinehart turned back to the sensation novel for the main ingredients of *The Spiral Staircase*—characters who deliberately withhold evidence, an abandoned orphan, seemingly doomed loves, disguise, a secret room, abduction, an isolated setting, and a deathbed confession. All of that plus mysterious nightly threats to the seemingly helpless residents of Sunnyside, the ironically named mansion central to the novel. Rinehart does introduce both professional and amateur detectives in *The Circular Staircase*, including Rachael

Innes the narrator, and as events unfold Rinehart peppers the dialog with questions posed by Miss Innes; thus this series:

> Why did Arnold Armstrong come back after he had left the house the night he was killed?
> No answer. Was it on the mission Louise had mentioned?
> Who admitted him?
> Gertrude said she had locked the east entry. There was no key on the dead man or in the door. He must have been admitted from within.
> Who had been locked in the clothes chute?
> Some one unfamiliar with the house, evidently. Only two people missing from the household, Rosie and Gertrude. Rosie had been at the lodge. Therefore—but was it Gertrude? Might it not have been the mysterious intruder again?
> Who had accosted Rosie on the drive?
> Again—perhaps the nightly visitor. It seemed more likely, some one who suspected a secret at the lodge. Was Louise under surveillance?
> Who had passed Louise on the circular staircase?
> Could it have been Thomas? The key to the east entry made this a possibility. But why was he there, if it were indeed he?
> Who had made the hole in the trunk-room wall?

The answers to these and the other questions raised in order to solve the two mysteries in the novel (who killed Arnold Armstrong and who has been trying to break into the house), however, are not provided by the detectives' investigations but by adventitious events. In *The Circular Staircase* Rinehart depends on foreshadowing rather than clues for the book's major effect upon its readers, and the book and its author have become known as the fountainhead of the had-I-but-known school of detective fiction. This reputation comes from passages like this one:

> I record this scrap of conversation, just as I have tried to put down anything and everything that had a bearing on what followed, because the gardener Hal they sent the next day played an important part in the events of the next few weeks— events that culminated, as you know, by stirring the country profoundly. At that time, however, I was busy trying to keep my skirts dry, and paid little or no attention to what seemed then a most trivial remark.

While passages like this one (and there are a lot of them) help Rinehart to establish a tame gothic atmosphere—things seem bad and confusing now, but they will be all right in the end—they are also part of her portrait of her hero which combines gentle comedy with the determination and grit of a middle aged, middle class single woman.

R. Austin Freeman

After dabbling with note-book fiction as Clifford Ashdown and rogue fiction with his Romney Pringle stories, R. Austin Freeman settled down to write detective stories about medico-legal savant Dr. John Thorndyke, first in a novel, *The Red Thumb Mark* (1907), and then in a series of short stories published in *Pearson's Magazine* beginning in 1908 and later in the U.S. in *McClure's Magazine*. The first set of these stories, nine in all, was then published as *Dr. Thorndyke's Cases* in 1909. They reprise the characters from Freeman's novel—narrator, Dr. Jervis, impresario, Dr. Thorndyke, and lab assistant, Polton. In many ways Freeman's first set of stories is markedly Sherlock Holmesey. First of all, they run on the genius detective and the obtuse narrator: thus the Holmes-Watson echo in this passage from "The Anthropologist at Large":

> "My dear fellow," he replied, "you have all the data. Enlighten yourself by the exercise of your own brilliant faculties. Don't give way to mental indolence."
> I endeavoured, from the facts in my possession, to construct the personality of the mysterious burglar, and failed utterly; nor was I more successful in my endeavour to guess at the nature of the stolen property; and it was not until the following morning, when we had set out on our quest and were approaching Limehouse, that Thorndyke would revert to the subject.

And in the stories Thorndike's combination of superior perception, faultless logic, and encyclopedic knowledge evoke the same wonder and awe for those in the world of the fiction as in Conan Doyle's stories:

> I gazed at my friend in blank astonishment, for these events befell in the days before I had joined him as his assistant, and his special knowledge and powers of inference were not then fully appreciated by me ["The Man with the Nailed Shoes"].
> As Thorndyke's description proceeded, the inspector's mouth gradually opened wider and wider, until he appeared the very type and symbol of astonishment. But its effect on Mrs. Haldean was much more remarkable. Rising from her chair, she leaned on the table and stared at Thorndyke with an expression of awe—even of terror ["The Stranger's Latch Key"].

And, as in the models, the genius detective makes the most labyrinthine problem seem easy: "This explanation, like the others, was quite simple when one had heard it" ("The Stranger's Latch Key"). But the solutions Freeman invents are also regularly both surprising and novel—like the accident involving a steer's horn in "The Blue Sequin" or the missile used in "The Aluminum Dagger." With all these similarities, Freeman, nevertheless, intended to differentiate his detective stories from all of those others in the pages of contemporary magazines and newspapers, first by zeroing in on the science. It wasn't that contemporary detective stories had no science in them—Conan Doyle and L.T. Meade's collaborators, after all, were physicians—but that they didn't contain very precise science. Freeman intended to change that:

> But the interest of so-called "detective" fiction is, I believe, greatly enhanced by a careful adherence to the probable, and a strict avoidance of physical impossibilities; and, in accordance with this belief, I have been scrupulous in confining myself to authentic facts and practicable methods. The stories have, for the most part, a

medico-legal motive, and the methods of solution described in them are similar to those employed in actual practice by medical jurists. The stories illustrate, in fact, the application to the detection of crime of the ordinary methods of scientific research. I may add that the experiments described have in all cases been performed by me, and that the micro-photographs are, of course, from the actual specimens [Introduction, *Dr. Thorndyke's Cases*].

The aforesaid micro-photographs (in "A Message from the Deep Sea"), and the paragraphs describing Polton's use of Marsh's test for arsenic in "The Moabite Cypher" represent better science than British readers could find elsewhere in the genre at the time. But a portion of the portrayal and the fascination with science comes from Thorndyke's toys. The hero carries with him a "magazine knife, containing, among other implements, a railway-key" ("The Moabite Cipher") as well as in "his pocket a small metal box which he always carried, and which contained such requisites as cover-slips, capillary tubes, moulding wax, and other 'diagnostic materials'" ("A Message from the Deep Sea"). He has a fancy camera kit and its bicycle carrying case. And then there is Polton's hardware, including

> a singular appliance, of his own manufacture, somewhat like a miniature vacuum cleaner. It had been made from a bicycle foot-pump, by reversing the piston-valve, and was fitted with a glass nozzle and a small detachable glass receiver for collecting the dust, at the end of a flexible metal tube ["The Anthropologist at Large"].

In addition to his attention to scientific detail, Freeman moved to differentiate himself from the horde of detective story writers by means of what he called "the inverted detective story"—narratives which begin with a description of the crime being committed followed by a description of how the detective reads the crime-scene and uncovers the criminal. These began with "The Case of Oscar Brodski" in *Pearson's* (December 1910), and included "A Case of Premeditation," "The Echo of a Mutiny," and "A Wastrel's Romance," all of which Freeman published (along with a non-inverted story, "The Old Lag") in *The Singing Bone* in 1912. In the introduction to that volume Freeman explains how he came to write this variant of the detective story:

> In the conventional "detective story" the interest is made to focus on the question, "Who did it?" The identity of the criminal is a secret that is jealously guarded up to the very end of the book, and its disclosure forms the final climax.
> This I have always regarded as somewhat of a mistake. In real life, the identity of the criminal is a question of supreme importance for practical reasons; but in fiction, where no such reasons exist, I conceive the interest of the reader to be engaged chiefly by the demonstration of unexpected consequences of simple actions, of unsuspected causal connections, and by the evolution of an ordered train of evidence from a mass of facts apparently incoherent and unrelated. The reader's curiosity is concerned not so much with the question "Who did it?" as with the question "How was the discovery achieved?" That is to say, the ingenious reader is interested more in the intermediate action than in the ultimate result.

The offer by a popular author of a prize to the reader who should identify the criminal in a certain "detective story," exhibiting as it did the opposite view, suggested to me an interesting question.

Would it be possible to write a detective story in which from the outset the reader was taken entirely into the author's confidence, was made an actual witness of the crime and furnished with every fact that could possibly be used in its detection? Would there be any story left when the reader had all the facts? I believed that there would; and as an experiment to test the justice of my belief, I wrote "The Case of Oscar Brodski." Here the usual conditions are reversed; the reader knows everything, the detective knows nothing, and the interest focuses on the unexpected significance of trivial circumstances.

Just because readers see the crime committed, however, does not mean that Freeman makes everything plain for his readers. In "A Case of Premeditation," for instance, he involves readers in wondering precisely what the criminal is up to as he plans his crime. Inverted or not, Freeman's stories, like so much contemporary detective fiction, are partly games:

"Now, my dear Jervis," said Thorndyke, shaking an admonitory forefinger at me, "don't, I pray you, give way to mental indolence. You have these few facts that I have mentioned. Consider them separately and collectively, and in their relation to the circumstances. Don't attempt to suck my brain when you have an excellent brain of your own to suck."

"But if you would like to take part in the competition, I am authorized to show you the photograph and the translation. I will pass them on to you, and I wish you joy of them" ["The Moabite Cipher"].

J.S. FLETCHER

J.S. Fletcher would make a name for himself in the 1920s with his detective novels. But two decades before *The Middle Temple Murder* he started out writing short stories about an eccentric elderly amateur detective named Archer Dawe and published eight of them as *The Adventures of Archer Dawe, sleuth-hound* (1909). All of these are atypically short and bear the marks of contemporary newspaper rather than magazine detective stories. Thus Fletcher repeats in each story a brief description of his dress in order to establish Archer Dawe as eccentric—and original:

Archer Dawe was a man of sixty—a little, squat-figured man who dressed, Sunday or week-day, in rusty black; was never seen, indoors or out, without a very high-crowned, wide-brimmed silk hat; and who wore old-fashioned, stick-up collars, held tightly to his wizened throat by swathes of black neck-cloth ["The Mystery at Merrill's Mill"].

And he supplies him with *bona fides* by a quick glance at his collection of books on crime, his curio cases full of mementos of mayhem, and by telling readers that Archer Dawe is a self-made criminologist:

Then it came out that for years and years he had spent all his spare time in making a study of criminology, had watched and studied men, had compared and classified and analyzed, and had invented a system of his own in the detection of crime which was soon to make his name a terror to evil doers ["The Mystery at Merrill's Mill"].

This sounds a lot more grandiose than the cases that Fletcher invents for his detective—while the first piece in the collection ("The Mystery of Merrill's Mill") concerns solving a murder, there are few real evil doers present and the majority of the stories depict Dawe finding lost, strayed, or stolen things, including jewels and jewelry in "An Innocent Receiver," "The Shy Young Man's Chocolates," "The Sea Captain's Snuff-Box" and "The Stolen Chalice and Cross," and cash in "The Man Who Stole His Own Money" and "A Mere Mater of Inadvertence." As if telling readers that Dawe is a "criminologist," that he has a "system," and that that he is recommended by the police makes him a detective were enough, Fletcher gives no insight into how his hero does what he does: typically the victim presents the detective a problem, he says that he will solve it but cautions the victim not to ask him how, and then he presents the solution. The only instance of tradecraft in the collection is in "The Contents of the Coffin" where Fletcher makes Archer Dawe a master of disguise—forgetting that he has depended on his eccentric manners and appearance to establish his character. Fletcher also wrote a series of stories about Paul Campenhaye in 1913–14 for the *Red Magazine* and *Top Notch*, ten of which were published in book form as *Paul Campenhaye, Specialist in Criminology* in 1918 (OCLC also lists a suspicious 1914 edition). Even if the hero bills himself as a "criminologist" and is called to the rescue by peers, the Campenhaye stories offer a dreary chronicle of ineptness and good luck. In "The Tobacco Box," for instance, he is hoodwinked by a sharper posing as an Oxford don, and in "The House on Hardress Hill" coincidence rather than intelligence saves his life.

CAROLYN WELLS

In 1913 The Home Correspondence School published Carolyn Wells' *The Technique of the Mystery Story*. In its twenty six chapters Wells goes from outlining the histories of ghost, riddle, and detective stories to advice about how to handle motive, evidence, structure, and plot in the detective story. When *The Technique* was published she had written four detective novels, but she would go on to write more—a lot more. Wells' first was *The Clue* (1909) and in it she introduced her own Sherlock Holmes look-alike, Fleming Stone: "He did not know the man personally, but he had read and heard of the wonderful work he had done in celebrated cases all over the country." But since surprise lies at the heart of the Wells' idea of the detective story and surprise is something readers have to wait for, in *The Clue* she does not introduce Fleming Stone until the last chapters—after the amateur sleuth spends 300 pages trying to sort out the mystery. Surprise is also connected to the way Wells deals with physical evidence. At the beginning of the investigation her amateur detectives pooh pooh the notion of physical evidence in solving crimes:

> "What kind of a thing do you expect to find?"
>
> "I don't know, I'm sure. In the Sherlock Holmes stories it's usually cigar ashes or something like that. Oh, pshaw! I don't suppose we'll find anything."
>
> "I think in detective stories everything is found out by footprints. I never saw anything like the obliging way in which people make footprints for detectives."
>
> "And how absurd it is!" commented Rob. "I don't believe footprints are ever made clearly enough to deduce the rest of the man from."
>
> "Well, you see, in detective stories, there's always that 'light snow which had fallen late the night before.'"
>
> "Yes," said Fessenden, laughing at her cleverness, "and there's always some minor character who chances to time that snow exactly, and who knows when it began and when it stopped."
>
> "Yes, and then the principal characters carefully plant their footprints, going and returning—overlapping, you know—and so Mr. Smarty-Cat Detective deduces the whole story."

At the end of the novel, however, the discovery of the murderer depends entirely on the discovery of a tiny breath mint. Additionally while she leads readers to believe that they are reading about a closed environment crime, at the end she reveals a secret passage by which the murderer had access to the scene of the crime. In addition to the ingenious surprises revealed by the great detective at the end of the novel, *The Clue* was the kind of detective story that would later cause S.S. Van Dine to issue a ban on love interest from detective fiction as his third rule. Looking for the motive for the murder of a woman on the night before her wedding, the majority of the novel focuses upon who loves (or doesn't love) whom—with three women fixated on the prospective bridegroom as well as the developing relationship between the lawyer-amateur detective and one of the house-guests. Several decades later, in "Why Women Read Detective Stories" (*True Detective Mysteries,* September 1930), after discussing women's superior reasoning powers, Wells spoke to this and came close to calling the detective story the new love romance:

> Another reason for feminine interest is the scope for the working of their emotions.
>
> A woman may read a dozen new novels without much catching of her breath or tightening of her heartstrings.
>
> But in a well-written detective story she finds someone to pity, someone to hate, someone to become enraged at, someone to love, and all with startling and inescapable reasons...
>
> She is up against a new phase of life and it intrigues her. As for the old love stories, she knew all seven of their plots and they held no surprises for her experienced interest.

Edwin Balmer and
William B. McHarg

In the first decade of the twentieth century Edwin Balmer and William B. McHarg wanted to change the world—or at least they wanted to use detective stories to change the way their readers saw evidence and the role of the detective. They tried to do this through nine stories about psychologist/detective Luther Trant published in 1909 in *Hampton's Magazine*—a crusading journal whose mission was "to expose evil wherever we can; ...to expose it calmly and truly; ...to expose it in order that it may be replaced by good"—and then in book form as *The Achievements of Luther Trant* in 1910. While in form the Balmer and McHarg's stories follow the problem-surprise solution formula of their contemporaries, their subject matter is different, even radically different. For one thing, even though some of the Luther Trant stories (like "The Empty Cartridges" and "The Private Bank Puzzle") concentrate on presenting and solving the same seemingly intractable domestic puzzles common to the detective stories of the day, others take a new direction and bring in crimes hot off the front pages of contemporary American newspapers hardly ever mentioned in earlier detective fiction: thus there is the gang-related murder of the prosecutor in "The Fast Watch," the fear of kidnapping for ransom in "The Red Dress," and illegal immigration in "The Eleventh Hour." The most anthologized of Luther Trant stories, "The Man Higher Up," has to do with the wide-spread climate of corporate corruption:

> To-day the enemies are the big, corrupting, thieving corporations like this company; and appreciating that, I am not ashamed to be a spy in their ranks, commissioned by the Government to catch and condemn President Welter, and any other officers involved with him, for systematically stealing from the Government for the past ten years.

In addition to this new subject matter, Balmer and McHarg didn't simply employ the traditional straw man tradition of presenting bumbling police as a contrast to the genius detective, they joined progressive, muckraking journalists and complained about police use of "the third degree"—both for its brutality and its ineffectiveness. Following the movement for modern policing inspired by August Volmer in California, Balmer and McHarg envisioned a new kind of detective police work in the Luther Trant stories, one that is more accurate:

> The numerous convictions of innocent persons are as black a shame to-day as burnings and torturings were in the Middle Ages; as tests by fire and water, or as executions for witchcraft. Courts take evidence to-day exactly as it was taken when Joseph was a prisoner in Egypt. They hang and imprison on grounds of 'precedent' and 'common sense.' They accept the word of a witness where its truth seems likely, and refuse it where it seems otherwise ["The Red Dress"];

and one that is accurate because it is scientific:

Daily I have been proving, as mere laboratory experiments ... that which—applied in courts and jails—would conclusively prove a man innocent in five minutes, or condemn him as a criminal on the evidence of his own uncontrollable reactions. And more than that, Dr. Reiland! Teach any detective what you have taught to me, and if he has half the persistence in looking for the marks of crime on *men* that he had in tracing its marks on *things,* he can clear up half the cases that fill the jail in three days ["The Man in the Room"].

That kind of detection is accurate and scientific because it goes beyond the natural sciences and uses the new science of psychology. Luther Trant, therefore, serves as the apostle of new methods of detection, methods that enable the detective to unerringly determine guilt and innocence through the use of physiological tests—most often with the aid of different machines. Thus the galvanometer is "'a simple way of registering the emotions shown through the glands in the palms of the hand,' Trant continued" ("The First Watch"). Trant also uses a chronoscope (in "The Man in the Room"), an automatograph (in "The Red Dress"), both a plethysmograph and a pneumograph (in "The Man Higher Up"), and a psychometer (in "The Eleventh Hour"). With these instruments

there is no room for mistakes, Mr. Eldredge, in scientific psychology. Instead of analyzing evidence by the haphazard methods of the courts, we can analyze it scientifically, exactly, incontrovertibly—we can select infallibly the true from the false ["The Red Dress"].

THOMAS HANSHEW

In 1910 Thomas Hanshew's Hamilton Cleek started out as a combination of Raffles and Sexton Blake but shortly changed into the medium through which Hanshew delivered surprising solutions to knotty crime problems— the stuff regular detective stories were made of. American actor turned writer, Hanshew began publishing Cleek stories in *Pearson's Magazine* on March 19, 1910. These led to *The Man of Forty Faces* later in the year and then to *Cleek of Scotland Yard being the record of the further life and adventures of that remarkable detective genius, the man of the forty faces, once known to police as the vanishing cracksman* in 1914. In the first Cleek story the hero is an epic criminal:

The man for whom Scotland Yard had been groping for a year—the man over whom all England, all France, all Germany wondered—close shut in the grip of his hands and then had let him go. The biggest and the boldest criminal the police had ever had to cope with, the almost supernatural genius of crime, who defied all systems, laughed at all laws, mocked at all the Vidocqs, and Dupins, and Sherlock Holmeses, whether amateur or professional, French or English, German or American, that ever had or ever could be pitted against him, and who, for sheer devilry, for diabolical ingenuity, and for colossal impudence, as well as for a nature-bestowed power that was simply amazing, had not his match in all the universe ["The Affair of the Man Who Called Himself Hamilton Cleek"].

Like Dante in the poem, however, Cleek meets his Beatrice in the form of Alisa Lorne:

> I have lived a life of crime from my very boyhood because I couldn't help it, because it appealed to me, because I glory in risks and revel in dangers. I never knew where it would lead me—I never thought, never cared—but I looked into the gateway of heaven last night, and I can't go down the path to hell any longer. Here is an even half of Miss Wyvern's jewels. If you and her father would have me hand over the other half to you, and would have 'The Vanishing Cracksman' disappear for ever, and a useless life converted into a useful one, you have only to say so to make it an accomplished thing ["The Affair of the Man Who Calls Himself Hamilton Cleek"].
>
> You know what redeemed me—a woman's eyes, a woman's rose-white soul! I said, did I not, that I wanted to win her, wanted to be worthy of her, wanted to climb up and stand with her in the light? ["The Wizard's Belt"].

And so in the first few stories Cleek fights his old companions in crime—assorted Parisian Apaches—and Hanshew deals in exotic backgrounds and gothic effects like

> the most loathsome-looking creature I ever saw; a huge, crawling, red shape that was like a blood-red spider, with the eyes, the hooked beak and the writhing tentacles of an octopus. It made no sound, but it seemed to know her, to understand her, for when she waved her hand toward the open door of her own room it crawled away, and, obeying that gesture, dragged its huge bulk over the threshold, and passed from sight ["The Problem of the Red Crawl"].

Beginning with the fourth story ("The Caliph's Daughter") he ditches most of the thriller paraphernalia and makes his hero more of a standard detective. Thus, while his capacity for impersonation plays a role in his life as a criminal, it has less utility for Cleek as a solver of enigmas, but Hanshew kept it (along with Cleek's secret identities as Captain Burbage and George Headland, the secret locale where he meets Mr. Narkon of Scotland Yard, and his enterprising young assistant Dollops) as embroidery on his increasingly problem-solution centered detective stories. It was not, however, that Hanshew spent a lot of time writing about how Cleek solved problems as opposed to the solutions themselves. Here the stories incline toward the locked room variety: there's even one entitled "The Problem of the Steel Room." And they strive for some of the most bizarre solutions—one involving a seamstress' cutting table ("The Riddle of the 5.28"), one involving sneezing powder ("The Lion's Smile"), and one involving x-ray martyrs ("The Divided House").

BARONESS ORCZY (AGAIN)

In 1910 Baroness Orczy introduced her second detective in *Lady Molly of Scotland Yard*, a collection of twelve short stories (the last two of which involve a continuous narrative) about Molly Robertson-Kirk. Three editions appeared in its first year of publication. In retrospect, it's hard to imagine why, for the Lady Molly stories have little to recommend them beyond a few brief patches of reticent feminism—feminism mostly based on women's superior intuition:

> We of the Female Department are dreadfully snubbed by the men, though don't tell me that women have not ten times as much intuition as the blundering and sterner sex; my firm belief is that we shouldn't have half so many undetected crimes if some of the so-called mysteries were put to the test of feminine investigation ["The Ninescore Mystery"].
>
> No doubt he began to feel that here, too, was a case where feminine tact and my lady's own marvellous intuition might prove more useful than the more approved methods of the sterner sex ["A Day's Folly"].

The collection begins by creating mystery about Lady Molly's real identity: "Well, you know, some say she is the daughter of a duke, others that she was born in the gutter, and that the handle has been soldered on to her name in order to give her style and influence" ("The Ninescore Mystery"). Forgetting parentage, it's a title, the stories contend, that she earned. Orczy appoints Lady Molly head of a fictitious Female Department of Scotland Yard, and makes it her mission to prove the worth and to advance the fortunes of that department. Thus

> "Mary, don't you understand? It is the chance I have been waiting for—the chance of a lifetime? They are all desperate about the case up at the Yard; the public is furious, and columns of sarcastic letters appear in the daily press. None of our men know what to do; they are at their wits' end" ["The Ninescore Mystery"].

Although Orczy doesn't suggest that it's official policy, she mostly has Lady Molly solve cases involving the gentry and the transfer of wealth and titles. The one exception is "The Irish Tweed Coat," which concerns other countries' organized crime:

> You do not know its many clubs and bands of assassins, beside whom the so-called Russian Nihilists are simple, blundering children. The Mafia, which is the parent of all such murderous organisations, has members and agents in every town, village, and hamlet in Italy, in every post-office and barracks, in every trade and profession from the highest to the lowest in the land. The Sicilian police force is infested with it, so are the Italian customs.

Readers, however, see Lady Molly doing little investigation; she comes up with the solutions in at the end of the narratives. It's something one does not question:

> My dear lady had been pondering all through the journey, and even now she was singularly silent and absorbed. There was a deep frown between her eyes, and every now and then the luminous, dark orbs would suddenly narrow, and the pupils contract as if smitten with a sudden light.

> I was not a little puzzled as to what was going on in that active brain of hers, but my experience was that silence on my part was the surest card to play ["A Day's Folly"].

And the narrator being an awestruck servant (Mary Granard, a minor member of the department until she resigns to serve Lady Molly exclusively, narrates all of the stories) makes this possible. The last two stories ("Sir Jeremiah's Will" and "The End"), however, turn all of the professionalism and feminism of the previous ten on their heads and explain that Lady Molly became a detective solely to exonerate her husband imprisoned for a murder he did not commit—a deed she accomplishes largely by flirting with two of the most likely suspects.

WILLIAM HOPE HODGSON

In January 1910 William Hope Hodgson began publishing stories about Thomas Carnacki in Robert Barr and Jerome K. Jerome's magazine *The Idler*. In 1913 nine of the Carnacki stories were collected and published as *Carnacki the Ghost-Finder*. More than a decade earlier Meade and Eustace anticipated Hodgson's excursions into the supernatural with their stories about John Bell who claims to be a ghost-buster detective, but regardless of Bell's claims which are never borne out in the stories, Carnacki is the real article. Hodgson gives him esoteric erudition: he says things like "You had better read Harzam's Monograph, and my Addenda to it, on Astral and Astarral Co-ordination and Interference" ("The Gateway of the Monster"). More importantly, the stories all begin with Carnacki investigating some sort of real or artificial supernatural occurrence—usually one sort of house haunting or another (doors banging in "The Gateway of the Monster," whistling rooms in "The Whistling Room," horse's hoof beats in "The Horse of the Invisible," wandering spirits in "The Searcher of the End House"). Rather than being an exorcizing zealot, Carnaki is methodical, painstaking, and open-minded in his work:

> But in that somewhat brief and general search, I found nothing; and decided to begin my usual exact examination of every square foot of the place—not only of the hall, in this case, but of the whole interior of the castle.
> I spent three uncomfortable weeks, searching, but without results of any kind. And, you know, the care I take at this period is extreme; for I have solved hundreds of cases of so-called "hauntings" at this early stage, simply by the most minute investigation, and the keeping of a perfectly open mind ["The House Among the Laurels"].

Carnacki carries with him not only a kit of tools for investigating the mundane world (including a camera and flash equipment) but the latest "scientific" protection against evils from the beyond: thus he both draws pentacles but knows that it was only a partial "Defense" there and I nearly died in the pentacle. After that I came across Professor Garder's "Experiments with a Medium." When they surrounded the Medium with a current, in vacuum, he lost his power—almost as if it cut him off from the Immaterial. That made me think a lot; and that is how I came to make the Electric Pentacle, which is a most marvellous "Defense" against certain manifestations. I used the shape of the defensive star for this protection, because I have, personally, no doubt at all but that there is some extraordinary virtue in the old magic figure ["The Gateway of the Monster"].

While all of the stories run on sensation—invariably Carnacki fears for his life in the middle of the narratives—only some of them deal with genuine supernatural powers—"The Gateway of the Monster" and "The Whistling Room," for example. Others turn out to be detective stories in which the hero finds clues which expose evil doers regardless of the gothic atmosphere. In "The House Among the Laurels," for example, a criminal gang has rigged up special effects to frighten people and in "The Horse of the Invisible" a thwarted lover does the same in an attempt to frighten off his rival. In most of these stories, however, regardless of discovering human agents who have manufactured eerie effects Hodgson leaves his readers with a suggestion that not everything has been explained and that supernatural forces may have also been present. Thus the ending of "The Horse of the Invisible":

> "The look on Parsket's face, and the thing he called out, when he heard the great hoof-sounds coming down the passage, seem to show that he had the sudden realisation of what before then may have been nothing more than a horrible suspicion. And his fear and appreciation of some tremendous danger approaching was probably more keenly real even than mine. And then he did the one fine, great thing!"
>
> "And the cause?" I said. "What caused it?"
>
> Carnacki shook his head.
>
> "God knows," he answered, with a peculiar sincere reverence. "IF that thing was what it seemed to be, one might suggest an explanation, which would not offend one's reason, but which may be utterly wrong. Yet I have thought, though it would take a long lecture on Thought Induction to get you to appreciate my reasons, that Parsket had produced what I might term a kind of 'induced haunting,' a kind of induced simulation of his mental conceptions, due to his desperate thoughts and broodings. It is impossible to make it clearer, in a few words."

Perhaps Hodgson's intent in the Carnacki stories shows up most clearly in their context—his hero is not just detective and ghost buster, he's also a storyteller. In "The Thing Invisible" the nominal narrator tells his readers about the impact of listening to Carnacki talk:

> I and his three other friends, Jessop, Arkright, and Taylor, would receive a card or a wire, asking us to call. Not one of us ever willingly missed; for after a thoroughly sensible little dinner, Carnacki would snuggle down into his big armchair, and begin to talk. And what talks they were! Stories, true in every word; yet full of

weird and extraordinary incidents that held one silent and awed until had made an end of speaking. And afterwards, we four would shake him silently by the hand and stumble out into the dark streets, fearful even of our own shadows, and so with haste to our homes.

Augusta Groner

Perhaps in response to the interest raised in literary circles by the publication of *The Lock and Key Library: Classic Mystery and Detective Stories of All Nations,* in December 1909 *The Bookman* published "German and Scandinavian Detective Stories" by Grace Isabel Colbron. Her survey begins with a long discussion of Austrian writer Augusta Groner and ends with the judgment that "Mrs. Groner's work is excellent and entitles her to be named with the best of other lands." Several months later Grossett and Dunlap published Colbron's translation of Augusta Groner's *Joe Muller, Detective: Being the Account of Some Adventures in the Professional Experience of a Member of the Imperial Austrian Police* (1910). The stories in the collection don't disguise the fact that *Joe Muller* is a response to the Sherlock Holmes. Indeed, Groner is so conscious of the fact that she writing detective stories that she supplies an introduction in which she provides a biography of her hero which begins by noting that Joe Muller is in part a reverse of the conventional detective character.

> He has neither the impressive authority of Sherlock Holmes, nor the keen brilliancy of Monsieur Lecoq. Muller is a small, slight, plain-looking man, of indefinite age, and of much humbleness of mien ["Introduction"].

And the author carries some of this out in each of the stories when she repeats that he is physically unimpressive and makes clear that he occupies a decidedly subordinate position in the Austrian Secret Service (an organization Groner essentially describes as a detective branch of the police). Further, she makes modesty one of Muller's defining traits—as witnessed by his description of detective work:

> "What I have done is only what any one could do who has that particular faculty. I do only what is in human power to do, and the cleverest criminal can do no more. Besides which, we all know that every criminal commits some stupidity, and leaves some trace behind him. If it is really a crime which we have found the trace of here, we will soon discover it" ["The Case of the Lamp That Went Out"].

Modesty of the character, of course, is a thin disguise for the author's disingenuousness: the entire law enforcement establishment of the Austro-Hungarian Empire holds Muller in awe, and, in the manner of all genius detectives, he solves crimes that no one else can. But Groner really wanted to set Joe Muller apart by means of pathos. Condemned to forever serve in the lowest, most ill-paid position in the service by a past miscarriage of justice, as well as in a world governed by inherited rank and privilege, Joe Muller's most prominent characteristic is humility. In addition, each of the stories emphasizes Muller's compassion:

> And at other times, Muller's own warm heart gets him into trouble. He will track down his victim, driven by the power in his soul which is stronger than all volition; but when he has this victim in the net, he will sometimes discover him to be a much finer, better man than the other individual, whose wrong at this particular criminal's hand set in motion the machinery of justice. Several times that has happened to Muller, and each time his heart got the better of his professional instincts, of his practical common-sense, too, perhaps,... at least as far as his own advancement was concerned, and he warned the victim, defeating his own work ["Introduction"].

And in "The Case of the Golden Bullet" his sympathy with the criminal causes him to lose his job: "Even the friendliness of the kind old chief could not keep him in his position after this new display of the unreliability of his heart." Along with this emphasis on sentiment, the Joe Muller stories stand out because of their depiction of the police. Not only is it rare to find a government officer as the hero in the detective stories of the period, but Groner also reflects a more realistic portrait of the police than any of her contemporaries. This ranges from scenes at headquarters and admissions of fallibility, to the passage in "The Pocket Diary Found in the Snow" where even an out of factory worker won't take a job as a detective:

> "If you have the talent for that sort of thing, you may find permanent work here."
> A gesture and a look from the workingman showed the detective that the former did not think very highly of such occupation. Muller laid his hand on the other's shoulder and said gravely: "You wouldn't care to take service with us? This sort of thing doesn't rate very high, I know. But I tell you that if we have our hearts in the right place, and our brains are worth anything, we are of more good to humanity than many an honest citizen who wouldn't shake hands with us."

G.K. CHESTERTON

In his role as a pundit G.K. Chesterton had thought more than a bit about detective stories before he actually wrote one. In his 1901 piece in *The Defendant* ("A Defense of Detective Fiction") Chesterton made them sound like thrillers:

> By dealing with the unsleeping sentinels who guard the outposts of society, it tends to remind us that we live in an armed camp, making war with a chaotic world, and that the criminals, the children of chaos, are nothing but the traitors within our gates. When the detective in a police romance stands alone, and somewhat fatuously fearless amid the knives and fists of a thieves' kitchen, it does certainly serve to make us remember that it is the agent of social justice who is the original and poetic figure; while the burglars and footpads are merely placid old cosmic conservatives, happy in the immemorial respectability of apes and wolves.

But then in 1905 he introduced his own detective, Rupert Grant, in his Sherlock Holmes send up *The Club of Queer Trades*. By 1908 he began to talk about detective stories as puzzle pieces instead of thrillers: "Now a whole department of popular fiction exists simply to give people riddles rather than romances; I mean the things commonly called detective stories" ("Why Books Become Popular," *The Bibliophile*, September 1908). And then he turned to writing his Father Brown stories, beginning with "Valentin Follows a Curious Trail" (aka "The Blue Cross") published first in *The Saturday Evening Post* (July 23, 1910) and then in Britain in *The Story Teller*. In 1911 Chesterton collected twelve Father Brown stories and published them as *The Innocence of Father Brown*. This would be followed by four more collections, ending with *The Scandal of Father Brown* in 1935. Chesterton also continued to write about detective stories with pieces such as "How to Write a Detective Story" (1925) and "The Ideal Detective Story" (1930).

Chesterton made the Father Brown stories out of several components— some of which were more unique than others. First he made his detective hero different; instead of a Sherlock Holmes knock-off, Chesterton chose a

> little priest was so much the essence of those Eastern flats; he had a face as round and dull as a Norfolk dumpling; he had eyes as empty as the North Sea; he had several brown paper parcels, which he was quite incapable of collecting ["Valentin Follows a Curious Trail"].

Chesterton's priest, however, does more than violate the superficial conventions of the detective hero. First of all, Father Brown was Chesterton's version of his friend Rev. John O'Connor, the Roman Catholic pastor of St. Cuthbert's in Bradford who, over a decade, inspired and guided the author's conversation into the Roman Catholic Church. His first impression of O'Connor, however, was of his encyclopedic knowledge of crime and criminals. Chesterton's most remarked upon departure from contemporary conventions of detective fiction, however, was not simply having his hero be an inconspicuous Roman Catholic priest with a lot of insider knowledge of crime, but making his Father Brown stories into Christian homilies, by wrapping the conclusions around either priestly functions or the conflict between spiritual and mundane views of reality. Thus, in "The Blue Cross," there is this point about faith and reason:

> "Oh, by being a celibate simpleton, I suppose," he said. "Has it never struck you that a man who does next to nothing but hear men's real sins is not likely to be wholly unaware of human evil? But, as a matter of fact, another part of my trade, too, made me sure you weren't a priest."
>
> "What?" asked the thief, almost gaping.
>
> "You attacked reason," said Father Brown. "It's bad theology."

It is no coincidence, moreover, that an atheist appears as the antagonist in "The Secret Garden," and a priest of a new religion is the villain in "The Eye of Apollo," and that "The Hammer of God" depends upon humility. Nor is it a coincidence that the police and courts have nothing to do with the execution of justice in the Father Brown stories. Chesterton's detective stories also depend upon the same impulse that put the "queer" into *The Club of Queer Trades*. Just as his initial description of Flambeau in "Valentin Follows a Curious Trail" emphasizes the outsized peculiarities of his crimes, Chesterton often made his detective stories revolve around unusual, even bizarre combinations of circumstances and facts. This comes up in a number of places such as the superficially impossibilities in the locked room environments in "The Secret Garden" and "The Invisible Man"; in "Valentin Follows a Curious Trail" where Chesterton strings curious events together; and in "The Honour of Israel Gow" where he presents readers with odd and disparate evidence.

ARTHUR B. REEVE

What with newspaper reporter Walter Jamison playing Watson to Craig Kennedy's Holmes, it's not hard to tell where the Craig Kennedy stories came from. But, beginning with "The Case of Helen Bond" (*Cosmopolitan*, December 1910), Arthur B. Reeve also made himself into the American apostle of scientific detection, and he continued in that role through eighty one more stories about Craig Kennedy, Professor of Chemistry (or Professor of Criminal Science after "The Deadly Tube, *Cosmopolitan* March 1911) at Columbia University. At the beginning of the first story (and then reprinted as "Craig Kennedy's Theories" in *The Silent Bullet* [1912]), Reeve's detective articulates his dedication to combining science and detection:

> I mean exactly what I say. I am going to apply science to the detection of crime, the same sort of methods by which you trace out the presence of a chemical, or run an unknown germ to earth ["The Case of Helen Bond"].

Nothing particularly new here. What is new is Reeve's connection of scientific detection to colleges and universities. He sees the detection of crime as an unmet obligation of the university:

> Colleges have gone a long way from the old ideal of pure culture. They have got down to solving the hard facts of life—pretty nearly all, except one. They still treat crime in the old way, study its statistics and pore over its causes and the theories of how it can be prevented. But as for running the criminal himself down, scientifically, relentlessly—bah! we haven't made an inch of progress since the hammer and tongs method of your Byrnes ["The Case of Helen Bond"].

And since the faculty is the heart of the collegiate system, finding new approaches to "running the criminal himself down" are up to them:

> "You must remember, Walter," he pursued, warming up to his subject, "that it's only within the last ten years or so that we have had the really practical college professor who could do it. The silk-stockinged variety is out of date now. To-day it is the college professor who is the third arbitrator in labour disputes, who reforms

our currency, who heads our tariff commissions, and conserves our farms and forests. We have professors of everything—why not professors of crime?" ["The Case of Helen Bond"].

With a college professor in charge, the narrative heart of Reeve's Craig Kennedy stories is the laboratory demonstration: invariably, at the end of the stories suspects gather (usually in the lab at Columbia) and watch Professor Kennedy perform a demonstration with scientific apparatus that answers the questions of how and who raised in the story. As in Balmer and McHarg's Luther Trant stories, Reeve features wonderful new scientific machines—usually introducing them mysteriously at the visit to the crime scene and then explaining them later at the demonstration. Indeed, by 1912 *Cosmopolitan* began to feature the two most prominent scientific inventors of the age, Nikola Tesla and Thomas A. Edison, in their advertisements for Reeve's stories: thus "Thomas A. Edison is reading these Craig Kennedy stories and thinks they are 'great'" (epigraph from "The Poisoned Pen," May 1912). The Craig Kennedy stories not only feature a scientist as a detective, they feature villains who are scientists as well—these range from Helen Bond who travels to Paris to learn new techniques of safe-cracking, to Vanderdyke who comes back from South America with a stash of curare in "The Azure Ring," or Professor Poissan with his thermit in "The Diamond Maker."

In addition to a continuing string of Craig Kennedy stories, in 1913 Reeve experimented with two female heroes, Constance Dunlap and Clare Kendall. The twelve semi-connected Constance Dunlap stories fall into the category of rogue fiction, but Clare Kendall, who has the same initials as Reeve's scientist hero, is on the right side of the law:

> Clare Kendall was a clear, gray-eyed girl, dark of hair, tall, striking, self-reliant. Alert of mind and energetic of nature, she had fought her way unaided to a position of keen rivalry with the best men in the detective profession. And yet, for all that, she was as eternally feminine as the harshest of critics of the "new" woman might wish. For it was simply that Clare was one of those girls who "do things"—do well the thing for which they find they are fitted ["The Crimeometer"].

She appeared in five stories from May to November 1913 syndicated in numerous American newspapers—usually in Saturday or Sunday supplements—and in one story ("The Crimeometer") in *Pearson's* September 1914 issue. Kendall, like Craig Kennedy, solves crimes with the aid of science—indeed, in "The Crimeometer" she uses the same blood pressure cuff and word association gambit that Kennedy used in his first cases.

SAMUEL HOPKINS ADAMS

In 1911 Samuel Hopkins Adams published a collection of ten detective stories (one of which has two parts) entitled *Average Jones*. It displays a number of new emphases in the development of detective fiction. To take the most

American factor first, a prominent motif of muckraking runs through the volume. Several of the stories ("The B-Flat Trombone" and "The One Best Bet") center on corrupt politicians, and, keeping in mind that Muckrakers helped pass the U.S. Pure Food and Drug Act of 1906, "Open Trail" deals with quack patent medicine and "Red Dot" the processed meat industry. The sidebar to this in all of the stories is contempt for the police:

> The police (with the characteristic stupidity of a corps of former truck-drivers and bartenders, decorated with brass buttons and shields and without further qualification dubbed "detectives") vacillated from theory to theory. Their putty-and-pasteboard fantasies did not long survive the Honorable William Linder's return to consciousness and coherence ["The B-Flat Trombone"].

Adams ties the hero's development into progressive consciousness-raising. He begins the series of stories with the background of Jones' corrupt politician uncle's last joke—bequeathing his nephew his fortune acquired by graft:

> He will squander his unearned and undeserved fortune, thus completing the vicious circle, and returning the millions acquired by my political activities, in a poisoned shower upon the city, for which, having bossed, bullied and looted it, I feel no sentiment other than contempt ["The B-Flat Trombone"].

His friend Waldemar, "the owner and at times operator, of an important and decent newspaper," however, convinces the idle and bored young Jones (Adrian Van Reypen Egerton Jones) to take up investigating bogus and predatory advertisements printed in his and others' papers. Throughout the collection Waldemar appears in stories that rely in one way or another on exposing political or corporate corruptions. While indictments of turn of the century corporate and political corruption color the Average Jones stories, they do not reflect their central purposes. One of those is the posing of zany conundrums for readers. These include a falling asteroid, a man who speaks only Latin, and a strolling trombone player, along with problems compounded by clues written in Braille and misread chemical formulas. In the stories in which cleverness takes center stage Jones is accompanied by his friend, "Robert Bertram, the club idler, slender and languidly elegant." And Bertram opens yet another of Adams' purposes. The opening paragraph of "Big Print" holds more than one clue:

> IN the Cosmic Club Mr. Algernon Spofford was a figure of distinction. Amidst the varied, curious, eccentric, brilliant, and even slightly unbalanced minds which made the organization unique, his was the only wholly stolid and stupid one. Club tradition declared that he had been admitted solely for the beneficent purpose of keeping the more egotistic members in a permanent and pleasing glow of superiority. He was very rich, but otherwise quite harmless. In an access of unappreciated cynicism, Average Jones had once suggested to him, as a device for his newly acquired coat-of arms, "Rocks et Praeterea Nihil."

The atmosphere of the Average Jones stories sets them apart—Bertram, the club, Latin quotes in the stories, facetious diction, allusions to college life ("Are you conversant with the Baconian system of thought, which Old Chips used to preach to us at Hamilton?" countered Average Jones. "Forgotten it if I ever knew it," returned Kirby ["Blue Fires"]), a letter from said Francis Bacon commenting on Shakespeare. All of these anticipate the worlds created by Margery Allingham and Dorothy Sayers more than a decade later.

MELVILLE DAVISSON POST

The year after publishing G.K. Chesterton's Father Brown stories, *The Saturday Evening Post* published "The Broken Stirrup Leather" (aka "The Angel of the Lord") on May 20, 1911, the first of a series of stories about life and law in rural Ante-bellum Virginia told by Martin about his uncle, Abner. Their author, Melville Davisson Post, had already made a significant contribution to crime fiction with his stories about unscrupulous lawyer Randolph Mason written in the late 1890s. Between 1911 and 1914 Post wrote ten stories built around Uncle Abner either for *The Saturday Evening Post* or *The Metropolitan Magazine*. These, along with eight stories written during the War, were collected and published as *Uncle Abner Master of Mysteries* in 1918. Hardly Conan Doyle's (or Chesterton's) detective stories, Post's Uncle Abner stories take place on the edge of civilization—in the isolated, mountainous part of Virginia that would become West Virginia. And there Post often emphasizes the harshness and sinister qualities of the land:

> The very aspect of the land was sinister. The house stood on a hill; round its base, through the sodded meadows, the river ran—dark, swift and silent; stretching westward was a forest and for background the great mountains stood into the sky. The house was very old. The high windows were of little panes of glass and on the ancient white door the paint was seamed and cracked with age ["The Wrong Hand"].

One of the first things Abner's nephew Martin tells readers in "The Broken Stirrup Leather" is that "it was a wild country. There were no banks." This kind of setting precludes much of the furniture of the detective story as it was coming to be known—no libraries for bodies to be in, no diamond tiaras to be stolen, no collections of suspects, and no police or detectives. Mirroring the land, harshness characterizes the lives of many of people in the stories:

> He was a cattleman named Dix. He had once been a shipper, but he had come in for a good deal of bad luck. His partner, Alkire, had absconded with a big sum of money due the grazers. This had ruined Dix; he had given up his land, which wasn't very much, to the grazers. After that he had gone over the mountain to his people, got together a pretty big sum of money and bought a large tract of grazing land. Foreign claimants had sued him in the courts on some old title and he had lost the whole tract and the money that he had paid for it ["The Broken Stirrup Leather"].

With these contexts, evil is more elemental than in other turn of the century detective stories, and more apparent. The narrator can see it in characters' faces. Thus, in "The Riddle,"

> there was everything fine and distinguished in his face, but the face was a ruin. Made for the occupancy of a god, the man's body was the dwelling of a devil. I do not mean a clean and vicious devil, but one low and bestial, that wallowed and gorged itself with sins ["The Riddle"].

Abner is the patriarch of this community:

> I ought to say a word about my Uncle Abner. He was one of those austere, deeply religious men who were the product of the Reformation. He always carried a Bible in his pocket and he read it where he pleased.... Abner belonged to the church militant, and his God was a war lord ["The Broken Stirrup Leather"].

In the stories Abner enters possessed of knowledge of the crime or criminal intent, but instead of summary judgment he pays precise attention to argument and physical evidence in confronting the guilty and ensuring the safety of his community.

FRANCIS LYNDE

While Melville Davisson Post pushed the corrosive effects of corporate greed found in his Randolph Mason stories into the background of the pieces he wrote about Uncle Abner, it became a constant theme in Francis Lynde's *Scientific Sprague* (1912). Principally a writer about the American West, Lynde used the thrill and romance of railroading as the principal background of the six stories in the volume, but he also included the naked aggression of corporate barbarians from the East Coast (the Big Nine) anxious to swallow up the plucky Nevada Short Line Railroad as another focus of the stories in the collection. Hence at their core the crimes in the stories are crimes against the railroad—interfering with telegraphic communication ("The Wire Devil"), stealing proxy votes ("High Finance in Comarty Gulch"), attempting to sabotage rail lines ("The Electrocution of Tunnel Number Three"), and fomenting labor unrest ("The Mystery of the Black Blight") for example—and the criminals are the faceless East Coast monopolists who suborn locals to do their dirty work. And that dirty work, of course, means that the Nevada Short Line needs a crack detective. Like every railroad, the Short Line employs detectives accustomed to violence: "You have a division detective of some sort, haven't you?—a fellow who does the gun-play act when it becomes necessary?" But what the line really needs is Calvin Sprague, someone with brains. Sprague is a chemist (and former star collegiate football player) who works for the Department of Agriculture where his job extends beyond the laboratory:

> "I don't mind piping myself off to you, Dick, though the full size of my job isn't generally known," the athletic-looking stop-over guest was saying. "You got the

first part of it right; I'm down on the Department of Agriculture pay-rolls as a chemistry sharp. But outside of that I've half a dozen little hobbies which they let me ride now and then. You'll guess what one of them is when I tell you that I was the man who fried out the evidence in the post-office cases last winter" ["The Wire Devil"].

...

"My name never appears. That is the high card in the game. So far as that goes, I never mess or meddle in the police details. My part of the job is always and only the theoretical stunt. They come to me and I tell 'em what to do. And just about half the time they haven't the least idea why they are doing it" ["The Wire Devil"].

Although here it seems as if Sprague is a covert government detective, later in the stories he sings the praises of being an amateur:

"A man does his best work as an amateur—in any line. As long as the manhunting comes in the way of a recreation, I enjoy it keenly. But if I had to make a business of it, it would be different" ["High Finance in Comarty Gulch"].

While the hero's training as a chemist plays a role in the "The Electrocution of Tunnel Number Three" where the solution rests on the hero's chemical analysis of a spot on the criminal's clothes, Sprague routinely couples detection with observation and the scientific method—both of which he demystifies in "High Finance in Comarty Gulch":

"I'm not sure that I can explain it so that you will understand, but I'll try. In the first place, it is necessary to go at these little problems with a perfectly open mind— the laboratory mind, which is neither prejudiced nor prepossessed nor in any way concerned with anything but the bare facts. Reason, and the proper emphasis to be placed upon each fact as it comes to bat, are the two needful qualities in any problem-solving—and about the only two."

Frank Gelett Burgess

Frank Gelett Burgess wrote a lot of different kinds of things—satire, nonsense verse, juvenile stories. And in 1912 he tried his hand at detective stories with *The Master of Mysteries*, a collection of twenty-four stories about Astro, a palm reader who solves people's problems through mundane rather than esoteric means. In the stories Burgess explored a variety of facets of the detective story. There are stories centering on solving serious crimes including kidnapping, murder, and espionage. Additionally Burgess displays an up-to-date interest in forensics. Thus several of the stories ("The Lorsson Elopement" and "The Calendon Kidnaping Case") contain detailed passages about fingerprints and, most astonishingly, in "The Heir to Soothoid," Burgess's detective uses retinal scans to establish identity. He also shares with other American writers an inclination to muckraking. Thus in "The Trouble with Tulliver" Astro's assistant points out that helping a distressed but honest District Attorney is a noble calling:

> "Oh!" she exclaimed, taking his hand, "why can't you help him, if there is a plot? I'd like to see you try your hand at something more worth while than mere murders and jewel mysteries. You're wasting your talents on such ordinary detective work. Why not offer your services? Why not take up the fight for him, and with him, if it's possible, and help him win? You'll never have a more worthy cause!"

And apropos to the fakery that led to the Pure Food and Drug Act in 1906, Soothoid in "The Heir to Soothoid" is the

> "biggest fake on earth," said the colonel, "and the most remunerative. My old uncle invented it, you know. Conceived the brilliantly vile idea of doping ordinary chicle with a tincture of opium and making chewing-gum of it. 'It soothes the nerves,'— I should say it did!—'Children cry for it,' and all that sort of thing! It's monstrous, of course. It ought to be suppressed by law, and it's only a question of time when this pure-food agitation will knock it out of business. It's a crime against civilization."

Even in stories involving heinous crimes Burgess tends to add a light touch— as he does in "The Calendon Kidnaping Case" where the kidnapped child is found in a closet happily eating a pot of jam. And he has more than a bit of fun with his detective's vocation. Astro's day job is being a palm reader to the carriage set—and in a semi serious vein Burgess does supply information at the start of each story to demonstrate that his detective's familiarity with things esoteric. But none of this knowledge figures in solving people's problems: that mostly has to do with observation and knowledge of human nature. This his assistant makes clear in "The Denton Boudoir Mystery":

> "Are you sure you can do it?" she asked, raising her golden brows.
> "My dear," he replied, taking up his water-pipe again, "am I not a Mahatma of the Fourth Sphere, and were not the divine laws of cosmic life revealed to me while I was a chela on the heights of the Himalayas?"
> Valeska broke into a silvery laugh. "Do you know," she said, "that patter of yours is almost as becoming as that turban and robe. But, to be serious, have you any clue as yet?"

A significant number of the stories in *The Master of Mysteries* involve relationships—"The Lorsson Elopement," "Priscilla's Presents," "The Two Miss Mannings," "Missing John Hudson," "Why Mrs. Burbank Ran Away," "Vengeance Of The Pi Rho Nu," and "Mrs. Stellery's Letters" each presents Astro's detective work as vital in making romantic relationships whole. Indeed, part of the structure of the collection is the growth of the relationship between Astro and his assistant Valeska Wynne. In the stories up to "Priscilla's Presents" there is a teacher-student relationship between them, but after that story their love for one another is revealed in increments until it reaches fruition in the last story, "Black Light."

Charles Felton Pidgin

Charles Felton Pidgin had been writing about Quincy Adams Sawyer all the way back to *Quincy Adams Sawyer and Mason's corner folks; a novel; a picture of New England home life* in 1900. In 1912 he made his character into a detective with the seven somewhat miscellaneous short stories included in *The Chronicles of Quincy Adams Sawyer, Detective*. In the first story in the collection, "The Double Thumb Print," Pidgin drew a brief sketch of the making of a detective. Apropos to the emphasis on police reform in the U.S. at the time, this centers on describing the only worthwhile elements in Sawyer's early experience as hanging out with cops and learning about criminology. Science, Pidgin tells readers, was Sawyer's first ticket to the detective dance:

> Quincy, purely in the pursuit of his own inclinations, had made friends with the police inspectors and had entered upon an exhaustive study of police matters, a study to which many subjects in his school curriculum, as he early discovered, lent a wealth of information that was invaluable. For instance, he early made the discovery that, if one were able to deal out, in grudgingly small amount, scientific information concerning chemical analysis and kindred subjects, it was easy to secure in return information concerning the more ordinary points of police work. Thus Quincy's four years in the high school passed with mutual profit to himself and to the police inspectors ["The Double Thumb Print"].

Once in college the emphasis turned to sociology:

> By the time he had finished his sophomore year he knew police work and methods from Alpha to Omega. Also, he had exhausted the resources of his university so far as sociology was concerned and had browsed about casually through what few other courses chanced to appeal to him ["The Double Thumb Print"].

Just as in his relationship with the police, at college Sawyer encounters tension between knowledge and authority, but finds that his professors are not as anxious to learn from him as police inspectors and he is asked to exercise his inclination for police work and adventure in other precincts—which he does by setting himself up as a private detective. Throughout the stories Pidgin depicts the differences between private and public detectives with the continuing character of Sawyer's friend Detective Gates of the Boston Department. Through the Sawyer/Gates combination Pidgin contrasts knowledge and titular authority as well as freedom and routine:

> "I'm sick of routine work, Sawyer," he complained. "I've been chasing through pawn shops for weeks, doing nothing more important than discovering the thieves of fake diamonds and cheap watches, until I'm sick and tired of it all" ["The Unreachable Island"].
>
> "Gee, Sawyer," he muttered, rising to depart, "you free lances certainly do get all the fun out of life, while we regulars scrape along on the secondaries" ["The Unreachable Island"].

The stories themselves reflect several tends in contemporary detective fiction. There is the forensic trend—not so much from the passing references to science in Sawyer's adolescence but in the new interest in fingerprints. Thus "The Double Thumb Print" turns on fake and faking fingerprints. Then there is the legal conundrum story—the legal concept of double jeopardy forms the basis of "The Affair of Lamson's Cook." While the first story, "The Double Thumb Print" details Sawyer's setting up shop in Boston and turns on his knowledge of the Boston underworld, the majority of the stories in the collection take place in the New England countryside and feature aspects of New England gothic, including an isolated colony of pirates living with their treasure in Vermont. And in the Sawyer stories violence—including fist fights and gun play—not only characterize life in the city, it has become an adjunct of the detective's life wherever he goes.

HARVEY O'HIGGINS

In 1911 Harvey O'Higgins landed the plumb assignment of writing up a series of stories for *McClure's* about detective William J. Burns, who was then fresh from solving the *Los Angeles Times* bombing case. So it was with more than a touch of pride that *Collier's* announced in the epigraph to "Detective Barney" (November 9, 1912) that the following was

> the first of a series of six stories in which the author who wrote of Burns's greatest successes and collaborated with him on the play "The Argyle Case," will throw upon the screen of fiction the picture of a real detective at work.

It took O'Higgins until 1913 to finish the six pieces. The following year he added the last Barney story ("Barney has a Hunch"), and in 1915 published them together as *The Adventures of Detective Barney*. They describe detection as mostly finding and arresting professional criminals rather than identifying criminals from clues at crime scenes. True to the editorial promise of providing a picture of a real detective at work, in the Babbing Detective Agency the Barney stories depict the operations of a thinly disguised Burns Agency. In part O'Higgins did this by viewing detective work through the distorted point of view of sixteen year old Barney Cook whose imagination has been overheated by dime novels: thus this juxtaposition of Barney's fantasy and the reality:

> As, for example:—Babbing, in his sanctum, at a make-up table, gumming a false mustache his lip; his dresser waiting to hand him a wig and a revolver; the room picturesquely hung with costumes and disguises, handcuffs and leg-irons, dodgers that offered rewards for desperate captures ("dead or alive") and sets of burglar's tools and the weapons of outlawry...

And Barney's better judgment accepted that picture from his inebriated young imagination without really knowing that he had accepted it—until he was called from the outer public office of the bureau into Babbing's private room, and found the famous detective sitting at a table-desk, in a swivel chair, reading his morning mail like the manager of any successful business at work in the office of any successful business manager ["Padages Palmer"].

After cadging his way into Babbing's employment, Barney experiences both the exhilaration and the boredom of being a detective. Thus, at the end of the first story, O'Higgins presents his hero's ebullient joy of being a detective in spite of the gory aftermath of a criminal's suicide:

> Barney, slamming the door behind him, fled down the hall, frightened, aghast, but with a high exultant inner voice still crooning triumphantly: "I'm a de-*tec*-tive! I'm a de-*tec*-tive!" Through the mouth! The back of his head out! Even in his horror there was a pleasurable shudder for he had all a boy's healthy curiosity about murder, shootings and affairs of bloodshed ["Detective Barney"].

But in each story O'Higgins makes sure to demonstrate that detective work contains a generous portion of drudgery. For Barney in some ways it's as bad as being in school:

> But he had also to make out daily reports of his hours on duty, the items of his expenses, and those incidents of his day's work that concerned the case on which he was engaged. And no school-room compositions could have been more tedious. At first he had been allowed to narrate his report to a stenographer, who put it into shape and typed it for him; later, he was required to write it out, for the stenographer to correct and typewrite; but now he had to type it himself, and retype it when the stenographer had revised his spelling and his punctuation, and then type it again if the office manager edited it ["The Anonymous Letters"].

As the stories progress, in spite of his belief that detection is an art—"It isn't a science. It's an art. You can't reduce it to rules. It's intuitive. All the science in the business can't take the place of the 'hunch'" ("Barney Has a Hunch")— Detective Babbing teaches Barney some of the tradecraft of the business. More importantly, he makes sure that Barney understands the moral equilibrium that the detective must find:

> "As a detective, you're allowed to do a great many things that would be punished in the private individual. You're expected to swindle, and steal from, and lie to, and betray the enemies of society in any way you can, in order to defeat them and defend society. It's your duty to do it, and do it diligently. If you don't, You're as bad as the criminal. And that's the only moral law that binds you, professionally."
>
> "But, in your private life,"—He wagged an emphatic forefinger—"you're bound by all the moralities that bind every one else.... When I send you out to get a man, You 're a crook if you don't use every means to bring him in, no matter what sympathy you feel for him or his mother or his sweetheart or any one else. Understand?" ["The Dummy"].

VICTOR LORENZO WHITECHURCH

Canon Victor Lorenzo Whitechurch had been writing shortish short stories about railways at least since October 1905 when "Sir Gilbert Murrell's Picture" appeared in *The Royal Magazine*. In 1912 fifteen of his railroad pieces appeared as *Thrilling Stories of the Railway*. Most of them feature Thorpe Hazell, Whitechurch's entry into the eccentric detective contest. Several things make Whitechurch's hero stand out. One is that technically he is not a detective but a "book-collector and railway enthusiast, a gentleman of independent means, whose knowledge of book editions and bindings was equaled only by his grasp of railway details." The other is that "he was a strong faddist on food and 'physical culture.' He carried vegetarianism to an extreme, and was continually practicing various exercises of the strangest description" ("Peter Crane's Cigars"). In the stories Hazell's book collecting hardly appears, but the latter qualities serve as frequent light-hearted digressions. Thus, for example, there is this bit of zaniness in "The Tragedy on the London and Mid-Northern" where the hero

> broke his journey at a farmhouse, where he begged for a glass of milk and a dry crust of bread. When he had partaken of this he astonished the woman who had given it to him by lying down flat on his back and rubbing his chest violently.

Indeed "How the Bishop Kept His Appointment" revolves around both a chase to catch a scheduled train and the Bishop's promise to try vegetarianism for a fortnight—which ends with him writing to Hazell, "I am much looking forward to resuming my ham for breakfast tomorrow, and rejoice that Providence provided the animal necessary for its production." Reflected in this contretemps, throughout the stories Whitechurch's hero maintains a sense of humor, in part because of his enthusiasm. Having a "railway enthusiast" as a hero gave Whitechurch access to an area that held significant promise for writers, especially writers of detective stories. Railroads and their workings provided a specific, technically complicated, interesting microcosm as well as a set of interdependent, precise scheduled times, both of which possess the appearance of permanence and predictability but both of which can be tampered with and manipulated. Thus Whitechurch's stories rest on presenting railroad related conundrums such as how can a car in the middle of a train disappear ("Sir Gilbert Murrell's Picture"), how can a crash be averted when an engine runs away out of control ("The Adventure of the Pilot Engine"), and how can a properly running train be prevented from keeping its schedule ("The Ruse that Succeeded")? Solving these posers depends on Hazell's encyclopedic knowledge of railroads as well as his enthusiasm for the chase. But only nine of the stories in the collection feature Thorpe Hazell. And while all of them strive to be thrilling, not all of the stories in *Thrilling Stories of the Railway*, strictly speaking, are detective stories—i.e. stories involving problem solving and crimes against persons. Six of the stories in *Thrilling Stories of the Railway* center on spies and espionage—"The Tragedy on the London and Mid-Northern," "The Affair of the German Dispatch-box," "The Adventure of the Pilot Engine," "The Mystery of the Boat Express," "Winning the Race," and "The Ruse that Succeeded." And several, such as "A Case of Signaling" and "The Strikers," focus on suspense rather than detection.

HARRISON JEWELL HOLT

In 1912 Harrison Jewell Holt introduced detective Stephen Garth in his novel *Midnight at Mears House*. Then he took to short stories and published three stories featuring Garth in *Pearson's Magazine* ("The Disappearance of the Japanese Envoy" [December 1912], "The Missing Sense" [January 1913], and "The Scattered Violets" [February 1913]). A fourth was promised ("The Mystery of the Bungalow Ghost") but did not appear in the March *Pearson's* as advertised. They all focus on the fact that Stephen Garth is blind. "He was then collecting material for a projected book on sociological problems, which necessitated his living largely among the poor, and familiarizing himself through actual experience with their ways of life.... He was helping a little lame boy in the slums set off some fireworks, and a Roman candle exploded in his hand and blinded him" ("The Disappearance of the Japanese Envoy"). Through Garth Holt chose to center his stories on one of the principal elements of contemporary detective fiction, the exploration of the senses, exemplified in the almost infinitely repeated variations on Conan Doyle's vignettes showing that Holmes sees more than Watson. Of course Holt makes his detective very smart:

> One secret of his success was his ability to banish all such worries from his mind, and to devote himself wholly to finding a plausible solution for whatever problem confronted him. The lightning-like rapidity with which he would invent, examine, and reject theory after theory until he hit upon one that stood the test of his hypercritical analysis has always been a marvel to me. I felt sure, therefore, that he had already evolved several hypotheses to account for what had happened; but curious as I was to learn what they were, I thought it wiser to wait until we were alone before attempting to gratify my curiosity; for I knew he would not care to take Galbraith into his confidence—the Inspector had already shown himself too skeptical ("The Disappearance of the Japanese Envoy").

But more than exceptional intellectual processes, Holt makes his blind hero's extraordinary senses the key to his ability to solve knotty problems—and the key to the stories. Thus in "The Disappearance of the Japanese Envoy" Garth feels a single hair on a chair he occupies and his extraordinary sense of smell comes to the center in "The Scattered Violets." And there is also hearing:

> Garth's unusual ability in this respect can be attributed in a large measure no doubt to his truly wonderful sense of hearing, which enabled him to distinguish and

interpret sound with an unerring, almost uncanny skill. Especially was this the case as regards the tones, inflection and timbre of the human voice. From this he was able to deduce an astonishingly large number of facts concerning the speaker—such as his age, nationality, occupation, physical and mental state of health, disposition and character ["The Disappearance of the Japanese Envoy"].

ANNA KATHERINE GREEN (AGAIN)

Almost as a reminder of her prominence in mystery circles, in 1913 Dodd and Mead gathered together nine pieces by Anna Katherine Green and published them under the title of *Masterpieces of Mystery*. Three of them ("Midnight in Beauchamp Row," "The Gray Lady," and "The Staircase at Heart's Delight") they reprinted from her 1900 collection *A Difficult Problem*, two more (*The Amethyst Box* and "The Ruby and the Caldron") are from Green's *Amethyst Box* (1905), one (*The House in the Mist*) was a stand alone publication in 1905, and one ("Room No. 3") appeared in *Woman's Home Companion* in 1909. Several of these (*The Amethyst Box, The House in the Mist,* and *Room No. 3*) are novellas. Focused on sentiment and melodrama, "Midnight at Beauchamp Row" and "The Thief" have no detectives in them and have to do with revelations aimed to evoke pathos rather than solutions to problems— the first having to do with the unintentional death of a husband and the second with a revelation of hidden poverty. Inspector Gryce, the detective Green invented in 1878, appears in two of the stories: one of them, "The Staircase at Heart's Delight," is a reprinted bit of note book fiction regarding the danger faced by policemen, and the other is "The Ruby and the Caldron" in which someone other than the detective solves the crime. In "The Little Steel Coils" Green included a nod or two to the contemporary detective story. The narrator is a successful private detective ("I was told that you had the credit of seeing light where others can see nothing but darkness"), faced with bizarre puzzles (an obituary appearing before a man's death along with no obvious evidence of foul play on the corpse), who finds fulfillment in doing his job—

> I was confident that his death was not a natural one, and entered upon one of those secret and prolonged investigations which have constituted the pleasure of my life for so many years.

—and who discovers the technical and trendy (using curare) method of murder. But most of this, following the practice of the sensation novel, becomes subservient to unraveling the emotion-laden motive of the bridegroom jilted at the altar.

MELVILLE DAVISSON POST

From May through October 1913 Melville Davisson Post published his latest take on the detective and the detective story with four stories about

French police detective Monsieur Jonquelle published in *The Saturday Evening Post*. After the war these were issued with eight other stories as *Monsieur Jonquelle Prefect of the Paris Police* (1923). With all of the contemporary interest in the history of the detective story, as context for these stories Post used the century-old discussion of the difference between law and police practice in England and France. In "Found in the Fog," for instance, Post makes the point as part of Monsieur Jonquelle's continuing argument with the criminal:

> Now in France, and among all Latin peoples a mystery, a riddle, a problem is forgotten like any other event if the answer is not found within the proverbial seven days of public notice. But to all Saxon races, to the Germans and to the English, a mystery is an eternal challenge. If a thing have an explanation it is immediately forgotten, but if it cannot be explained it will abide forever. Moreover the Saxon mind will never cease to consider it and will never give it up.

And then, much to the criminal's surprise and dismay, Post bases the denouement on a difference between French and English law. Unlike Post's earlier stories which stress the theme of justice from several perspectives, however, the prewar Monsieur Jonquelle stories depend more upon the mechanics of surprise than presenting perspectives on justice. The first two ("Alien Corn" and "The Haunted Door") feature a gullible narrator who is duped into abetting criminal actions only to have his concepts of people and events suddenly reinterpreted when the criminals depart and Monsieur Jonquelle appears to briefly sum up his mistakes. The other two stories ("Found in the Fog" and "The Ruined Eye") present contests between Jonquelle and a criminal which combine both argument and guile on the detective's part which lead the criminal into a trap in the final paragraphs. Two years after creating Monsieur Jonquelle, in February 1915, Post added an English detective, Sir Henry Marquis, to his stable of characters

HESKETH VERNON HESKETH-PRITCHARD

Hesketh Vernon Hesketh-Pritchard played cricket with Conan Doyle, Hornung, Kipling, H.G. Wells, and P.G. Wodehouse. With his mother he wrote the Flaxman Low stories for *Pearson's* and traveled in exotic places for the *Daily Express*. In 1913 he published *November Joe: Detective of the Woods*, containing sixteen stories which take place in Canada and Alaska. Part-time backwoods hunting guide and part-time consultant for the provincial police, November Joe is Pritchard's variation on the theme of Sherlock Holmes:

> "He is a most skilled and minute observer, and you must not forget that the speciality of a Sherlock Holmes is the everyday routine of a woodsman. Observation and deduction are part and parcel of his daily existence. He literally reads as he runs. The floor of the forest is his page. And when a crime is committed in the woods, these facts are very fortunate" ["Sir Andrew's Advice"].

Each of the stories in the collection depends upon November Joe reading the signs of human passage in the wilds of North America. Most often these are footprints, but Pritchard adds variety by occasionally shifting the setting from the backwoods to camp sites, homes, and railway cars. Thus this passage from "The Looted Island":

> "I think they was man and wife. She's a smallish woman; I'd guess she's maybe weakly, too. And he's fond of reading; anyway, he can read."
> Stafford stared at November half suspiciously.
> "What?" he shouted. "Are you kidding me? Or how did you get all that?"
> "That's easy," replied November. "There are two or three traces of a little flat foot in front of the stove, and a woman couldn't run this job on her own, so it's likely there was a man, too."
> Stafford grunted. "You said she was weakly!"
> "I thought maybe she was, for if she hadn't spilt the water out of the kettle most times she took it off the stove there wouldn't be any track, and here is one near on top of the other, so it happened more'n once on the same spot. She found your kettle heavy, Mr. Stafford," Joe said seriously.

Additionally, Pritchard includes a number of stories in which his hero must not only find and read clues, but (as in "The Seven Lumberjacks" and "The Black Fox Skin") he needs to discern real from fabricated clues. While exploring the possibilities of the application of the detective's art to crime problems set in the wilds of North America, as a minor theme Pritchard portrays life in the wilderness as more elemental than that portrayed in conventional detective stories. The people in the stories are principally trappers and lumberjacks. Justice is immediate and compassionate. Thus, for example, in "The Crime at Big Tree Portage" November Joe frees a killer whose victim abused his wife, and in "Miss Virginia Planx" he declines to report a false kidnapping to allow a woman to escape an demanding and irrational father. As Pritchard would have it, the elemental quality of the setting adds definition to both the stories and their hero:

> I have been present at many trials and the most dangerous witnesses that I have ever seen have been men of the November Joe type, that is, practically illiterate woodsmen. Their evidence has a quality of terrible simplicity; they give minute but unanswerable details; they hold up the candle to truth with a vengeance, and this, I think, is partly due to the fact that their minds are unclouded by any atmosphere of make-believe; they have never read any sensational novels; all their experiences are at first-hand; they bring forward naked facts with sledge-hammer results ["Sir Andrew's Advice"].

ERNEST BRAMAH

In the Fall of 1913 Ernest Bramah wrote a series of stories about a blind detective that appeared serially in the *News of the World*. The next year those eight stories appeared in book form in London as *Max Carrados*. Bramah introduced his detective a year after Dodd and Mead published *Midnight at Mears House* in New York and six months after Harrison Jewell Holt's three stories about his blind detective, Stephen Garth, in *Pearson's*. Coincidentally or not, Bramah gave his blind detective some American connections. His name and (like Samuel Hopkins Adams' Average Jones) his personal wealth, for instance, come from the States:

> Practically everything I possess was left to me by an American cousin, on the condition that I took the name of Carrados. He made his fortune by an ingenious conspiracy of doctoring the crop reports and unloading favourably in consequence. And I need hardly remind you that the receiver is equally guilty with the thief ["The Coin of Dionysus"].

Max Carrados' blindness, however, is not quite as superficially central to Bramah's stories as it is to Holt's. Bramah does draw upon the notion of the heightened senses of the blind:

> "Yes; but other people heard the voice as well. Only I had no blundering, self-confident eyes to be hoodwinked."
>
> "That's a rum way of putting it," said Carlyle. "Are your ears never hoodwinked, may I ask?"
>
> "Not now. Nor my fingers. Nor any of my other senses that have to look out for themselves."
>
> "Blindness invites confidence," replied Carrados. "We are out of the running—human rivalry ceases to exist" [The Coin of Dionysis"].

Bramah provides a foil for his hero in the form of disgraced lawyer turned private inquiry agent, Louis Carlyle, who is Max Carrados' entry into the world of detectives as well as a means of showing the uses of the senses and the superiority of thinking versus "seeing." None the less, the author also gives his hero a valet with a photographic memory who sees things that need to be seen. Either to alleviate or magnify the pathos of his hero's blindness, Bramah contrasted stories with serious outcomes—like "The Knight's Cross Signal Problem" which turns upon British mistreatment of Indians—with a zany treasure hunt story ("The Comedy at Fountain Cottage"). In the stories themselves he sometimes adds overtly comic gags, such as

> "Paris, egad?" he grunted. "Something in your line that France can take from us since the days of—what's-his-name—Vidocq, eh? Clever fellow, that, what? Wasn't it about him and the Purloined Letter?" ["The Clever Miss Straithwaite"].

While the term "Criminology" occasionally enters into Carrados and Carlyle's discussion of crime problems, it is as imprecise as in other contemporary fiction where it is used as a shibboleth for readers of detective stories. More than as social science, Bramah has Max Carrados consistently treat his cases like games. In "The Game played in the Dark" the hero supplies an extended comparison of detection and cricket and in "The Tragedy at Brookbend Cottage" Max says,

> "In a game of this kind one has to take sides and we have taken ours. It remains for us to see that our side wins."

In the first story, moreover, Bramah links his hero's desire to be a detective with something more than the employment of heightened senses or the intellectual and physical focus of playing games when he has his hero reflect on his reasons for wanting to join Carlyle as a detective:

> "It might be merely a whim, but it is more than that," replied Carrados. "It is, well, partly vanity, partly *ennui*, partly "—certainly there was something more nearly tragic in his voice than comic now—"partly hope."

HUGH C. WEIR

Four years after Baroness Orczy's Lady Molly stories, Hugh C. Weir created detective Madelyn Mack in the U.S.. But with Madelyn Mack there is a "which came first?" question: the 1914 Page Company's first edition of *Miss Madelyn Mack, Detective* contains photos of actress Alice Joyce playing the part of Weir's detective in a [now lost] Kalem Moving Picture Company film of "Madelyn Mack," which means that Weir may have created his character for the screen before he made her the hero of the four short stories and one novella included in *Miss Madelyn Mack, Detective*. It also means that Madelyn Mack was among the first fictional detectives to appear on film—antedating Gillette's film version of *Sherlock Holmes* by two years. On page or stage, Weir made his Madelyn Mack stories a paean to women detectives real and imaginary. The book begins with a dedication to Mary Holland, of the Holland Detective Agency, one of the first fingerprint experts in the U.S.:

> It is you, woman detective of real life, who suggested Madelyn. It was the stories you told me from your own note-book of men's knavery that suggested these exploits of Miss Mack. None should know better than you that the riddles of fiction fall ever short of the riddles of truth.

And his made-up biography for Madelyn Mack echoes the actual path taken by real women who became detectives:

> The college girl confronted suddenly with the necessity of earning her own living; the epidemic of mysterious "shop-lifting" cases chronicled in the newspaper she was studying for employment advertisements; her application to the New York department stores, that had been victimized, for a place on their detective staffs, and their curt refusal; her sudden determination to undertake the case as a free lance, and her remarkable success, which resulted in the conviction of the notorious Madame Bousard, and which secured for Miss Mack her first position as assistant

house-detective with the famous Niegel dry-goods firm ["The Man with Nine Lives"].

From these modest beginnings Weir creates a nation-wide, even international detective agency for his character to lead. Typically the stories begin when Madelyn arrives back to New York from another city or country, and she attributes her success to

> hard work and common sense—not uncommon sense such as we associate with our old friend, Sherlock Holmes, but common, *business* sense. And, of course, imagination! That may be one reason why I have made what you call a success ["The Man with Nine Lives"].

But, of course, she is very much like Sherlock Holmes, finding clues, withholding evidence and inference, besting the police detectives, and solving puzzles. In fact she is called "Miss Sherlock Holmes at work" in "The Bullet from Nowhere." Her friend, and the narrator of the stories, Nora Noraker, is every bit a Watson character. And detective plots of the stories mirror those in the Conan Doyle tradition: "The Man with Nine Lives" and "The Bullet from Nowhere" turn on understanding mechanical devices, "The Missing Bridegroom" and "The Purple Thumb Print" depend on domestic relationships gone awry, and "Cinderella's Slipper," like other American stories of the time, is an anti-trust story. In them all, Weir makes a point of depicting his hero as a woman as well as showing her as a detective. He makes an issue of femininity and the notion that solving crimes is a man's (or "manish") vocation. Thus the belief that a woman detective "wore men's collars, thick-soled shoes, and brushed her hair back straight in a little knot!" ("The Purple Thumb Print"): he takes on this stereotype early in the first story—"I had vaguely imagined a masculine-appearing woman, curt of voice, sharp of feature, perhaps dressed in a severe, tailor-made gown. I saw a young woman of maybe twenty-five, with red and white cheeks, crowned by a softly waved mass of dull gold hair, and a pair of vivacious, grey-blue eyes that at once made one forget every other detail of her appearance" ("The Man with Nine Lives"). To further "feminize" her, Weir provides Madelyn with a cozy retreat, redolent with flowers, and opera records playing on the Victrola.

Reprise

For the 1890s, other than Anna Katherine Green's slow fade and Ottolengui's innovations, the short detective story was pretty much a British concern. That was not the case after the turn of the century. Not only were American magazines luring away British talent from Conan Doyle to Chesterton who sold their first publication rights to them, but American writers were also beginning to outnumber their British counterparts in the production of short fiction about detectives: well over half of the new writers who created series stories about detectives between 1901 and 1914 were Americans. Additionally, while there were certainly overtly anglophile writers like Thomas Hanshew among the Americans and others who followed Conan Doyle's patterns in lock step with the master, American detective stories also began to differ from those by British writers, differ in the crimes upon which their stories were built, and differ in the characteristics of their detectives—detectives like Lewis' Inspector Val or Adams' Average Jones, who displayed the kind of wit, sophistication, and insouciance which ironically came to be identified with British detective heroes in the 1920s.

The search for a new kind of detective hero became another defining characteristic of the new century. As in the previous decade, very few official police officers were featured in short detective fiction—and one of them is Orczy's head of the imaginary female department at Scotland Yard. And while some American writers mention the contemporary movement for police reform, it has only minor impact on their stories. As in the 1890s, women heroes continued to appear, but remained a decided minority. Primitive rather than exotic settings gave rise to a new kind of character with Uncle Abner and November Joe. The role of the senses in problem solving led to the creation of two blind detectives and consideration of crime as sin lay under the life and works of both Father Brown and Uncle Abner. But more than anything, science loomed large: the combination of fiction, crime and science became almost unavoidable in the stories of the first decade of the twentieth century. Moving away from the vague diagnoses of Meade and her physician partners, after the turn of the century science in detective stories got more precise. One finds writers on the lookout for actual diseases with weird symptoms in which to wrap the conundrums in their stories—thus, for instance, ailments like Meniere's disease pop up in Butler's "The Tragedy at the Colonial." Diagnosing them was a new crop of specialist scientist detectives—medico-legal experts like Thorndyke and Kennedy began to offer real competition in the hero department to the polymath amateur or consulting detectives of the previous decade. Countering them is a spate of villains using esoteric means to accomplish their foul ends—thus the repeated use of curare (wourali) and x-rays in period stories. In addition to more frequent use of actual medical or pharmacological facts to complicate stories, period writers quickly latched on to the real world advances in forensic science occurring at the turn of the century. Fingerprinting—and devious means around fingerprint identification—was the making of numerous plots, as was examination of the unique properties of bullets. The new fiction continued to insert of lectures about the efficacy and efficiency of the scientific method, but in the new century these were backed up my machines, unbiased and infallible scientific machines that made intransigent clues readily understandable—Balmer and McHarg, among others, made careers out of using and explaining technical gismos with Latin-sounding names. Finally, there was the advent of the social sciences. Psychology, criminology, and sociology all gained academic and popular recognition at the turn of the twentieth century—as part of Progressives' desire to observe, define, and ameliorate individual and collective human misery. These new disciplines also provided labels for fictional detectives which writers used to establish their bona fides—often without providing particulars about what a "criminologist" or "psychologist," for instance, does.

5

Criminal Heroes

Going back to the Greeks and tales about Autolycus, Prince of Thieves, there has always been something about bad boys. From picaros to highwaymen, the history of literature is full of them—a point emphasized at the beginning of the twentieth century when Professor Frank Chandler published *The Literature of Roguery* (1907). A puckish element has accompanied crime literature almost from its beginning, stretching from unrepentant sinners in Newgate calendars to slippery singing highwaymen in Bulwer-Lytton and Ainsworth. While they stood outside of the society they preyed upon and had formerly been associated primarily with ballads and romances, at the end of the nineteenth century those who committed crimes morphed into new kinds of heroes in several different kinds of stories. One of the oldest rogue heroes, Robin Hood, was given a significant boost in 1883 with the publication of Howard Pyle's illustrated novel *The Merry Adventures of Robin Hood of Great Renown in Nottinghamshire*, a book that stressed the hero's redistribution of wealth. Stories patterned on the career of Dick Turpin, emphasizing capture and escape as well as the redeeming and redeemed qualities of criminals formed a pattern passed on from Bulwer-Lytton and Ainsworth to later writers. The pirate as a central character (if not a hero) gained currency in the late nineteenth century after Gilbert and Sullivan's *Pirates of Penzance* (1879) and Robert Louis Stevenson's *Treasure Island* (1883). And then three years later, Stevenson's *Strange Case of Dr. Jeckyll and Mr. Hyde* popularized the dual identity character which was then domesticated into the milquetoast/avenger hero in Baroness Orczy's play and novels about the Scarlet Pimpernel (1903). At the turn of the century the caper story, showing the accomplishment of an "impossible" task by a clever individual became popular. Caper stories, it was quickly seen, were kinds of inverted detective stories where the hero's intelligence (and the narrative's interest) is directed to the difficulty of committing the crime versus the difficulty of solving it—significantly R. Austin Freeman wrote his Romney Pringle stories before his "inverted" detective stories. Indeed the aforesaid Professor Chandler ended his study of rogues in literature with a chapter on "The Literature of Crime Detection." This connection of detectives and rogues got a boost when E.W. Hornung dedicated *The Amateur Cracksman*, the most popular collection of gentleman crook stories of the era, to his brother-in-law, Arthur Conan Doyle. But the connection between detectives and suave criminals was there before Hornung invented A.J. Raffles.

It was one of the ramifications of the transition from the pseudo-autobiographical notebook story to the new detective story inspired by Poe and brought up to date by Conan Doyle and Sherlock Holmes. Thus the new emphasis on problem solving as the narrative's defining action (versus hunting and chasing) placed great value on complexity and cleverness—sometimes on the part of both the detective and the perpetrator of the crime. Going back to the beginning, the antagonists in Poe's stories were either bizarre circumstance or very smart people: critics are quick to bring up the archetype of the double when it comes to Minister D—in "The Purloined Letter." Conan Doyle gradually picked up on the fact that if one is going to have a genius detective as the hero, then either one will have to reinvent perverse circumstances again and again, have the detective stoop to deal with dopey criminals, or invent a worthy antagonist for that hero. But that was not the only implication of the genius detective hero. Almost as soon as Sherlock Holmes appeared in print, the genius detective became the subject of a lot of burlesques, satires, and parodies—responding to the hyperbole of the newly popular character. The rogue hero became part of this equal and opposite reaction to the too smart, always right detective hero.

And then there was real life. Astor, Carnegie, Flagler, Vanderbilt, Stanford, and a lot more: the end of the nineteenth century saw the rise of the robber barons—entrepreneurs who accumulated unimagined wealth and displayed it both in philanthropy and, more commonly, in ostentation. At the same time that epic wealth drew the attention of an awestruck public, there emerged a group of larger than life confidence men. At the turn of the century in the U.S. Reed Waddell and Tom O'Brien, for example, sold rubes "gold bricks," the latter collecting $500,000 from victims at the Columbian Exposition of 1893. William McCloudy and Waddell both sold the Brooklyn Bridge to newcomers to New York City. The phrase "there's a sucker born every minute" was attributed to nineteenth century con man Joseph Lewis. Their successes cried out for chronicling. And there was also technology. At the turn of the century burglar alarms, uncrackable safes, time locks, rapid communication by telephone, and other inventions arrived to help protect property. According to E. W. Hornung in *The Crime Doctor*, these led to a new kind of criminal:

> Your twentieth-century criminal, with his telephone and his motor-car—for professional purposes—his high explosives and his scientific tools, has got to be an educated person, to begin with; and I am afraid there's an increasing number of educated people who have got to be criminals or else paupers all their lives.

For readers fascinated with technology, showing how the clever felon could overcome even the most contemporary challenges was as gratifying as the moral or scientific analyses of criminals. But increasingly a lot of writers found that they could both exploit the rogue hero's cleverness and turn their narratives into melodramas in which the hero redeems him or her self.

The Survey

FLORENCE ALICE PRICE JAMES

In 1884 Florence Alice Price James, under the name Florence Warden, published *The House on the Marsh*, a novel that stayed popular for several decades—it was made into a film in 1920. The novel, a bit *Jane Eyrey* and a bit Wilkie Collinsish, is the narrative of 18 year old governess Violet Christie whose first job is caring for the children of Mr. and Mrs. Rayner, residents of a particularly boggy corner of England. Mrs. Rayner is a mysterious recluse isolated in her bedroom in the dampest part of the house while Mr. Rayner is an affable, suave, accomplished, and (apparent to all but the narrator) flirtatious gentleman. Even Violet, though, senses there's something not quite right about him:

> Perhaps I am wrong. I really have no proof that he is anything but what he wishes every one to think him—a light-hearted accomplished man, of idle life and pleasant temper. It is not his fault that, with all his cleverness, his ease of manner is not quite the ease of a gentleman.

For a member of the county elite, however, Rayner expresses some unorthodox opinions on the subjects of crime and criminals in conversations with Violet:

> "I believe you have more sympathy with the thieves than with the policemen," said I, laughing.
> "I have, infinitely more. I have just the same admiration for the successful diamond-robber that you have for Robin Hood and Jack Sheppard, and just the same contempt for the policeman that you have for the Sheriff of Nottingham and Jack's gaol."
> "Oh, but that is different!" I broke in hotly—for I always put down "Robin Hood" in confession-books as "my favourite hero," and I was not without a weakness for Jack.
> "Oh, yes, it is very different, I know!" said Mr. Rayner maliciously. "Robin Hood wore Lincoln green and carried a picturesque bow and arrow, while Sheppard's costume, in coloured prints, is enough of itself to win any woman's heart. And then the pretty story about Maid Marian! Jack Sheppard had a sweetheart too, hadn't he? Some dainty little lady whose mild reproaches for his crimes proved gentle incentives to more, and who was never really sorry for her lover's sins until he was hanged for them."
> "Well, Mr. Rayner, their very appearance, which you laugh at, shows them to be superior to the modern burglar."

"Have you ever seen a modern burglar?"

"No; but I know what they look like. They have fustian caps and long protruding upper lips, and their eyes are quite close together, and their ladyloves are like Nancy Sikes."

"I see. Then you don't sympathise with a criminal unless he is good looking, nicely dressed, and in love with a lady of beauty and refinement?"

As the novel proceeds, house robberies occur in the district, Violet falls for one of the neighborhood beaus, and Rayner's favorite servant becomes increasingly hostile and threatening to the narrator. Finally Jane, the servant, tries to murder Violet but instead badly injures herself. In her delirium she reveals a number of facts about the recent burglaries (including the fact that some of the stolen items are in the house's cellar). Detectives turn up, and with the help of Violet's lover (not the detectives), it comes out that Rayner is a gentleman burglar:

"Pretty fellow you are to be hoodwinked like that, and drink and sleep quietly under the very roof of one of the greatest scoundrels unhung!"

"Who?" said the other, startled. "Mr. Rayner?"

"Mr. Rayner! Yes, 'Mr. Rayner' to simple folk like you; but to me and every thief-taker that knows his business—the missing forger, James Woodfall!"

Rayner/Woodfall, however, eludes capture, but accidentally drowns in one of the district's ponds.

Charles L. Young

About the time that readers encountered forger James Woodfall in *The House on the Marsh,* Sir Charles L. Young was reading up on a real forger: James (Jim the Penman) Townsend Saward, an English barrister who was convicted and sentenced to transportation in 1857 for leading a forging ring and fencing the proceeds of the Great Gold Robbery of 1855. Young's reading inspired his play *Jim the Penman* which debuted at the Haymarket Theatre on March 25, 1886, had a triumphant run in New York, inspired Dick Donovan's *Jim the Penman: The Life Story of One of the Most Astounding Criminals that Have Ever Lived* (1910), and became a silent film in 1915. The Turner Classic Movie synopsis of the film's plot can serve as a summary of all three fictional versions of Jim the Penman's life and loves:

Nina L'Estrange chooses to marry Louis Percival over his rival and friend, bank cashier James Ralston. After Percival goes to Chicago to take care of his inheritance, Ralston forges a letter to Nina from Percival breaking the engagement. She marries Ralston and they move to London, where Ralston begins a forging operation with Baron Hartfeld and amasses a fortune, though no one suspects that he is the notorious "Jim the Penman." After Ralston and Hartfeld successfully steal the famous Drelincourt necklace, Ralston learns that his daughter is engaged to Lord Drelincourt. He tries to return the necklace, but Hartfeld refuses to give it up. Captain

Redwood, an English aristocrat and amateur detective, overhears their disagreement. He recovers the necklace and obtains $75,000 "hush money" from Ralston, which he gives to Percival, whom Jim the Penman earlier robbed. Although Nina learns about Ralston's forgeries, she overlooks them for the sake of their daughter who is about to marry. On the eve of the wedding, Ralston, now remorseful, dies of heart failure while arguing with Hartfeld. Redwood then apprehends Hartfeld [www.tcm.com].

As seen above, the various versions of Jim the Penman helped establish some of the characteristics of the Victorian conception of the Gentleman Crook story as one containing double identity, multiple crimes, crimes requiring skill, and tragic consequences.

Elizabeth Phipps Train

A decade after *Jim the Penman* drew crowds to theaters in London and New York, Elizabeth Phipps Train published *A Social Highwayman* (1896) in *Lippincott's Magazine*; in the same year it was remade as a play, and was converted to film in 1916. The short novel chronicles the fall of Courtice Jaffrey from social lion to self-confessed jewel thief. And it carried with it motifs from earlier gentleman crook stories to the world after Sherlock Holmes. As in earlier works, the hero has a double identity. Jaffrey has all of the signs of class:

> I soon found that he was quite a celebrity. He was widely known in New York, and his reputation as a dude was almost national. He was a member of all the best clubs, and, notwithstanding his many absurdities of dress and manner, he seemed to be popular with both men and women. Yet, though popular with all, he was intimate with none, and while he had hosts of acquaintances he had no close comrades. This seemed somewhat strange to me, as he had many qualities calculated to attach people to him. For instance, he was generous to a fault and lavish to a degree. I supposed that he inherited money, for he was always in funds, and his hospitality was ever abundant and ready. His tastes were luxurious, and he gratified them without stint. During my whole term of service with him I never knew him to refuse a loan, while I could name hundreds of cases which his bounty relieved. As far as courtesy and good breeding are concerned, he was the most perfect gentleman I have ever known, and I have been in the employ of some of the best-bred of several nations.

And yet he's a jewel thief. While he doesn't use it as an excuse, Jaffrey brings the traditional Robin Hood argument in to explain his crimes:

> This man, who tomorrow possibly may be under the ban of your scorn, and—er contempt, who has for ten years led a life of fraud and deceit, has never (I can swear this, gentlemen, for he has opened his heart to me, and I have every reason

to believe his statement) robbed a being who could not well afford to lose what he has taken, and that two-thirds, at least, of his ill-gotten gains have gone to the relief of the poor and destitute. The persons who have suffered from his depredations are persons who have—er no bowels of compassion; who—er never extend a helping hand to the unfortunate, and who are amply able to—er spare the amount which he has—er—has appropriated without their permission.

But there are some differences in *The Social Highwayman*. Of these perhaps the chief is the point of view. Jenkins Hanby, Jaffrey's valet, narrates the story. He is a crook by training and inclination, just coming off a prison term at the start of the novel. And Jaffrey both understands and values his valet's larcenous leanings:

Of course you are lying to me, Hanby, but—er—but a good servant is—er—is a luxury worth paying something for, and though you are a—er—a scoundrel, Hanby, you-er—you are a clever one.

As the action progresses, Hanby becomes in effect Jaffrey's protector, using his wits to keep his boss from being identified as a criminal. Throughout the course of the novel Hanby's narrative voice also allows Train to insert bits of social satire, like this:

Then came two of the leaders of New York society, Mrs. I. Noble-Revere and Mrs. Munyon Pyle,—"Money-Pile" Wall Street called her husband,—women with magnificent establishments, stupendous fortunes, immense social power, and—husbands. The latter, however, like well-trained servants, knew enough to minister to, without obtruding upon, the comfort and welfare of those who had acquired the right to command them. They were social nonentities, though financial magnates, and one never considered them.

And it also allows Hanby to make the novel's principal point—thief though he may be, Jaffrey is more of a gentleman than the others who populate the world of the New York elite.

MELVILLE DAVISSON POST

In the main, however, *The Social Highwayman*, like its predecessors, is a mawkish, sentimental melodrama, more about traditional character values than about real rogues or problem solving. Melville Davisson Post's stories about Randolph Mason were not mawkish, sentimental melodramas. Attorney Post published three collections of short stories about criminal lawyer Randolph Mason: *The Strange Schemes of Randolph Mason* (1896); *Man of Last Resort, or The Clients of Randolph Mason* (1897); and *The Corrector of Destinies* (1908). By 1908 Randolph Mason had become almost civil—probably due to the stories' publication in *Pearson's Magazine*—but he wasn't that way at the start. He was a nasty piece of work, just as Post wanted him to be, because at the start the Mason stories were a response to detective stories in general and

Sherlock Holmes in particular. Post talks a bit about this in his introduction to the first Randolph Mason book:

> Perhaps, of all things, the human mind loves best the problem.... It propounds this riddle to the writer: Create mind-children, O Magician, with red blood in their faces, who, by power inherited from you, are enabled to secure the fruits of drudgery, without the drudgery. Nor must the genius of Circumstance help. Make them do what we cannot do, good Magician, but make them of clay as we are. We know all the old methods so well, and we are weary of them. Give us new ones.
>
> Exacting is this taskmaster. It demands that the problem builder cunningly join together the Fancy and the Fact, and thereby enchant and bewilder, but not deceive. It demands all the mighty motives of life in the problem. Thus it happens that the toiler has tramped and retramped the field of crime. Poe and the French writers constructed masterpieces in the early day. Later came the flood of "Detective Stories" until the stomach of the reader failed. Yesterday, Mr. Conan Doyle created Sherlock Holmes, and the public pricked up its ears and listened with interest.
>
> It is significant that the general plan of this kind of tale has never once been changed to any degree. The writers, one and all, have labored, often with great genius, to construct problems in crime, where by acute deduction the criminal and his methods were determined; or, reversing it, they have sought to plan the crime so cunningly as to effectually conceal the criminal and his methods. The intent has always been to baffle the trailer, and when the identity of the criminal was finally revealed, the story ended.

Post's idea of something new in the field of crime fiction was to create stories to show that social propriety, morality, and, most importantly, the law were impediments that could be overcome in solving problems. Thus in the Randolph Mason stories Post uses actual laws (he cites legal precedents at the start of each story) to enable characters to commit acts that readers assume are illegal—and which are certainly immoral—allowing blame and consequences to be either avoided or shifted. The most egregious example of this is in "Corpus Delecti," the first story in the first Randolph Mason book, where Mason instructs a character on how he can commit a murder without suffering any consequences. Subsequent stories center on lesser crimes from fraud, to partnership malpractice, forgery, robbery, and embezzlement. While in many of the stories Mason's clients have sympathetic motives, often concerned with helping others, but following the lawyer's advice they shift losses from themselves to innocent third parties. While he only briefly appears in each story, Randolph Mason is at the center of this. In some of the stories there is more than a bit of the Master Criminal about him—more than a bit of Professor Moriarty. Post repeatedly compares Mason to Napoleon and includes descriptions like this one from the judge in "The Men of the Jimmie":

> "I feel," he continued, "for the first time the utter inability of the law to cope with the gigantic cunning of Evil. I appreciate the utter villainy that pervaded this entire transaction. I am convinced that it was planned with painstaking care by some

master mind moved by Satanic impulse. I now know that there is abroad in this city a malicious intelligence of almost infinite genius, against which the machinery of the law is inoperative" ["The Men of the Jimmie"].

In others, however, Post presents him as an aloof, reclusive, melancholic, even Poe-like genius:

> "He turned up suddenly in his ancient haunts about four months ago," said Walcott, "as grand, gloomy, and peculiar as Napoleon ever was in his palmiest days. The younger members of the club call him 'Zanona Redivivus.' He wanders through the house usually late at night, apparently without noticing anything or anybody. His mind seems to be deeply and busily at work, leaving his bodily self to wander as it may happen ["Corpus Delecti"].

And rather than abetting crime and criminals, Mason finds purpose in solving challenging problems:

> What miserable puppets men are! moved backward and forward in Fate's games as though they were strung on a wire and had their bellies filled with sawdust! Yet each one has his problem, and that is the important matter. In these problems one pits himself against the mysterious intelligence of Chance, —against the dread cunning and the fatal patience of Destiny. Ah! these are worthy foemen. The steel grates when one crosses swords with such mighty fencers ["The Error of William Van Broom"].

In the Randolph Mason stories, then, Post's search for something new in the way of crime problem stories led him to play with new character types from Randolph Mason, who is sometimes a Master Criminal and sometimes just a genius, to his clients who Mason assists in becoming gentleman crooks who successfully commit crimes to maintain their places in society.

GRANT ALLEN

Grant Allen's "A Deadly Dilemma" was the lead story in the first issue of *The Strand Magazine* in 1891. His "The Great Ruby Robbery" appeared in the same issue as Conan Doyle's "Silver Blaze." But most of Allen's stories are fringe detective stories, often more interested in things other than clues and puzzles. That is certainly the case of his collection of twelve strung-together short stories that comprised *An African Millionaire* (1897). They are narrated by "Seymour Wilbraham Wentworth ... brother-in-law and secretary to Sir Charles Vandrift, the South African millionaire and famous financier." The first ten stories are accounts of Vandrift being tricked out of thousands of pounds per story by assorted confidence tricks perpetrated by the notorious "Colonel Clay." The last two concern the capture and trial of Colonel Clay.

> "Who is Colonel Clay?" Sir Charles asked.
> "That's just what I want to know," the Commissary answered, in his curious American –French—English. "He is a Colonel, because he occasionally gives him-

self a commission; he is called Colonel Clay, because he appears to possess an india-rubber face, and he can mould it like clay in the hands of the potter. Real name, unknown. Nationality, equally French and English. Address, usually Europe. Profession, former maker of wax figures to the Musee Grevin. Age, what he chooses. Employs his knowledge to mould his own nose and cheeks, with wax additions, to the character he desires to personate" ["The Episode of the Mexican Seer"].

In the stories he appears as Mexican Seer Antonio Herrarra, Curate Brabazon, Scotsman David Granton, Professor Schleiermacher, American Elihu Quackenboss, and detective Medhurst. Often, in various disguises, his companion "Madame Picardets" accompanies him. The stories become guessing contests in which Wentworth and Vandrift seek to spot Colonel Clay before he defrauds Vandrift of yet another thousand pounds—guessing contests in which the answers become increasingly obvious to readers. In addition to accomplishing coup after coup, at the conclusion of Clay's capers he sends the millionaire a letter which both taunts and attempts to instruct. Thus at the end of "The Episode of the Drawn Game" his sermon to Vandrift is

> Well, that's just how I view myself. *You* are a capitalist and a millionaire. In *your* large way you prey upon society. *You* deal in Corners, Options, Concessions, Syndicates. You drain the world dry of its blood and its money. You possess, like the mosquito, a beautiful instrument of suction—Founders' Shares—with which you absorb the surplus wealth of the community. In *my* smaller way, again, I relieve you in turn of a portion of the plunder. I am a Robin Hood of my age; and, looking upon *you* as an exceptionally bad form of millionaire—as well as an exceptionally easy form of pigeon for a man of my type and talents to pluck —I have, so to speak, taken up my abode upon you.

This message receives particular attention at the close of the book; the last two chapters describe the arrest of Colonel Clay (with the help of an enhanced photographic technique) and his trial. At the conclusion of the trial the judge has harsher words for Vandrift than for the confessed confidence man:

> The judge summed up in a caustic way which was pleasant to neither party. He asked the jury to dismiss from their minds entirely the impression created by what he frankly described as 'Sir Charles Vandrift's obvious dishonesty.' They must not allow the fact that he was a millionaire—and a particularly shady one—to prejudice their feelings in favour of the prisoner. Even the richest—and vilest—of men must be protected. Besides, this was a public question. If a rogue cheated a rogue, he must still be punished. If a murderer stabbed or shot a murderer, he must still be hung for it. Society must see that the worst of thieves were not preyed upon by others. Therefore, the proved facts that Sir Charles Vandrift, with all his millions, had meanly tried to cheat the prisoner, or some other poor person, out of valuable diamonds—had basely tried to juggle Lord Craig-Ellachie's mines into his own hands—had vilely tried to bribe a son to betray his father—had directly tried, by underhand means, to save his own money, at the risk of destroying the wealth of others who trusted to his probity—these proved facts must not blind them to the

truth that the prisoner at the bar (if he were really Colonel Clay) was an abandoned swindler.

This, however, was noting new to readers—Allen had introduced his notion much earlier—half way through the book. Thus in "The Episode of the Drawn Game" he gives his readers this exchange from and about his characters:

> "I hardly know whether I'm exactly the man to make the hero of a novel," Charles murmured, with complacence. And he certainly didn't look it.
>
> "I was thinking rather of Colonel Clay as the hero," the poet responded coldly.
>
> "Ah, that's the way with you men of letters," Charles answered, growing warm. "You always have a sneaking sympathy with the rascals."
>
> "That may be better," Coleyard retorted, in an icy voice, "than sympathy with the worst forms of Stock Exchange speculation."

ARTHUR MORRISON

Three years after introducing detective Martin Hewitt, his replacement for Sherlock Holmes, in *The Strand Magazine*, Arthur Morrison wrote a series of six stories about Horace Dorrington that ran from January to June 1897 in *The Windsor Magazine*. The same year Ward and Lock published them as *The Dorrington Deed Box*, an incomplete book that begins with a nascent frame story about the theft of James Rigby's identity, proceeds to Rigby's examination of documents related to the firm of Dorrington and Hicks, private inquiry agents, which unfold five "episodes" or "cases," but then simply ends without wrapping up the frame story. The six stories that comprise *The Dorrington Deed* box all recount ingenious stratagems designed to make Dorrington money. These center on identity theft ("The Narrative of Mr. James Rigby"), theft ("The Case of the Mirror of Portugal"), and extortion ("The Affair of the Avalanche Bicycle & Tyre Co., Ltd."). All of them contain elements of standard detective stories. Morrison frequently turns his narratives on close observation and Dorrington's discovery of minutiae—fragments of a bottle in "The Mirror of Portugal" and bits of adhesive tape in "The Affair of the Avalanche Bicycle & Tyre Co., Ltd.," for example. Furthermore he includes and uses clues in the stories in the same teasing manner that was becoming standard in contemporary detective stories. Thus

> then he turned his attention to the chair. It was, as I have said, a light chair made of flat iron strip, bent to shape and riveted. It had seen good service, and its present coat of green paint was evidently far from being its original one. Also it was rusty in places, and parts had been repaired and strengthened with cross-pieces secured by bolts and square nuts, some rusty and loose. It was from one of these square nuts, holding a cross-piece that stayed the back at the top, that Dorrington secured some object—it might have been a hair—which he carefully transferred to his pocket-book. This done, with one more glance round, he betook himself to the pavilion ["The Affair of the Avalanche Bicycle & Tyre Co., Ltd."].

Hicks of the firm of Dorrington and Hicks makes only a cameo appearance in the stories; the star of them is charming, articulate, intelligent, and utterly unscrupulous Horace Dorrington: "I may as well tell you that I'm a bit of a scoundrel myself, by way of profession. I don't boast about it, but it's well to be frank in making arrangements of this sort" ("The Narrative of Mr. James Rigby"). Dorrington possesses the talents and skills of the standard contemporary fictional detective—curiosity, discipline, imagination, knowledge, etc. But instead of using them to serve justice he uses them to serve himself:

> For it was an important thing in Dorrington's rascally trade to get hold of as much of other people's private business as possible, and to know exactly in what cupboard to find every man's skeleton. For there was no knowing but it might be turned into money sooner or later ["The Narrative of Mr. James Rigby"].

There is, however, a difference between the rascal and the villain, and Morrison comes close to stepping over the line in the opening stories in *The Dorrington Deed Box*. In them Dorrington contemplates and in fact plans murder, the murder of James Rigby whose identity he plans to steals. Then things change. In one of the later stories, "The Case of Mr. Loftus Deacon," Dorrington acts as a conventional detective, and in two of the final four stories Morrison pits his hero against criminals. These reenact the motif of the biter bit. In "The Affair of the Avalanche Bicycle & Tyre Co., Ltd.," for example, because of his skill as a detective, Dorrington is able to extort money from a businessman when he uncovers his plans to dupe the public by selling stock in a dummy corporation. And then there is "The Case of the Mirror of Portugal" which posits more moral complexity. In that story the thieves Dorrington hopes to beat choose to throw a priceless diamond into the Thames rather than let him best them. So whether it was the choice of *The Windsor Magazine* or Morrison's own desire to move on to other characters, Dorrington is a variety of rascals rather than one consistent character.

GUY BOOTHBY

From January through June 1897 Guy Boothby took a break from his Dr. Nicola novels and published six stories in *Pearson's Magazine* with the generic title "A Prince of Swindlers" and an additional sub-title—thus "A Prince of Swindlers: The Duchess of Wiltshire's Diamonds," etc. These were collected and published as *A Prince of Swindlers* in 1900 and later as *The Viceroy's Protégé, or A Prince of Swindlers*. They provide episodes from the career of Simon Carne who takes advantage of a chance encounter with the Viceroy of India and, through his influence, becomes a social lion back in England. Carne, however, is not the wealthy aesthete he pretends to be—nor is he Detective Klimo, his alter ego. He is a gentleman crook. Boothby dresses his Simon Carne adventures in an underdeveloped frame story involving Carne's relationship with "the famous Trincomalee Liz, whose doings had made her notorious from the

Saghalian coast to the shores of the Persian Gulf, [and who] was at the prime of her life and beauty—a beauty such as no man who has ever seen it will ever forget" ("Introduction"). Right out of Rider Haggard, in the beginning Liz advances Carne the immense sum of cash he requires to set himself up in London, and in the last story, "An Imperial Finale," Liz warns Carne that a detective is on his trail, thus allowing him to sail off with his spoils. Other than that help from Liz, Carne is on his own with only the assistance of his Indian craftsman servants and Belton his valet-assistant. While some of *The Dorrington Deed Box* stories (running at the same time) have elements of the caper story in them, describing ingenious, seemingly impossible, and dangerous crimes is the principal focus of the *Prince of Swindlers* tales. Like all of the stories, "The Duchess of Wiltshire's Diamonds" begins with a knotty (and criminal) problem to solve:

> "I have cracked a good many hard nuts in my time," he said reflectively, "but never one that seemed so difficult at first sight as this. As far as I see at present, the case stands as follows: the box will be brought from the bank where it usually reposes to Wiltshire House on the morning of the dance. I shall be allowed to have possession of it, without the stones of course, for a period possibly extending from eleven o'clock in the morning to four or five, at any rate not later than seven, in the evening. After the ball the necklace will be returned to it, when it will be locked up in the safe, over which the butler and a footman will mount guard."
>
> "To get into the room during the night is not only too risky, but physically out of the question; while to rob Her Grace of her treasure during the progress of the dance would be equally impossible. The Duke fetches the casket and takes it back to the bank himself, so that to all intents and purposes I am almost as far off the solution as ever."

Boothby shows his hero stealing diamonds, horsenapping the Derby favorite, cracking a millionaire's safe, and robbing an Austrian nobleman of his gold plate. In four of the episodes, then, the victims fall easily into the Robin Hood category—to the Duke of Wiltshire, for instance, the loss of his wife's priceless diamonds hardly makes a dent in his bank balance. In "A Service to the State," a story which deals with the Sinn Fein bombings, Carne thwarts Irish American bombers and walks away with their money. And, almost in compensation for that good deed, in "A Case of Philanthropy" at gun point Carne steals a fund for the relief of earthquake victims in the Canary Islands. In each case much of the readers' gratification rests on seeing Simon Carne accomplish the impossible, much like a magician: "It was as clever a conjuring trick as any he had ever seen" ("The Duchess of Wiltshire's Diamonds"). The stories, however, do not rest simply on fascination with the mechanics of "impossible" crimes, they also convey the gratification Carne derives from planning and executing perfect crimes. Thus

> though the business which was taking him out would have presented sufficient dangers to have deterred many men who consider themselves not wanting in pluck,

it did not in the least oppress Simon Carne; on the contrary, it seemed to afford him no small amount of satisfaction. He whistled a tune to himself as he drove along the lamplit thoroughfares, and smiled as sweetly as a lover thinking of his mistress when he reviewed the plot he had so cunningly contrived ["A Service to the State"].

FREDERICK MERRICK WHITE

1897 was the year for gentleman crooks. From June to May 1898 Frederick Merrick White published twelve stories in *The Ludgate* that were collected as *The Master Criminal*. Although seriously off the mark, White prefaced his stories with a brief explanation of his intent:

> The history of famous detectives, imaginary and otherwise, has frequently been written, but the history of a famous criminal—never.
>
> This is a bold statement, but a true one all the same. The most notorious of rascals know that sooner or later they will be found out, and they therefore plan their lives accordingly. But they are always found out in the end. And yet there must be many colossal rascals who have lived and died apparently with the odor of sanctity. Such a character would be quite new to fiction, and herein I propose to attempt the history of the Sherlock Holmes of malefactors.
>
> Given a rascal with the intellect of the famous creation in question, and detection would be reduced to a vanishing point.

White's *Ludgate* stories chronicle the exploits of Felix Gryde. An unassuming and anonymous individual, Glyde looked like "the poplar conception of a minor poet, save for the fact that Gryde was clean of garb and kept his hair cut." White makes him a master of disguise and his hero appears in a new identity in most of the stories. Indeed, White shows a lot more interest in portraying the alternate identities his hero assumes than explaining why he dedicates his life to felony or how he lives in his proper persona. In other words, White is more interested in the criminal than the gentleman part of the formula. Gryde, granted, wants to be at the top of his profession: "I can see in this the elements of the most remarkable and daring crime in the history of matters predatory." At the same time, however, White plays down the notion of genius as being part of the make-up of the gentleman crook when Gryde says, "Fortune always does seem to favor the man who has capital, energy, and an amazing faculty for taking pains." Essentially caper stories, White's tales center on his hero pulling off one gigantic coup after another—from robbing Windsor Castle, to fixing a famous race meeting, to holding the body of a deceased emperor for a £100,000 ransom. He has minions all over Europe who help him with his coups, but (other than occasional women companions) they are anonymous and disposable. Significantly, there are no detectives flummoxed in the stories primarily because there are no detectives in them—White simply ends them with Gryde's triumphs.

E.W. HORNUNG

A year after stories about Horace Dorrington, Simon Carne, and Felix Gryde ended their magazine runs, *Cassell's Magazine* published a story about another gentleman crook, "The Ides of March" by Ernest William Hornung. Hornung followed this up with a half dozen other stories about cricketer turned burglar A.J. Raffles which appeared together in 1899 as *The Amateur Cracksman*, a volume the author dedicated to his brother-in-law, Arthur Conan Doyle. Very quickly Raffles became one of the most popular characters of the era, and Hornung continued writing about him for ten years in the short story collections *The Black Mask* (aka *Raffles: Further Adventures of the Amateur Cracksman*) (1901), *A Thief in the Night* (1905), and in the novel *Mr. Justice Raffles* (1909). Watson-like, one of Raffles' old school mates, "Bunny" Manders, narrates the tales—and comes off as one of the most servile and besotted of the contemporary companion stereotype. Thus

> nor was this simply because Raffles had the subtle power of making himself irre-sistible at will. He was beyond comparison the most masterful man whom I have ever known; yet my acquiescence was due to more than the mere subjection of the weaker nature to the stronger ["The Ides of March"].

Raffles and Manders turn to crime because they have run out of money. Several times Raffles says that his crimes are just a phase: "I've never brought off a really big coup yet; when I do I shall chuck it up" ("The Ides of March"). "The Ides of March" recounts their burglary of a jewelry store; "A Costume Piece" narrates a botched jewel robbery; "Gentlemen and Players" again turns on burgling jewels; "Le Premier Pas" follows how mistaken identity ushers Raffles into a life of crime; "Willful Murder" turns on protecting their secret identity by murder; "Nine Points of the Law" concerns Raffles and Bunny stealing and returning a painting to its rightful owner; "The Return Match" shows the gentlemen crooks saving a professional burglar from the police; and "The Gift of the Emperor" ends the first series with Raffles' theft of a rare and valuable pearl, his narrow escape from Detective Mackenzie, and Bunny's arrest. In most of the stories things simply do not turn out the way Raffles plans them. The Raffles stories, then, are hardly caper pieces; rather they place great emphasis on the hero's insouciance, ingenuity, and motivation. Hornung, in fact, provides readers with a catalog of explanations for Raffles' (and Bunny's) vocational choices. There is, of course, want—both men turn to crime because they have lost all of their cash. And Hornung even tips in an aside on socialism in the first story:

> Of course it's very wrong, but we can't all be moralists, and the distribution of wealth is very wrong to begin with.

But Hornung pays more attention to other motives. In "A Costume Piece" he brings in the idea of art for art's sake:

Does the writer only write when the wolf is at the door? Does the painter paint for bread alone? Must you and I be *driven* to crime like Tom of Bow and Dick of Whitechapel? You pain me, my dear chap; you needn't laugh, because you do. Art for art's sake is a vile catchword, but I confess it appeals to me. In this case my motives are absolutely pure, for I doubt if we shall ever be able to dispose of such peculiar stones. But if I don't have a try for them—after tonight—I shall never be able to hold up my head again.

Highlighted by Raffles' fame as a cricketer, Hornung also links crime and sport. In "Gentlemen and Players" Raffles explains that

> cricket ... like everything else, is good enough sport until you discover a better. As a source of excitement it isn't in it with other things you wot of, Bunny, and the involuntary comparison becomes a bore. What's the satisfaction of taking a man's wicket when you want his spoons? Still, if you can bowl a bit your low cunning won't get rusty, and always looking for the weak spot's just the kind of mental exercise one wants. Yes, perhaps there's some affinity between the two things after all.

Sport, to be sure, depends upon mastery of technique, as Bunny observes in "The Ides of March":

> And there I stood, shining my light and holding my phial with a keener interest than I had ever brought to any honest avocation. And there knelt A. J. Raffles, with his black hair tumbled, and the same watchful, quiet, determined half-smile with which I have seen him send down over after over in a county match!

More importantly, however, sport generates excitement, and Hornung mentions excitement as a motive in each of the stories, for example:

> The truth is that I was entering into our nefarious undertaking with an involuntary zeal of which I was myself quite unconscious at the time. The romance and the peril of the whole proceeding held me spellbound and entranced. My moral sense and my sense of fear were stricken by a common paralysis. And there I stood, shining my light and holding my phial with a keener interest than I had ever brought to any honest avocation ["The Ides of March"].
>
> His eyes were brighter than I had known them for many a day. They shone with the perverted enthusiasm which was roused in him only by the contemplation of some new audacity ("Gentlemen and Players").

Indeed the desire for concentrated excitement even extends to a contemplation of the thrill experienced by murderers:

> I've told you before that the biggest man alive is the man who's committed a murder, and not yet been found out; at least he ought to be, but he so very seldom has the soul to appreciate himself. Just think of it! Think of coming in here and talking to the men, very likely about the murder itself; and knowing you've done it; and wondering how they'd look if *they* knew! Oh, it would be great, simply great! ["Wilful Murder"].

Raffles, however, never commits the murder he contemplates in "Willful Murder" and Hornung instead shows his readers the soul-destroyed and pitiable character of the real murderer.

DAVID CHRISTIE MURRAY

In 1899 David Christie Murray, who had dabbled in detective fiction four years earlier, published *A Rogue's Conscience*—a simplified moral homily on the subject of the rogue as hero. The novel begins with the description of the complicated and clever escape from arrest contrived by James Mortimer and his Scottish partner, Alexander Ross, who have stolen a large quantity of the paper upon which the Bank of England notes are printed and are counterfeiting and passing notes which the Bank must honor. Mortimer is the brains of the partnership—indeed he is an aristocrat among rogues:

> There are people who find the idea of an aristocracy absurd. As if there were not an aristocracy in every rank and walk of life! As if a dozen men could ever live together for a month without making one of one sort or another—of brains, or money, or muscle, or daring, or cunning, or goodness, or cruelty, or anything in which some one of their number was uppermost. James was an aristocrat in his own walk of life, and, even with the full consciousness that the supreme moment was close at hand, he was proud and pleased to have his position recognized.

For Mortimer, at least, the rogue's uncertain and dangerous life has its compensation:

> His active rogue's mind shot out defensive thoughts this way and that; examined, criticised, and found all complete. It was an hour of supreme invention, supreme importance, and he felt glorious and like a hero.

Throughout the early parts of the novel Murray provides Mortimer with speeches on his way of life, like this one:

> You see, sir, that when a man is what people call a scoundrel he runs some danger. All men, I find, estimate all other men by themselves. I never betrayed a partner, but that is not my form of scoundrelism; and I am not only a scoundrel, but a philosopher. I will do, for gain and an easy life, what a great many other people will not do.

The counterfeiters escape to Canada with their swag which they continue to disburse in the colonies. In a frontier town they settle down. With the discovery of gold, a forest fire, the kindling of young love, a vigilante mob, and the danger of the exposure of his past in the background, Mortimer engages in a discussion of roguery. Among his points is a thinly disguised, self-aggrandizing self-portrait:

> He gave them as the experiences of an old school fellow—"a man of the highest family," he said; "a man of charming manners and of various accomplishments."

This person, according to his historian's account, had deliberately chosen "a life of what most people would call crime." James, who could tell a story admirably, held his listener enthralled with the history of his acquaintance's escapes, which he professed to have received at first hand from the lips of the adventurer as he lay upon his last bed.

"He was a good rascal," said James. "He had a variety of excellent qualities. He gave away the greater portion of his ill-got gains. I have never heard of his passing a case of distress without relieving it, when he had money in his pocket. He regarded himself as a sort of modern Robin Hood taking toll from the rich for the benefit of the humble."

His listener, however, counters with

I don't fancy I was thinking of your kind of wickedness... if you have any to boast of. I was thinking of the really wicked—the cruel, the heartless the selfish people; such people, for example, as those who ruined my father. Of course, at the very bottom of their hearts, they are ignorant to begin with.... A dense and impenetrable ignorance of other people's feelings, of other people's hopes and despairs; an ignorance black and absolute; a dark and total isolation of the heart.

Whether it is these arguments or a renewal provided by the New World and being surrounded by good, hard working, honest people, in the end Mortimer gives up the scoundrel's life and even reinforces Ross' determination to go straight by making him feel what their victims have felt.

R. Austin Freeman and
John J. Pitcairn

Having yet to invent Dr. Thorndyke, in 1902 R. Austin Freeman and John J. Pitcairn, writing as Clifford Ashdown, published *The Adventures of Romney Pringle*, a collection of six stories, some of which, at least, had appeared in *Cassell's Magazine*, beginning with "The Assyrian Rejuvenator" in June of 1902. Five more Pringle stories appeared in *Cassell's* in 1903 but had to wait until the 1960s to be published as *The Further Adventures of Romney Pringle*. More reminiscent of Dorrington than of Raffles, Romney Pringle's nominal profession perhaps hints at a wry approach to the stories: he is a writers' depiction of a literary agent. Pringle is a literary agent who does nothing concerning getting manuscripts read or published. Rather he is an opportunist who appropriates the plans and schemes of others when legal or illegal gain is to be made. Most of the stories recount how opportunities to make illicit profits quite literally fall into Pringle's hands—thus the dropped letter in "The Assyrian Rejuvenator," the chance meeting with Redmile in "The Foreign Office Dispatch," the mistaken identity in "The Lizard's Scale," etc. Frequently these accidents lead into biter bit plots, plots in which Pringle outsmarts criminals and walks of with their profits. In "The Assyrian Rejuvenator," for example he frightens off the sellers of fake patent medicine and cashes the postal orders sent to them for new orders, and there is the same kind of tables turned in "Paste Diamonds." Other than his capacity for innovation, the skill Romney Pringle most often displays is that of disguise. Indeed, in each story he removes the artificial port wine stain from his cheek, a facial feature of Pringle the nominal businessman, and assumes one disguise or another with wig, hair coloring, etc. Freeman-like the stories also pay attention to the description of processes. Here is how Pringle forges a government seal he later uses to manipulate international stock markets:

> On a table in one corner stood a glass vessel containing a clear blue solution. In this, well-coated with black lead, was immersed the seal abstracted from the waste-paper basket, which with a plate of copper, also hanging in the solution, was connected to wires of a detached electric lamp; in the course of the night the potent electricity had covered the wax with a deposit of copper sufficiently thick to form a perfect intaglio of the seal ["The Foreign Office Dispatch"].

While there is detail aplenty regarding how Pringle's capers work, Freeman and Pitcairn give readers scant information about their hero, particularly about whether he has (or does not have) thoughts or feelings about his less than wholesome livelihood. The closest they come is this quick glance in "The Kailyard Novel":

> At the very least it might prove an agreeable holiday, and in any case would lead to a new and probably amusing experience of human nature. Smiling at the ludicrous audacity of the idea, Pringle strolled up to the mantelpiece and interrogated himself in the Venetian mirror. Minus the delible port-wine mark, a pair of pince-nez, blackened hair, and a small strip of easily applied whisker would be a sufficient disguise. He thoughtfully lighted another cigarette.

But readers never know what those thoughts were; all the writers allowed them to see was the cleverness of their rogue hero's plot and counterplot.

MIRIAM MICHELSON

In 1903 Miriam Michelson's *In the Bishop's Carriage* was a best seller in the United States. Its popularity had little to do with the rage for Raffles or the character of the gentleman burglar. First of all, it was a story about a woman criminal and not a man, and secondly it had more connection with melodrama than with the conventions of crime or detective fiction. In the novel Nance Olden tells her story to her friend Mag Monohan, both of whom were orphans raised together at the Society for the Prevention of Cruelty to Children—or "the Cruelty" as the women call it. Nance has partnered with Tom Dorgan stealing whatever, wherever, and whenever opportunity arises. She is clearly the brains of the operation, living by her wits—hiding from the police, for instance, in the Bishop's carriage and playing the part of a college girl with amnesia in the opening scenes of the novel. While Tom is arrested and sent to prison (where he becomes more brutish and savage), Nance escapes arrest both through her wits and especially with the help of benevolent friends, including theater owner Overmuller, who turns her talents to acting. Along the way Nance has words with one of her benefactors on crime and the distribution of wealth:

> Your clown-criminal don't jump into the ring because he's so full of fun he can't stay out. He goes in for the same reason the real clown does—because he gets hungry and thirsty and sleepy and tired like other men, and he's got to fill his stomach and cover his back and get a place to sleep. And it's because your kind gets too much, that my kind gets so little it has to piece it out with this sort of thing. No, you don't know it quite all.

With success, however, instead of economic musings on crime, Nance boils success down to redirecting talents:

> After all, Miss Monahan, this graft of honesty they all preach so much about hasn't anything mysterious in it. All it is, is putting your wits to work according to the rules of the game and not against them.... And first thing you know, 'pon honor, Mag, it was as much fun planning how to "earn it now" as any lifting I ever schemed. It's getting the best of people that always charmed me—and here was a way to fool 'em according to law.

The second part of the novel concerns Nance's success as a comic actor and Impresario Overmuller's fight with the Theater Trust which intends to drive him out of business. The redeemed Nance gains the confidence of the head of the trust and steals a document which will reveal the Trust's illegal restraint of trade. The Trust capitulates, Overmuller and Nance marry, and she commits herself to good works—especially at the orphanage where she was housed.

Sidney Paternoster

It is a stretch to include Sidney Paternoster's *The Motor Pirate* (1904) with books written for adult audiences. In it one James Sutgrove tells the story of how he, accompanied by Inspector Forrest of Scotland Yard, seeks the identity and capture of the individual who possesses a preternaturally fast motor car and who stops and robs other motorists, including a Royal Personage who has gone out for a spin. From very early on it is apparent to all but the characters in the novel that the Pirate is Mannering, one of the neighboring gentry and Sutgrove's rival for the hand of Evie Maitland. Paternoster acknowledges that his story has some roots in romances about English highwaymen:

> His deeds were quite black enough without further blackening with printer's ink, and it would be a pity if the real Motor Pirate were lost sight of in mythical haze such as has gathered about the name of his great prototype, Dick Turpin.

Largely the narrative describes the hero and his Scotland Yard companion scouring rural byways or engaging in futile chases which reach speeds up to

60 miles per hour. At the end they look into Mannering's workshop, find a prototype of an even faster car powered by "liquid hydrogen." The story ends with the Pirate purposely driving his car off a cliff into the ocean. The only reflection on why a member of the gentry would take to crime is Sutgrove's brief comment that

> by that tragedy the world lost a brilliant thinker and inventor, though unfortunately these great talents were accompanied by an abnormal condition of mind, which led the owner to utilise his invention in criminal pursuits.

Henry Hering

Henry Hering's *The Burglar's Club: A Romance in Twelve Chronicles* (1906) aims at a different audience altogether. Originally published in *Pearson's Magazine*—beginning with "Sir John Carder's Cigars" (January 1905)—*The Burglar's Club* collects twelve lightly ironic stories concerning the exploits of a club of bachelor aristocrats based on a unique purpose:

> You see, we are men who've pretty well exhausted the pleasures of life. We've all been in the Army or the Navy, all of us are sportsmen, and we are bachelors; so there isn't much excitement left for us. We've started a Burglars' Club to help things on a bit. The entrance fee is a town burglary, the subject to be set by our President, and every other year each member has to keep up his subscription by a provincial line.

The items to be burgled in the series begin with a box of expensive cigars, but Hering quickly raises the stakes by making the burglars' targets famous and priceless items from a bishop's jeweled crozier, to the manuscript of *Pilgrim's Progress*, to an ounce of Radium, to the Great Seal of England. Each item is returned to its owner after display at a club meeting: these are gentleman burglars, after all. Indeed Hering ignores the moral implications of crime and provides his readers with what amounts to a series of college pranks. Rather than examining the emotional rush noted in the description of the Burglar's Club, the focus in each narrative lies in the individual hero's demonstration not only of inventiveness and sang froid, but also suavity and noblesse oblige. The stories in *The Burglar's Club* in part may be caper stories, but they also contain surprises. In "An Ounce of Radium," for instance, readers don't know that the burglar has brought a lead-lined container to hold the radium and feigns symptoms of sickness to dupe the sadistic scientist. Charwomen thwart the burglary when they mistakenly use Bunyan's manuscript to start the morning fires in "The Bunyan MS." Both "The Luck of the Illingworths" and "The Great Seal" have the heroes come upon other burglars with the same objects in mind. And in several of the stories, the unintended consequences of the burglaries involve preventing greater crimes—as the revelation at the close of "Sir John Carder's

Cigars" that Carder had been cheating on government contracts, and Birket Rivers' discovery of clandestine negotiations for a treaty between Russia and Persia. All of the stories in the collection, moreover, highlight what amounts to grace under pressure—the ability to respond to changing situations by thinking quickly and accurately.

ARTHUR STRINGER

Before R. Austin Freeman's Dr. Thorndyke stories or Arthur B. Reeve's Craig Kennedy tales, Arthur Stringer made explaining technology applied to crime one of his aims. Thus in *The Wire Tappers* (1906) Stringer showed that he was up to date on the newest ways to make a dishonest living. Take safe cracking:

> Now, once more, speaking as an expert, by lighting a small piece of sulphur, and using it as a sort of match to start and maintain combustion, I could turn on a stream of liquid oxygen and burn through that safe-steel about the same as a carpenter bores through a pine board. But the trouble is in getting the oxygen. Then, again, if it was a mere campaign of armour against the intruder, I could win out in quite a different way. I could take powdered aluminum, mixed with some metallic superoxide, such as iron-rust, and get what you'd call thermit. Then I could *take* this thermit, and ignite it by means of a magnesium wire, so that it would burn down through three inches of steel like a handful of live coals through three inches of ice. That is, if we wanted to be scientific and up-to-date. Or, even a couple of gallons of liquid air, say, poured on the top of the safe, ought to chill the steel so that one good blow from a sledge would crack it.

Stringer even has his hero invent an electric drill to aid in burglarous acts. But the principal focus on technology in *The Wire Tappers* is something more up to date than cracking safes: it's the ways and means of stealing data by tapping telegraph and telephone lines. Here is one of them:

> When Durkin leaned out of the window for the second time he held in his hand something that looked peculiarly like a fishing-rod. From it dangled two thin green wires, and with the metal hook on the end of it he tested and felt carefully up among the slovenly tangle of wires running out past the overhanging eave.
>
> It was a silly and careless way of doing things, he inwardly decided, this lazy stringing of wires from house-top to house-top, instead of keeping them in the tunnels where they belonged. It was not only violating regulations, but it was putting a premium on "lightning-slinging." And he remembered what Frances had once said to him about criminals in a city like New York, how the careless riot of wealth seemed to breed them, as any uncleanness breeds bacteria; how, in a way, each was only a natural and inevitable agent, taking advantage of organic waste, seizing on the unguarded and the unorderly. She had even once argued that the criminal could lay claim to a distinct economic value, enjoining, as he did, continual alertness of attention and cleanliness of commercial method.
>
> Yet the devil himself, he had somewhere read, could quote Scripture for his pur-

pose; and his fishing-pole moved restlessly up and down, like a long finger feeling through answering strings. For each time, almost, that his hook rested on one of the wires the little Bunnell relay on the table behind him spoke out feebly. To the trill and clatter of these metallic pulsations Durkin listened intently, until, determining that he had looped into the right wire, he made secure his switch and carefully drew down the window to within an inch of the sill.

Stringer based *The Wire Tappers*, in part, on depicting a series of technology-based capers. The heroes are Jim Durkin, a telegraph operator from the provinces with ambitions to invent revolutionary communication devices, and Frances Candler, an English woman unfairly fired from her job as a governess, both of whom become swept up by organized crime in New York. Readers see the pair tap telegraph and telephone lines in order to win money betting on horse races, buying cotton futures, cracking a jeweler's safe, and trying to stay a step ahead of their underworld nemesis, McNutt, and the police. Running in the background, Stringer follows Frances Candler's struggles with conscience. She feels the pull of excitement that crime brings:

> Some mysterious touch of his excitement at last communicated itself to the listening woman, almost against her will. She was as fluctuant, she told herself, as the aluminum needle of a quadrant electrometer.... Yet, as she comprehended Durkin's plot, point by point, she began to realize the vast possibilities that confronted them, and, as ever before, to fall a victim to the zest of action, the vital sting of responsibility. Nor did she allow herself to lose sight of the care and minuteness of the continued artfulness and finish, so teeming with its secondary aesthetic values, with which he had reconnoitered his ever-menacing territory and laid his mine. And added to this, she saw, was the zest of stalking the stalker: it carried with it an ameliorating tang of dramatic irony, an uncouth touch of poetic justice.

Frances, however, also feels repugnance from their criminal acts and becomes an increasingly hesitant partner. Throughout the novel Stringer shows both Frances' struggle with her conscience and her attempts to wean Jim from the life of crime to which he becomes increasingly addicted. In the end, of course, she wins and the couple sail away from the corrupt city to begin a new life together.

GEORGE RANDOLPH CHESTER

George Randolph Chester began writing stories about J. Rufus Wallingford in *The Saturday Evening Post* on October 5, 1907; these continued in the magazine until February 27, 1909. In 1908, in book form, Chester published *Get Rich Quick Wallingford*, a casually connected series of narratives about his larger than life confidence man. These begin with J. Rufus convincing his mark to invest in a scheme to manufacture colored carpet tacks, an idea which the mark believes to be original—but which is not. He then moves to another town where he takes over a fraternal order's insurance program and turns it into a ponzi scheme. Next he steals an inventor's invention and patent which he sells for immense profit. Traveling in the West, Wallingford stops in a small town and engages in land speculation. After a hasty exit, he undertakes to manipulate the market for wheat futures, and then tries to create a local monopoly of tobacconists. Throughout all of this, Wallingford lives in a world of profligate luxury—none of which he actually pays for, in part because he looks like he is rich:

> As the cab door opened and out of it stepped one of those impressive beings for whom the best things of this world have been especially made and provided. He was a large gentleman, a suave gentleman, a gentleman whose clothes not merely fit him but distinguished him, a gentleman of rare good living, even though one of the sort whose faces turn red when they eat; and the dignity of his worldly prosperousness surrounded him like a blessed aura.

In the first five episodes Wallingford enters with no money to invest (or live on), but leaves with a great deal, duping not only his original mark but also the friends and acquaintances who the mark draws into Wallingford's con. In the last two, however, Wallingford loses, first to a dishonest broker who does not follow his instructions and defeats Wallingford's plans, and then to a politician who edges Wallingford out of the way and takes over his money-making scheme. Wallingford's world runs on cycles of dishonesty:

> Here you go out West and trim a bunch of come-ons for twenty-five thousand, and what do you do next? Oh, just tarry here long enough to tuck that neat little bundle into the pocket of a bucket-shop broker that throws away the bucket! You'd think he was the wise boy, after that, but he'll drop your twenty-five thousand on a wire-tapping game, and the wire tapper will buy gold bricks with it. The goldbrick man will give it to the bookies and the bookies will lose it on stud poker. I'm a Billy goat myself. I clean up ten thousand last week on mining stock that permits Mr. Easy Mark to mine if he wants to, and I pay it right over last night for the fun of watching a faro expert deal from a sanded deck!

Chester's sub title for *Get Rich Quick Wallingford* was "a cheerful account of the rise and fall of an American business buccaneer." Throughout the book Wallingford repeats that nothing he does is against the law, that others provide him with opportunities and wealth because they are naïve or innocent or ignorant or greedy. As the episodes proceed, however, some of his victims become more sympathetic to the readers, and his wife's counsel to settle down becomes more articulated—and ignored. At the end, when Wallingford is arrested, Chester makes his point about Wallingford clear:

> You're not an individual criminal at all. You're only the logical development of the American tendency to 'get there' no matter how. It is the national weakness, the national menace, and you're only an exaggerated molecule of it. You think that so long as you stay inside the *law* you're all right, even morally; but a man who habitually shaves so close to the narrow edge is going to slip off some time.

E. Phillips Oppenheim

One of the most prolific writers in an age of prolific writers, E. Phillips Oppenheim's main claim to fame is being one of the inventors of espionage fiction. On October 1909 in the American edition of *Pearson's Magazine* he began a series of stories about Peter Ruff which concluded in 1911. In 1912 the twenty one stories appeared as *Peter Ruff and the Double Four*. The first half of the stories in the collection concern Peter Ruff as a reformed gentleman crook, and stories of the second half substitute international intrigue for crime. This switch has to do with the changing role of the "Double Four": in the first stories "The Double Four" is an international criminal syndicate, and in the later it becomes an international organization dedicated to preventing dirty work between nations. As the series begins, Oppenheim's hero is about to give up his life of crime—which encompasses both burglary and embezzlement— and settle into respectable, law-abiding suburban life with Maud Barnes. Inspector John Dory of the Yard, however, smashes this idyl by entering to arrest Spencer Fitzgerald. Escaping, Fitzgerald vows that "'I have no alternative,' he answered. 'The law has kicked me out from the respectable places. The law shall pay!'" Changing his name to Peter Ruff, he is too wise to return to his felonious ways. Instead he calls himself a private investigator and commits himself to a particular mission:

> Have you not sometimes come into contact with people driven into a situation from which they would willingly commit any crime to escape if they dared? It is not with them a question of money at all—it is simply a matter of ignorance. They do not know how to commit a crime. They have had no experience, and if they attempt it, they know perfectly well that they are likely to blunder. A person thoroughly experienced in the ways of criminals—a person of genius like myself— would have, without a doubt, an immense clientele, if only he dared put up his signboard. Literally, I cannot do that. Actually, I mean to do so! I shall be willing to accept contracts either to help nervous people out of an undesirable crisis; or, on the other hand, to measure my wits against the wits of Scotland Yard, and to discover the criminals whom they have failed to secure ["Introducing Mr. Peter Ruff"].

In the first two episodes Peter Ruff remains faithful to this calling—in both cases providing a live person for one thought to have been dead. And in almost all of the stories in the first half, Ruff's minor goal is to embarrass Inspector John Dory, the policeman who interrupted his dreams of a middle class life in Streatham and married his former fiancée. As the first half stories proceed, however, Ruff increasingly associates with the carriage trade, as in "The Indiscretion of Letty Shaw." In the first half, too, the Double Four enters and demands that Ruff accept a position on its council of leaders, a demand from which Ruff escapes by claiming to be married to his secretary, Violet Brown, a claim he turns into a fact. Violet had been with Ruff from the assumption of his new persona and profession. She understands its Robin Hood element:

> I am not over-scrupulous, you know. I hate wrongdoing, but I have never been able to treat as equal criminals the poor man who steals for a living, and the rich financier who robs right and left out of sheer greed. I agree with you that crime is not an absolute thing. The circumstances connected with every action in life determine its morality or immorality ["Introducing Mr. Peter Ruff"].

And she also understands the role of excitement in their new profession:

> "I came to you," she continued, looking at him earnestly, "for two reasons. The personal one I will not touch upon. The other was my love of excitement. I have tried many things in life, as you know, Peter, but I have seemed to carry always with me the heritage of weariness. I thought that my position here would help me to fight against it" ["Vincent Cawdor Commission Agent"].

MAY EDGINTON

In its June 1912 number, *Pearson's Magazine* began another run of tales about a rogue with "Nap Goes It Alone" ("The first adventure in which Napoleon Prince, engaging rogue, played a lone hand"). Thus began a series of stories by May Edginton featuring Napoleon Prince and his retinue (his sister, Jim Luck, his valet, and eventually his old flame Gerda) which became *The Games of Napoleon Prince* later in 1912. They center on Napoleon Prince's ingenious capers. Clearly he is in it for the fun and for the art:

> "Lord!" said he wearily. "What child's play! What rubbish! I had hoped for intricacies. If it wasn't for my artistic interest in my work we'd just bolt with this right now." He regarded the packet sombrely. "Here it is in our hands, and here it will remain, in our hands. But no! we won't be crude. We want to produce bankers' receipts, and have cut-glass locked into an official safe, and insured for thousands of pounds. We must get an element of subtlety into this farce. But really, saving your presence, Mary—how damn easy!" ["Johnny Luck"].

There had been plenty of smart rogues before Edginton, so the display of her hero's gifts and talents in solving knotty problems and leaving with the prize was hardly new. What was new was that until the final story in the collection in which his paralysis is cured, Napoleon Prince is wheelchair bound:

> Darn fine, he was. Crissen name 'Napoleon.' He'd got a head worth all the diplomatic services and Parliaments in Europe. He made the plans and we were to share the swag. He couldn't do much himself—got a sort o' creepin' paral'sis comin' up his right side, but his brain—my word! ["Johnny Luck"].

And in the first episode in the collection he meets Jim Luck who, in the first half of the stories, does for Prince those things he cannot. Prince, however, will not have just anyone work for him, he has his own standards:

"You're the kind of man I like. I wouldn't work with a cad. You are a gentleman. I don't want to know your story or your antecedents. You carry your birthmark. If the world has used you hardly, so much the better. You will have no scruples about hitting back as I hit. Scruples of any sort must go—my partners may have honour, but not honesty; pride, but no principles; manners, no morals. You follow me?" ["Johnny Luck"].

While Edginton does give readers a powerful international criminal syndicate, The Cosmopolitans, it plays very little part in the stories. In most cases Edginton's heroes steal from those who either don't deserve the treasure they possess or have acquired it by dubious and devious means. The capers Napoleon plans all have to do with stealing rare and precious things—famous jewels, artwork, and even the crown jewels of a minor European country. It is not work or even gain, however, that draws Napoleon Prince or Jim Luck to face danger and commit crimes—it's the lure and promise of adventure:

> It's a fine good world for rogue or saint. Rogue or saint, too, they're only a matter of terms. How'd you like a pure adventure this time, Johnnie? How'd you like to bring back a Lost Cause? All for sheer altruism? And for love of a ripping adventure full of sport and danger and brazen cheek? ["The Restoration of the King of Balukia"].

Jim Luck goes off stage in the middle of *The Adventures of Napoleon Prince* to marry Prince's sister and take up his inherited lordship. Gerda, Prince's long lost love, reenters and Napoleon makes her his partner in crime. In December 1912 Edginton began a new series in *Pearson's*. In it Napoleon has regained his health and the wheelchair is a thing of the past. Nonetheless, the new series continues to frame Napoleon's capers as play, and the generic title of the new series was "The Games of Napoleon Prince."

Arthur B. Reeve

Arthur B. Reeve had already begun his stories about scientist-detective Craig Kennedy published in *Cosmopolitan*, but beginning in 1913, perhaps attuned to the marketplace, he wrote a series of stories about a criminal hero. His Constance Dunlap was not only a criminal hero, she was a woman. In an odd turn of events, Harper Brother's edition of *Constance Dunlap* was published before its constituent chapters appeared in *Pearson's Magazine* which published those short stories/chapters from September 1913 ("The Forgers") to August 1914 ("The Fugitives"). Technically, Constance Dunlap is only really a criminal in the first story ("The Forgers") in which her husband embezzles from his employer and Constance tries to help him by using her skill as an artist to "raise" checks—erase the original amounts and forge new ones in their place. This is, however, to no avail and the police are on their trail. Carleton Dunlap leaves New York and eventually commits suicide, leaving his wife to fend for herself. Constance, however, does not go back into a life of crime, but in the succeeding eleven stories uses her wits to help desperate persons who have become involved in crime. Significantly, Reeve connects most of the crime in the stories with urban life—specifically urban life in New York City. This begins with Carleton Dunlap's original entry into embezzling to support their middle class life style: as he tells his wife, "You know as well as I that five thousand does not meet the social obligations laid on us by our position in the circle in which we are forced to move." In the succeeding stories Reeve brings in big business (in the form of the stock market and board room manipulation), embezzling, shop lifting, drug addiction, gambling, spiritualism, and divorce. Indeed, it turns out that Constance is addicted to the City's bipolar allure:

> Life in New York had seemed even more bitter to Constance than before. Yet the great city cast a spell over her, with its countless opportunities for adventure. She could not leave it, but had taken a suite in a quiet boarding house overlooking the bay from the Heights in Brooklyn.

The dark side of the City resides in the temptations crowding in upon innocents, innocents like Constance's husband. So, after Carleton's suicide Constance returns to the city and essentially makes a profession out of saving innocents from the power of temptation, the power of criminal predators, and the power of the law—in the form of private detective Drummond. Thus each of the stories is essentially the same: Constance meets someone in financial, personal, or legal trouble and helps them find a way out. While it is not quite as routine as in the Craig Kennedy stories, Reeve being Reeve, Constance often uses gadgets to solve her friends' problems: electronic eavesdropping devices, sphygmomanometers, fish eye lenses, thermite, etc. With all of this, Reeve also puts a thread of excitement into Constance's endeavors. Thus, in "The Gun Runners,"

> The appeal was romantic, almost irresistible. Besides—no, at the outset she put out of consideration any thought of the fascinating young soldier of fortune himself.

Reeve even puts a whiff of anarchy into his hero's character:

> The spirit of defiance of law and custom was strong upon her. That was all.

Ultimately, most of Constance's emotional satisfaction comes from the repeated encounters with detective Drummond. Drummond appears in each of the stories, sometimes representing blind, heavy-handed law enforcement, and sometimes in collusion with criminals representing corruption.

> It was a keen pleasure to feel that she was outwitting Drummond when, as some apparently insurmountable difficulty arose, she would overcome it.

In the last story, "The Fugitives," Constance once more outwits Drummond who says "Mrs. Dunlap.... I take my hat off to you." That being done, she recognizes the cost of her avocation: "She had talked in a moment of confidence of the loneliness she had felt since she had embarked as a rescuer of amateur criminals," and she goes off into the sunset committed to a new lover and a new life.

JOHN A. MOROSO

While *Pearson's Magazine* was publishing Reeve's Constance Dunlap stories, they also began a run of three stories by John A. Moroso: "Cuttlefish Farrington" (April 1914), "The Song of the Little Flower" (May 1914), and "Into the Night" (June 1914). All three center on Sir Francis Arthur Farrington:

> Tall and thin, with reddish hair streaked with silver, the mildest blue eyes and the nose and jaw of a fighting man, Sir Francis was of such distinguished appearance that many people would give him a second glance as he passed in the streets. None, however, would have thought the excellent gentleman with his well-ironed silk hat, his silver-tipped stick and his dressy walking suit of dark material a subject for the surveillance of Scotland Yard ["Cuttlefish Farrington"].

The ne'er do well peer, chucked out of his club, pensioned off by his family, veteran of the French Foreign Legion, finally settled down to make a serious study of penmanship, paper, and ink, making himself into an expert forger, nicknamed "cuttlefish" because of that creature's use of ink as a defense. The first of the three tales is a caper story, turning on forged checks and disappearing ink. The other two are comedies, one about how a wily woman cons both Farrington and his Foreign Legion friend Major Charles Dudney out of the bundle Cuttlefish got in the first story. The last piece, "Into the Night," is a sentimental tale in which the two Englishmen are rescued from penury by the head of the New York Mafia who asks them to assist him in kidnapping a world renowned tenor to sing for his dying daughter. In the world that Moroso depicts in these stories the police are doltish and the criminals' victims are contemptible nouveaux rich:

> From this establishment the ex–Legionary sallied for his morning strolls and for his afternoons and evenings mingling with the gilded coterie of transients in the drawing-rooms, tea-rooms, concert halls and cabarets of the most palatial of the hotels. Slowly but surely he made a place for himself in the Peacock Alleys of the richest and most boastful of the cities of the earth. It was the time of the year when the strutting of the money-burdened visitors was at its finest, for it is in spring and in summer that the merchant princes of the great cities of the West, the lumbermen and cattlemen, the men who mine copper and gold and silver seek New York for a good time, bringing their women and their wads with them ["Cuttlefish Farrington"].

On the other hand, Cuttlefish and the other criminals (including the Mafia chief) display likeable insouciance and bonhomie.

LOUIS JOSEPH VANCE

After one story about gentleman burglar Michael Lanyard in *Munsey's Magazine* (March 1914) Louis Joseph Vance wrote a novel about him—*The Lone Wolf: A Melodrama*. And then came the deluge: four more Lone Wolf novels (*The False Faces* [1918], *Alias the Lone Wolf* [1921], *The Lone Wolf Returns* [1923], and the posthumous *The Lone Wolf's Last Prowl* [1934]); a novel about his daughter (*Red Masquerade: Being the Story of the Lone Wolf's Daughter* [1921]); and a series of films beginning in 1917 which extended years beyond Vance's death in 1933. Subtitled "A Melodrama," the first novel begins with Michael Lanyand as a foundling being left at a hotel in Paris. After his Oliver Twistish beginning, Bourke, an Irish burglar, took the young Lanyard under his wing:

> Michael Lanyard learned many things; he became a mathematician of considerable promise, an expert mechanician, a connoisseur of armour-plate and explosives in their more pacific applications, and he learned to grade precious stones with a glance. Also, because Bourke was born of gentlefolk, he learned to speak English, what clothes to wear and when to wear them, and the civilized practice with knife and fork at table. And because Bourke was a diplomatist of sorts, Marcel acquired the knack of being at ease in every grade of society: he came to know that a self-made millionaire, taken the right way, is as approachable as one whose millions date back even unto the third generation; he could order a dinner at Sherry's as readily as drinks at Sharkey's. Most valuable accomplishment of all, he learned to laugh. In the way of by-products he picked up a working acquaintance with American, English and German slang—French slang he already knew as a mother-tongue—considerable geographical knowledge of the capitals of Europe, America and Illinois, a taste that discriminated between tobacco and the stuff sold as such in France, and a genuine passion for good paintings.

Between chapters one and two Lanyard has become a successful international criminal who lives in Paris under the guise of being an art connoisseur and collector. Presenting Lanyard's success off stage, of course, means that Vance is not interested in the caper side of the gentleman burglar story. Instead *The Lone Wolf* is a capture and escape thriller. On one hand the police in the person of a Scotland Yard detective threaten Lanyard with exposure and capture. And then there is The Pack. Instead of the vaguely defined international criminal syndicates in earlier gentleman crook stories, Vance picks up on the idea and uses it as a continuing threat to his hero. His syndicate, The Pack, has four leaders:

> Here we have Mr. Wertheimer, representing the swell-mobsmen across Channel; Monsieur le Comte standing for the gratin of Paris; Popinot, spokesman for our friends the Apaches; and the well-known Mr. Goodenough Smith, ambassador of the gun-men of New York.

And so, after chapter five, Vance's novel becomes a series of threats and escapes involving both Lanyard and his love interest, culminating in an escape to

England by biplane which includes an aerial chase and combat with the villains.

FRANK L. PACKARD

In May 1914 Frank L. Packard's "The Gray Seal" appeared in *People's Ideal Fiction Magazine*. It was followed by a run of seven other short stories in *People's Magazine*. These were included with other stories centered on Jimmie Dale in *The Adventures of Jimmie Dale* in 1917. After the War Jimmie Dale's adventures continued both in four books and in pulp magazines. Packard's hero, in fact, has been seen as the inspiration for a number of pulp era heroes. Jimmie Dale is a clubman whose wealth came from his father's safe manufacturing business (which he learned from the ground up) and who went into amateur safe cracking for the thrill of it:

> "He was the most puzzling, bewildering, delightful crook in the annals of crime," said Carruthers reminiscently, after a moment's silence. "Jimmie, he was the king-pin of them all. Clever isn't the word for him, or dare-devil isn't either. I used to think sometimes his motive was more than half for the pure deviltry of it, to laugh at the police and pull the noses of the rest of us that were after him. I used to dream nights about those confounded gray seals of his—that's where he got his name; he left every job he ever did with a little gray paper affair, fashioned diamond-shaped, stuck somewhere where it would be the first thing your eyes would light upon when you reached the scene."

Dale is not only the Gray Seal, he also maintains another secret identity as minor criminal Larry the Bat in order to stay current on happenings in the underworld jealous of the Gray Seal's notoriety and success. In the Jimmie Dale stories, then, Packard gives readers more than enough excitement. They are caper narratives detailing how he executes difficult exploits with clocks ticking and exposure around the corner. There are also capture and escape motifs in which the police, newspaper reporters and the underworld threaten to unmask and to capture his hero. Characteristic of the era, Packard presents the police as brutal and corrupt and most newspapers (except that of Jimmie's friend) as superficial and clueless. Finally Packard includes detective interest (along with the overriding suspense) with episodes that center on clues and evidence. Indeed Packard's plotting combines the gentleman crook tradition with that of the thrill a minute plotting of the dime novels which were evolving into the pulps when he wrote. In terms of character, from the first Packard lets his readers know that Jimmie Dale is not, in fact, simply a thrill-seeker but is on the side of the angels dedicated not to theft but to righting wrongs. And the intervention of a mysterious woman led him to that mission. Soon after his youthful hi-jinx of cracking safes for the fun of it, Dale begins to receive letters from an anonymous woman who is aware of his criminal activities, instructing him to undertake specific robberies which invariably turn out to be good deeds which relieve the innocent and aggrieve the guilty. But revealing her identity and introducing his criminal syndicate, the Crime Club, both occurred in later stories.

E.W. HORNUNG (AGAIN)

Having finished his last Raffles book, E.W. Hornung took another crack at criminals in stories in *Everybody's Magazine* collected as *The Crime Doctor* (1914). Instead of being about a rogue hero, this time, perhaps in atonement for Raffles and Bunny, Hornung centered his new book on Dr. John Dollar, alienist, who treats people who have committed or who are about to commit crimes. Dr. Dollar, however, hardly presents a coherent picture of the causes of or cures for crime. At first he gives crime a physiological basis, illustrating it with his own experience in the Boer War. After receiving a head wound, Dollar recovered but began committing crimes:

> "Physically and even mentally—from a medical point of view—but not morally, Mr. Vinson! Something subtle had happened, some pressure somewhere, some form of local paralysis. And it left me a pretty low-down type, I can tell you! It was a case of absolute automatism—but I won't go into particulars now, if you don't mind."
>
> ...
>
> "It had destroyed my moral sense on just one curious point; but, thank God, I came to see the cause as well as to suffer unspeakably from the effect."

Then Dollar tells the Home Secretary the materialistic environment makes people, especially women, criminals:

> When society women making a living out of bridge, traffic in tickets for Royal enclosures, charge a fat fee for a presentation at Court, and a small fortune for launching an unlikely family in their own set, there must be some reason for it apart from their own depravity. They are no more naturally depraved than I am, but their purse is perhaps even smaller, and their wants are certainly ten times as great. Cupidity is not the motive power; it's simple shortage of the needful—from their point of view. Society increases and multiplies in everything but money, and transmits its expensive tastes without the means to indulge them. So we get our good ladies with their tariff of introductions, and our members of the best clubs always ready for a deal over a horse or a car or anything else that's going to bring them in a fiver. It's a short step from that sort of thing to a shady trick, and from a shady trick to downright crime.

And he also posits that there are "congenital" criminals. Among these, Hornung includes the suffragettes in the story, suffragettes who go on a window-breaking rampage in which a policeman is killed at the beginning and who attempt arson at the end of the book. Dr. Dollar maintains a small nursing home which he opens to those wishing to be cured of their criminal tendencies. In the book, however, the home has only one occupant described and his prognosis is problematic. During the course of the book Hornung inserts an episode in which Dollar saves a dissipated young man by identifying and separating him from his tempter, a tempter he then makes into a mastermind criminal. But most of Hornung's narrative interest is in Dollar and Lady Vera. The beginning of the book concerns Dollar's efforts to have the Home Secretary save a habitual criminal from being executed for a crime he apparently didn't commit which Lady Vera believes she accidentally committed during a suffragette demonstration. Enthralled both by her person and her class, Dollar convinces the Home Secretary to stop the hanging and also convinces him to take no action against Lady Vera. Then follows blackmail attempts, Lady Vera's action preventing her fellow suffragettes from committing arson, the machinations of the criminal mastermind, and the grand conclusion where conscience reveals what really happened at the start of the plot and removes Lady Vera's taint. None of which, however, has much to do with Dollar's talent or skill as a psychiatrist or any connection with the theories about crime Hornung rehearses at the beginning.

Reprise

Like the detective story, the gentleman crook story had international origins. Of the major writers before 1897, only Arthur Morrison was British; the others were American (Train and Post), Canadian (Allen), and Australian (Boothby). These were countries, it should be added, with laws based on English Common Law but with different systems of law enforcement, and different views on authority, crime, criminals, wealth, social status, and the make-up of the hero. As with the detective story, popular magazines encouraged writers to take up the form. Indeed *Pearson's Magazine*, a journal modeled after *The Strand*, regularly published crook stories as the war years approached. Especially as the war approached, melodramas featuring criminal heroes, often based on novels or short stories, became a favorite genre of the infant motion picture industry.

Perhaps it is best to say here, however, that there is actually no such thing as a gentleman crook story, but that there are stories about gentleman crooks; in the period between the invention of Sherlock Holmes and the First World War the character type of the gentleman crook certainly emerged and gained a modicum of popularity, but that character, unlike the character of the detective around whom a standard plot and structure developed, appears in a variety of different kinds of narratives with different kinds of themes. Furthermore, although the detective story plot, based on problem/enigma and solution/surprise, works in short stories and novels, that is not the case with the gentleman crook story. The gentleman crook caper plot works well in the short story or collections of short stories stitched together as pseudo novels. But when shifted into novels, the form demands character development which inevitably leads away from the focus on cleverness and toward sentiment and melodrama. Collectively gentleman (or gentlewoman) crooks do not even have a lot in common with one another—other than the fact that the heroes are not what they appear to be: they appear to be upright citizens but they are not, or (later in the period) they appear to be criminals but they are not.

6

Master Criminals

Other than miscellaneous devotees of the Fu Manchu stories, not many people have paid attention to the rivulet of fiction featuring master criminals published before World War I. For one thing, there are fewer, a lot fewer, master criminal tales than detective or gentleman crook stories published during the period—at least in adult oriented publications. Additionally, because they have a strong connection to the dime novels and penny dreadfuls which depend upon readers with very elastic credulity, they put off serious (or even semi-serious) readers and critics. Then too, on the parts of both writers and readers, the terminology is confused and confusing. Thus, while the meaning of the term "criminal" is reasonably clear, the term "master" means two different things: first, it means one who has learned and expertly practiced an art or craft, and second it means one who wields authority over an individual or group. These two meanings have, in turn, led to more than a bit of confusion, because writers (to say nothing of reviewers) have used the same term to describe both solitary gentleman burglars and mysterious leaders of gigantic criminal, political, or economic enterprises—the confusion places Raffles in the same category as Dr. Fu Manchu. And that can hardly be.

While, as noted above, readers could hardly tell it from reading detective stories, in Britain and the United States the world at the turn of the twentieth century was a disorienting, dangerous and frightening place. In spite of determined imperialist expansion around the globe, definite indications demonstrated that not every people welcomed European or American proprietorship of their counties. Thus the end of the nineteenth century witnessed periodic rebellions against Western rule in Africa, in India, and in Asia. And in addition to gunboats, the Western response was an upsurge in xenophobia and racism. Anti-Asian sentiment and fears of the "Yellow Peril" flourished in novels like M.P. Shiel's *The Yellow Danger* (1899), and a tragic history of anti–Semitism got worse with the fictitious *Protocals of the Elders of Zion* (1903) which pretended to reveal a plot for Jewish domination of the world. If the world had changed, crime had changed, too. There were now secret ethnic criminal syndicates: the Cammora, the Mafia, and the Chinese Tongs. Also crime got political. Political unrest on the Continent led to the formation of societies based on "revolutionary" politics—in Italy, in Serbia, in Russia, in Germany, and in Britain. And violence was one of the tools of the new politics. William McKinley and Arch Duke Franz Ferdinand were evidence of this. And in 1884 Fenian bombs exploded in Victoria Station, Scotland Yard, the Carleton Club, at the home of Sir Watkin Williams-Wynn, M.P., and on London Bridge; unexploded bombs were found at Charing Cross, Ludgate Hill, and Paddington stations, and at Nelson's Column. Fear that things were not what they seemed to be, that violence could suddenly be thrust upon innocents, that unknown forces affected one's life appeared to be more and more rational. And new kinds of literature responded to this.

First there was the late Victorian gothic revival, the literary movement that brought readers Robert Louis Stevenson's *Strange Case of Dr Jekyll and Mr Hyde* (1886), George du Maurier's *Trilby* (1894), Richard Marsh's *The Beetle* (1897), and finally Bram Stoker's *Dracula* (1897). Each piece presented readers with both a larger than life evil and a society incapable of restraining it. As thrilling as the new gothic fiction was, the thought of the butt of a Mauser rifle banging on the study door prompted by the wave of invasion fiction offered readers at the turn of the century a more practical kind of terror. This is the sort of horror imagined in George Chesney's *The Battle of Dorking* (1871) in which a Teutonic country invades Britain. This notion of unseen foreign powers plotting collective and individual conquest was carried on in William LeQueux's *The Great War in England in 1897* (1894) and his *The Invasion of 1910* (1906); Erskine Childers' *The Riddle of the Sands* (1903); Saki's *When William Came: A Story of London Under the Hohenzollerns* (1913); and H.G. Wells' *The War in the Air* (1907) and most emphatically in his earlier *War of the Worlds* (1898) which begins with

> No one would have believed, in the last years of the nineteenth century, that human affairs were being watched keenly and closely by intelligences greater than man's own...

That notion of superior intelligence—benevolent or malevolent—was tied into science fiction from its very beginnings in the late nineteenth century. One of the founders of the form, Jules Verne, peopled his works with misanthropic geniuses: there is Nemo in *20,000 Leagues Under the Sea* (1870) who sinks ships from imperialist countries, and Robur of *Robur the Conqueror* (1886) and *The Master of the World* (1904) who inclines toward world domination in his airships. And predating Wells, Edward Douglas Fawcett's *Hartmann the Anarchist, or the Doom of the Great City* (1893), combined invasion literature, and science fiction. Both gothic tales and invasion fiction contributed to the rise of the master criminal story.

While the detective and gentleman crook stories of the period involve readers in understanding the details of an enigmatic event (albeit from different perspectives), master criminal stories are episodic and use speed to gloss over credibility. They make personal and social terror combined with the peripatetic excitement of the adventure story their stock in trade. It was for these qualities that the terms "shocker" (1886 OED) and "thriller" (1896 OED) were invented during the period to describe certain kinds of popular fiction. They were the stories that depended upon a threat to law greater than that presented by any one individual crime; indeed they sometimes depended upon a threat to civilization itself. They centered on the struggle of a hero with an alien, larger than life villain (and his or her minions) who is exempt from the ordinary resources of law enforcement and is characterized by superior intelligence, grandiose ambition, proven planning and organizing ability, limitless funds, apparent omniscience, and extensive scientific knowledge. Searching in Victorian crime fiction for the literary origin of this type of villain, active in a plot with an atmosphere that mixes the rational and the irrational, leads pretty directly to Count Fosco in Wilkie Collins' *The Woman in White*.

Survey

The serial version of *The Woman in White* ran from 1859 to 1860. It traded on readers' responses to the suffering of women and the apparent impotence of justice, both of which involve Count Isidor Ottavio Baldassare Fosco. Collins' villain embodies most of the criteria that over the next decades would come to identify master criminals. Thus Fosco

1. is "immensely fat," and as an Italian, literally an alien, is separate from the world of the novel;
2. possesses a magnetic personality ("He looks like a man who could tame anything");
3. is likened to a dominant historical figure ("He is a most remarkable likeness, on a large scale, of the Great Napoleon. His features have Napoleon's magnificent regularity; his expression recalls the grandly calm, immovable power of the Great Soldier's face");
4. has significant scientific expertise:

> The best years of my life have been passed in the ardent study of medical and chemical science. Chemistry especially has always had irresistible attractions for me from the enormous, the illimitable power which the knowledge of it confers. Chemists— I assert it emphatically—might sway, if they pleased, the destinies of humanity;

5. has a relativistic attitude toward crime ("The fool's crime is the crime that is found out; and a wise man's crime is the crime that is not found out").

While he uses it for very different purposes, in *The Woman in White* Collins connects Fosco with a secret society, The Brotherhood, a feature that would be put to very different uses by later writers.

ARTHUR CONAN DOYLE

As memorable as Count Fosco was and is, the real inspiration for master criminal fiction at the turn of the century came when Conan Doyle decided to kill off Sherlock Holmes and invented Professor Moriarty to do it in "The Adventure of the Final Problem" (December 1893). Later he mentioned his master criminal in "The Adventure of the Empty House," "The Adventure of the Norwood Builder," "The Adventure of the Missing Three-Quarter," "The Adventure of the Illustrious Client," "His Last Bow," and *The Valley of Fear*. Eleven years after his first appearance, in *The Valley of Fear* (1914), Conan Doyle included a brief, tongue in cheek account of Moriarty's historical/literary origins, tracing him to Jonathan Wild (1682–1725), the head of organized crime in London at the start of the 18th century and the subject of a book by Henry Fielding:

> "Have you ever read of Jonathan Wild?"
> "Well, the name has a familiar sound. Someone in a novel, was he not? I don't take much stock of detectives in novels—chaps that do things and never let you see how they do them. That's just inspiration: not business."
> "Jonathan Wild wasn't a detective, and he wasn't in a novel. He was a master criminal, and he lived last century—1750 or thereabouts."

Although Moriarty is more talked about than seen in Conan Doyle's stories, Sherlock Holmes presents sketches of "his intellectual equal" in two long passages in "The Final Problem" and *The Valley of Fear*. Thus readers learn

1. Moriarty is a genius: "He is a genius, a philosopher, an abstract thinker. He has a brain of the first order" ("The Final Problem");
2. Moriarty is a mathematician: "He is a man of good birth and excellent education, endowed by nature with a phenomenal mathematical faculty" ("The Final Problem"); "Is he not the celebrated author of *The Dynamics of an Asteroid*, a book which ascends to such rarefied heights of pure mathematics that it is said that there was no man in the scientific press capable of criticizing it?" (*The Valley of Fear*);
3. Moriarty is "the Napoleon of crime, Watson" ("The Final Problem"); "this Napoleon-gone-wrong" (*The Valley of Fear*);
4. Moriarty is in charge of crime in London: "He is the organizer of half that is evil and of nearly all that is undetected in this great city" ("The Final Problem");
5. Moriarty is different from others in the world of the stories: "A criminal strain ran in his blood, which, instead of being modified, was increased and rendered infinitely more dangerous by his extraordinary mental powers" ("The Final Problem");
6. Moriarty is not answerable to ordinary law enforcement: "But the professor was fenced round with safeguards so cunningly devised that, do what I

would, it seemed impossible to get evidence which would convict in a court of law" ("The Final Problem");

7. Moriarty works though subordinates like Sebastian Moran who is his "chief of staff" ("The Adventure of the Empty House").

Although he provided his character with a set of master criminal credentials, nonetheless Conan Doyle's original purpose for introducing Moriarty was to provide himself with a definitive excuse for abandoning the Sherlock Holmes stories in order to write "better things" than detective stories. And when he brought the great detective back to life in 1903 others had taken up the character of the master criminal and had begun to refashion it in response to a world very different from that created in the early Sherlock Holmes stories.

GUY BOOTHBY

In 1895 Guy Boothby switched from using his native Australia as his subject and began writing a serial in *The Windsor Magazine* about one Dr. Nikola that was then published as *A Bid for Fortune*. In it Richard Hattaras, having made his pile in Australia, returns to England, and along the way saves a maiden in distress, a peer's son from drowning, and becomes mixed up in Dr. Nikola's unscrupulous machinations to own a Chinese/Tibetan talisman supposedly possessed of occult powers. The scene shifts from Australia to England and then back again with Hattaras and his friends repeatedly outmaneuvered by Nikola and his agents until the last scene of the narrative. Over the next six years Boothby published four more Dr. Nikola novels: *Dr. Nikola* (1896), *The Lust of Hate* (1898), *Dr. Nikola's Experiment* (1899), and *Farewell Nikola* (1901). While Hatteras returns in *Farewell Nikola*, new young men who find definition for their lives through adventure narrate the other novels.

And for more than a century Boothby's Dr. Nikola has been linked with the character of the master criminal—as seen in the titles of two fairly recent collections of Boothby's Nikola stories, *The Adventures of Doctor Nikola Criminal Mastermind* and *Dr. Nikola Master Criminal*. To be sure, Dr. Nikola shares some features with Conan Doyle's Professor Moriarty and later master criminals: he has a professional title and link to science (Nikola is a physician); he has a far-reaching network of agents (the point demonstrated in the opening chapter of the first novel); he gives the impression of possessing omniscience; he has connections with the occult; he has something vaguely foreign about him; he has the ability and reputation for inspiring awe and dread; and he has a sophisticated appearance but with a touch of eccentricity (a large black cat is his constant companion). However, except in *The Lust of Hate* in which he plays a cameo role and runs an assassination organization, Nikola's aims take him out of the ordinary world of crime or world conquest and connect him more with the doctor's experiments in *Frankenstein* than with Count Fosco in *The Woman in White*. Three of the five Nikola books in one way or another have to do with his search for rejuvenation and eternal life. While in *A Bid for Fortune* he resorts to criminal acts, Nikola's pursuit of his goals consistently also involve scientific means which Boothby details both in *Dr. Nikola's Experiment* and in a scene from *A Bid for Fortune*, one which looks forward to H.G. Wells' *The Island of Doctor Moreau* published the next year:

> On the other side of the hearth was a creature half ape and half man—the like of which I remember once to have seen in a museum of monstrosities in Sydney, where, if my memory serves me, he was described upon the catalogue as a Burmese monkey-boy. He was chained to the wall in somewhat the same fashion as we had been, and was chattering and scratching for all the world like a monkey in a zoo.
>
> But, horrible as these things were, the greatest surprise of all was yet to come. For, standing at the heavy oaken table in the centre of the room, was a man I should have known anywhere if I had been permitted half a glance at him. *It was Dr. Nikola.*
>
> When we entered he was busily occupied with a scalpel, dissecting an animal strangely resembling a monkey. On the table, and watching the work upon which his master was engaged, sat his constant companion, the same fiendish black cat I have mentioned on a previous occasion. While at the end nearest us, on tip-toe, in order to see what was going on, stood an albino dwarf, scarcely more than two feet eight inches high.

The search for eternal life, however, also includes Nikola's absorption with the occult. Thus Boothby centered both *A Bid for Fortune* and *Dr. Nikola* on his search for a talisman and its connection with a secret cult in Tibet. A useful adjunct to Nikola's connection with the occult is that it combines with the other exotic elements in Boothby's writing—travel to remote places (Australia, Africa, China, and remote Scotland)—to amplify the initiation theme basic to the young male heroes of his books.

While Boothby clearly intends Nikola to be seen as masterful, awe inspiring, and even at times dangerous, whether he presents him as a villain or a criminal is not altogether clear. While in *A Lust for Hate* Nikola arranges assassinations, in the next book he has become almost a philanthropist and "the most wonderful man with whom I have ever been brought in contact." In both *Dr. Nikola* and *Dr. Nikola's Experiment* he befriends and supports the narrators, and in the last book, *Farewell Nikola*, he has become Hattaras' friend, uses his talents as a physician to save a woman's life, and does not use his powers to punish a clearly villainous character who has done him a grave injury in the past. In spite of their titles, Nikola is only the principal figure in one book, *Dr. Nikola*, and he appears only briefly in *A Lust of Hate* and *Farewell Nikola*. And in all of them he serves more as a means to define the actual heroes of the books than as a model master criminal.

L. T. Meade and
Robert Eustace (Again)

L. T. Meade and Robert Eustace were clearer about the character of the master criminal when they created Katherine (aka Madame Klouchy) the head of "The Brotherhood of the Seven Kings." She appears first in a story with that title that ran in *The Strand* on January 1898. The short story begins with the following introduction:

> That a secret society, based upon the lines of similar institutions so notorious on the Continent during the last century, could ever have existed in the London of our day may seem impossible. Such a society, however, not only did exist, but through the instrumentality of a woman of unparalleled capacity and genius, obtained a firm footing. A century ago the Brotherhood of the Seven Kings was a name hardly whispered without horror and fear in Italy, and now, by the fascinations and influence of one woman, it began to accomplish fresh deeds of unparalleled daring and subtlety in London. By the wide extent of its scientific resources, and the impregnable secrecy of its organizations, it threatened to become a formidable menace to society, as well as a source of serious anxiety to the authorities of the law.

After this first story, Meade and Eustace wrote nine more in this series and these were published together as *The Brotherhood of the Seven Kings* (1899). For the first several paragraphs of the first story (aka as "At the Edge of the Crater") Meade and Eustace include a bit of detail about the secret society: it is led by a beautiful woman ("a scientist of no mean attainments"), it has "grotesque and horrible" initiation rites, it is responsible for "terrible" crimes which cannot be traced to it, and it has moved to England. The first half of the stories focus on Norman Head, a reformed member of the Society, and his largely futile attempts to thwart Mme. Kloucy and her plans which center on making huge illicit gains. These stories have the usual Meade and Eustace science-related endings: one turns on Mediterranean Fever, one on Tse Tse flies, one on x-rays, one on high frequency sound waves, and one on an thermometer-bomb booby trap. Working principally through minions in the early stories, Mme. Klouchy takes center stage in the final stories in which she attempts to murder Norman Head and his friends, and in which he (and Scotland Yard) try to arrest her. In the end Mme. Klouchy apparently commits suicide. The Mme. Klouchy stories repeat the characters of Meade and Eustace's Mme. Sara pieces without a lot of alterations. There are the bits of science tossed in at the denouement to wrap up the narratives, there is peril to innocents (in *The Seven Kings* two children are threatened, and helpless women, especially young women, are regulars), and many of the stories depend upon stolen inheritances and family secrets. They would soon use all of these again in the Sorceress of the Strand stories.

HUME NISBIT

Hume Nisbit also includes a woman criminal in *Comrades of the Black Cross* (1899), but Virginia Holt is a subordinate character, and she is what she is because of her father and then because of her husband, both of whom are bona fide master criminals in the old fashioned sense. First there was her dad:

> Her father was one of the most remarkable criminals in that land where remarkable atrocities and contradictions are engendered—New South Wales.... A clergyman by profession, and the younger son of an earl, influence alone had saved him from the hangman's noose for his first discovered crime. His after career in Sidney, as brilliant preacher, forger, poisoner and organizer of bushrangers, is historical.

But then Virginia found Apprasius Holt (aka Tiger)—who tops her father in the master criminal department. In that respect, both Apprasius and his father-in-law illustrate Nisbit's view of criminals and crime—that is, there are criminals:

> The visitor looked at No. 96 carelessly, for he bore the stamp of the ordinary and brutal criminal in every feature—the large outstanding red ears, the sugar-loaf shaped head and low brow, the short broken nose and enormous bull-dog jowl, the small, close-set eyes and high cheek-bones.

And there are criminals:

> The features were clearly chiseled and regular, and the ears small and flat against the long skull. The visitor noticed one peculiarity, however, about those small ears, they had no lobes and were pointed like the cut ears of a terrier dog.

The lethal combination is putting the brutal knuckle-draggers together with someone with brains, someone, indeed, who has extraordinary, even Napoleonic brains. That someone is Holt who puts together the Comrades of the Black Cross, a congregation of thieves, burglars, coiners, pickpockets, arm-twisters, and leg breakers. But Nisbit gives scant coverage to the crimes committed by this crew. Instead he allots considerable space to Holt and Virginia's attempts to divest a brother and sister of their fortune through a fraudulent stock market scheme. Indeed the narrator equates the actions of the stock exchange with those of the back alley thug:

> But when is the Stock Exchange to be handed over to the police? Where one fool is ruined at baccarat, or on the turf, thousands of innocent victims are sent to perdition by the ruthless company promoter. We don't do things consistently in England. We imprison housebreakers and pickpockets, but we permit worse thieves and deeper villains to flourish unchecked.

Along with the stock market scam—with the gang's conventional crimes added for variety—Nisbit gives his readers a detective story in the last quarter of the book. Gibson, "the most acute detective on the force," while investigating the jewel robbery described at the beginning of the book, finds the means to topple Holt and all of the Comrades of the Black Cross. But he does so entirely with the help of "little Paul," an orphan with second sight who tells Gibson what the criminals are planning.

L.T. MEADE AND
ROBERT EUSTACE (AGAIN)

L.T. Meade and Robert Eustace's six stories collected in *The Sorceress of the Strand* (*The Strand Magazine*, 1902–3) bring together the master criminal and the scientific detective. The Sorceress of the Strand, Madam Sara, "is a woman who stands alone as one of the greatest criminals of her day" ("The Face of the Abbot"). Here is the first description of her:

> "She goes by the name of Madame Sara, and knows London well. In fact, she confesses to having a shop in the Strand. What she has been doing in Brazil I do not know, for she keeps all her affairs strictly private. But you will be amazed when I tell you what her calling is."
>
> "What?" I asked.
>
> "A professional beautifier. She claims the privilege of restoring youth to those who consult her. She also declares that she can make quite ugly people handsome. There is no doubt that she is very clever. She knows a little bit of everything, and has wonderful recipes with regard to medicines, surgery, and dentistry. She is a most lovely woman herself, very fair, with blue eyes, an innocent, childlike manner, and quantities of rippling gold hair. She openly confesses that she is very much older than she appears. She looks about five-and-twenty. She seems to have travelled all over the world, and says that by birth she is a mixture of Indian and Italian, her father having been Italian and her mother Indian. Accompanying her is an Arab, a handsome, picturesque sort of fellow, who gives her the most absolute devotion, and she is also bringing back to England two Brazilians from Para. This woman deals in all sorts of curious secrets, but principally in cosmetics. Her shop in the Strand could, I fancy, tell many a strange history. Her clients go to her there, and she does what is necessary for them. It is a fact that she occasionally performs small surgical operations, and there is not a dentist in London who can vie with her. She confesses quite naively that she holds some secrets for making false teeth cling to the palate that no one knows of" ["Madam Sara"].

On the problem solving, surprise side, Meade and Eustace again employ their patent device of ending the individual stories by slinging in a bit of medico-scientific fact. In "The Talk of the Town," for example, there's a fake palm tree at the lecture hall:

> "Hollow, you see. Those are the tubes to convey the gas to the leaves, at the extremity of each of which is an orifice. Professor Piozzi was standing beneath a veritable shower-bath of that gas, which is odourless and colourless, and brings insensibility and death. It overwhelmed him, as you saw, and it was impossible for him to finish his lecture."

There's also a medication that affects the nature of mucus in "The Bloodstone" and, most memorably, a "poison is very like hyoscine" is inserted behind a temporary filling in a tooth in "Madame Sara." The detective work in *The Sorceress of the Strand* is done by the team of Dixon Druse (manager of "Werner's Agency, the Solvency Inquiry Agency of all British trade. Its business is to know the financial condition of all wholesale and retail firms, from Rothschild's to the smallest sweetstuff shop in Whitechapel"), and Eric Vandeleur, police surgeon of the Westminster District ("…one of the most astute experts of the day in medical jurisprudence, and the most skilled analyst in toxicological cases on the Metropolitan Police staff"). Smart as they may be, they are out gunned by Madame Sara. Nonetheless, in each of the stories her plots are thwarted at the last minute by Vandeleur even though he cannot quite explain things fully: "The more I considered it the more I felt that I was right; but by what fiendish cunning such a scheme could have been conceived and executed is beyond my power to explain" ("Madam Sara"). Until "The Teeth of the Wolf" her crimes are either carried out by surrogates or, as in the end of "Madame Sara," beyond the reach of an ineffectual legal system.

B. Fletcher Robinson and
J. Malcolm Fraser

In the winter of 1903 B. Fletcher Robinson and J. Malcolm Fraser published their six part serial, *The Trail of the Dead* in *The Windsor Magazine*. The narrator of the series, Dr. Robert Harland, explains the extraordinary nature of his tale at the start of the first episode ("The Hairy Caterpillar"):

> IT is with no intention of delighting the curious that I put my pen to paper. Only at the urgent desire of many members of my own profession have I undertaken a task necessarily disagreeable, and do now recall the details of a case which I take to be without parallel in the records of criminology. In the mental state of the afflicted being there was, indeed, little that was abnormal. Manias that are similar to his fill our asylums. But that laborious studies in the byways of science, rather than in her more frequented paths, had placed at the will of his disordered brain weapons of a deadly potency, transformed a personal misfortune into a great and urgent public danger.

Then follow narratives beginning with Harland and his cousin discovering a murder done by esoteric means at the German university where they are studying. They identify the murderer as Professor Marnac who has turned to killing people who criticize his published views, which puts them in deadly peril as they chase about Europe in pursuit of Marnac who is on the trail of other scholars to kill. Through Harland's narration, readers see that Marnac is an accomplished linguist and master of disguise, as well as one who can turn biology and chemistry to his own ends—there is the rare poisonous caterpillar in the first story followed by murders by a chemical used in curing ham, exploding ammonia, and conventional means such as revolver bullets. Indeed, as well as linking Robinson and Fraser's stories to the sources of master criminal stories, in its February 1904 issue *The Academy and Literature* singled out the ingenuity of Professor Marnac's murders:

> This book inevitably recalls Sherlock Holmes and Dr. Nikola, and those who enjoyed those stories will undoubtedly like "The Trail of the Dead." ...The escapes of the wily Professor are marvellous, while his methods of killing his victims are exceedingly ingenious. In fact, he is so ingenious that it seems a pity he could not kill a few more people before he came to an end. The story goes with a swing from start to finish [*The Academy and Literature*, February 1904].

EDGAR WALLACE

While he may not have been very good at financial details (like how much it would cost to pay off prize winners who guessed the solution to the serial version of *The Four Just Men* in *The Daily Mail* in 1905), Edgar Wallace knew his way around master criminals and thrillers. Indeed, *The Four Just Men* takes the idea of the master criminal and in effect stands it on its head. In the story Wallace created three master minds (and a fourth who has died) dedicated to committing difficult and elaborate crimes in order to preserve what they (plus the author and his readers) believe to be justice. Wallace includes a long list of assassinations they have accomplished in the text and outlines the current dilemma they face: a minister responsible for the passage of a bill deporting political refugees who will face punishment if returned to their home countries. Playing fair, the group repeatedly warns the minister, the police, and the newspapers about the consequences of passing the bill. The minister ignores their threat, signs the bill and then dies in a manner no one in the story can identify—although dozens of readers of the *Daily Mail* wrote in to explain how he was murdered by means of the telephone on his desk. Along with the thriller elements in *The Four Just Men*, Wallace includes several asides relevant to the master criminal story. First, there is an admission about the intended atmosphere of the tale:

> "I am tired of all this, tired of it "—he thrashed the edge of his desk with an open palm—" detectives and disguises and masked murderers until the atmosphere is, for all the world, like that of a melodrama."

Somewhat later the premier makes it sound as if the master criminal is yet another manifestation of early twentieth century life:

> "It is a poetical idea," said the phlegmatic premier, "and the standpoint of the Four is quite a logical one. Think of the enormous power for good or evil often vested in one man: a capitalist controlling the markets of the world, a speculator cornering cotton or wheat whilst mills stand idle and people starve, tyrants and despots with the destinies of nations between their thumb and finger—and then think of the

four men, known to none; vague, shadowy figures stalking tragically through the world, condemning and executing the capitalist, the corner-maker, the tyrant—evil forces all, and all beyond reach of the law."

SCOTT CAMPBELL

In 1906 in *Below the Dead Line* Scott Campbell once again paired a master criminal and Sherlock Holmes. But this time the action takes place in New York City and the famous Inspector Byrnes makes a cameo appearance. *Below the Dead Line* is a collection of twelve short stories strung together by a detective's search for a master criminal, but Felix Boyd is no run of the mill detective:

> Some few wiseacres, indeed, go as far as to openly assert that Boyd is neither more nor less than an American Sherlock Holmes, a man of most extraordinary detective ability in the secret employ of some of the great banking institutions, and their immediate resort in any great criminal emergency; but the opinion of these wiseacres, as a matter of fact, is not worth a whit more than that of many a less pretentious observer.

The stories in the collection all center on Wall Street—hence the title which refers to Inspector Byrnes' imaginary line drawn near New York's financial district below which suspected felons would be arrested on sight. They all concern financiers and financial instruments and Boyd solves each crime and apprehends the criminal. Early on, however, Boyd intuits that there is something more:

> "I do, indeed," said Boyd, with noticeable gravity. "It is my impression, Jimmie, that something seriously wrong exists down here below the 'Dead-Line.'"
>
> "Why do you think so?"
>
> "Don't ask me why; the grounds for my misgivings are still vague and indefinite. Yet I seriously believe that, somewhere in this wealthy locality, where millions change hands with each passing business hour, somewhere in the very heart of our great financial maelstrom, there exists a veritable genius for crime."
>
> "A genius for crime?" echoed Coleman.
>
> "A man whose obscure personality may be only vaguely discerned behind crafty operations executed by others, yet directed by him with all the evil ingenuity and consummate foresight of a master of knavery. I see only vague signs of this at present, Jimmie, now and then cropping out in crimes of new and peculiar originality, all of which point to a masterful and malignant genius hid in the background. As yet I have been unable to get the least definite line upon him; but some day I shall do so. Some day, Jimmie, one of these peculiar crimes will give me a clue to this master knave, who, I believe, lurks about here like a spider in its web, and conspires with and directs a well-organized gang of—"

For several stories Campbell keeps the power behind the crooks in the background, and then reveals in the fifth story that he is one Scanlon or "The Big

Finger." Campbell shows enough interest in master criminals that he describes part of their aesthetic in "The Case of the Big Finger":

> "A strangely potent factor, moreover, is the atmosphere of mystery with which a master criminal often surrounds himself. It both hides him from the sleuths of the law, like yourself, Jimmie, and inspires his confederates with an awe and subservience well calculated to prevent treachery. This element of mystery always has been recognized as a mighty power, Jimmie, and it has been applied for good or evil through centuries and by all classes, from the supreme dignitary of the church down to the most vicious denizen of the under-world."

Later on in the story Campbell describes Big Finger:

> It was a hard, stern face, that of a man over fifty, smoothly shaven, and with every line and feature denoting a powerful intellect and an invincible will. Yet the face was as brutal in its sinister austerity as that of a bulldog, and the man's huge head and broad shoulders could belong only to one of imposing frame and unusual physical prowess.

In the master criminal line there are not only his crimes and visage to describe him, but he also has minions and a secret lair. All of these supplement the detective plot of each story with a capture and escape melodrama in which either Boyd is lured into a trap and escapes or *vice versa*.

NEIL W. WILLIAMS

Neil W. Williams' master criminal in *The Electric Theft* (1906), Ivan Boleroff, *alias* Stavinski, diverts electricity from an electric company's turbines in Greece, stores it in large batteries ("accumulators") which he ships to England where he plans to sell it and manipulate the market for electricity— and then the plot morphs into a political battle about anarchy, a struggle for a young woman's hand, and a technological contest between the hero's newly invented loud speaker and Boleroff's conversion of the dome of St. Paul's cathedral into a gigantic sound-making machine. Why would a villain do these things? Williams explains it this way:

> Boleroff was at this time in the prime of life, with a tall, active, and well-developed figure. His countenance was Slavonic in its roundness of outline and snub nose. The eyes were dark, almond-shaped, and very brilliant and piercing; the teeth white and regular; the lower jaw massive and square. He wore a small black moustache, tightly waxed and upturned. Of Russian nationality, Boleroff was the well-educated son of a St Petersburg physician, who had apprenticed him at the age of seventeen to a firm of electrical engineers doing business on the banks of the Neva. The youth was clever, and progressed. A career was opening clearly and more clearly before him, when he took to dissolute habits. Peculation, with disgrace, followed. Ivan Boleroff was dismissed, and found himself idle and discontented. Presently he was wishing to be revenged upon a society from which he was now an outcast.

It was in this mood that Boleroff, still practically a youth, joined a secret revolutionary band. Its discipline proved irksome to a nature whose intense conceit placed no bounds upon its ambition. A quarrel with a superior, culminating in a blow over the right eye, marked him for life. He left the band as an anarchist, carrying with him a small group of disciples, and bent upon the destruction not alone of the Russian, but of all Governments, by a scheme of his own.

Since that scheme, at the beginning at least, rested on the theft and resale of electricity, Williams' hero, Reginald Burton, needs to be an electrical engineer—the engineer sent to the station from which power has been stolen. Burton is also an inventor, the creator of the electronic megaphone. Until the end of the novel most of the electricity business is secondary to Burton's repeated rescues of the lovely Blanche Green and his troubles with the Greek government. The end of the tale, however, tells of an epic battle between Burton and his megaphone and Boleroff's booming message of anarchy broadcast by means of a perverted use of the acoustic properties of the dome of St. Paul's cathedral. Burton, it goes without saying, wins.

Nelson Lloyd

Not long after Edgar Wallace combined genius, conspiracy, perfectly executed crimes, and hero-villains dedicated to social ideals in *The Four Just Men*, Nelson Lloyd wrote *The Robberies Company, LTD* (1906). At its core, *The Robberies Company* revolves around examining the unexamined life—in this case, the unexamined life of Captain Herberton Wade, a character who epitomizes the affluent leisure class of New York City. He is held hostage by a group that, posing as hired servants, takes over his house and sets in motion a scheme to bilk members of Wade's set out of a fortune. But this is no ordinary set of felons. They are expressly not from Wall Street:

> Do not for an instant suppose that any relation exists between it and those men whose actions have of late been the scandal of the financial world. They, violating the high trust imposed in them, violating the laws of the state and every principle of what you call common honesty are but vulgar thieves, and would not be employed as agents by the corporation of which I have the honor to be a director. Aside from the fact that they are not worthy of confidence, they have not the intellect required, and could be treated only with contempt.

Wade's captors are exceptional and international:

> The company, Captain, is managed by those who are as capable as you are in what you deem the accomplishments of a man of the world. Our vice president is one of the best polo players in England, but he goes refreshed from the field to his telescope to study the heavens and their countless mysteries. There is his real pleasure, there and delving into the minds of men, as well into the brain of the London cabby as into that of the member of the ministry. But you quit with your polo. And I take this man as an example. All our directors are of his order, as many-sided. In your

well-groomed way you are as much of a freak as the long-haired poet or musician in his—just as one-sided. Only such as know life and men are admitted to the councils of our company. Take, for instance, the rector of a large church on the Pacific slope, a most religious man. He saved me from a tiger's claws in the Indian jungle years ago, and for a strong hand and steady nerve has no equal, yet he can write a sonnet of the highest merit. There is in this house an agent of ours who is one of the most accomplished students of Oriental languages and literature in the world, but he is no spectacled pedant. He could outwrestle and outbox you with ease.

Intelligent and accomplished people join the Company motivated by a utopian social vision:

Do not think, however, that our company is composed of socialists or revolutionists. Quite the contrary is true. We do believe that society one hundred years hence will not hold the same absurd views as it does to-day. The revolution is going on now under our very eyes—the revolution of education. As education spreads through all classes, men will set more store by what they have in their heads than by what they have in their houses. People will not slave a lifetime to enjoy at its close the sight of a lot of useless impedimenta. Then we will revert to Rousseau's state of nature, but it will be the nature of the gods and not of animals. The useless luxuries and comforts will have been tried and found wanting. We will find more joy in hurling our imagination among the mysteries of the heavens than we do now in shooting our bodies along a dusty road in an automobile.

In the end, the Robberies Company's arguments prove so compelling that Wade becomes one of its members.

SIDNEY PATERNOSTER

Sidney Paternoster's *The Master Criminal* (1907) never really delivers in the master criminal department. To be sure the book does contain a character that Paternoster called a master criminal. He is Lynton Hora, the name assumed by Hartley Ruthven when he is expelled from the army and sent to prison for stealing regimental funds. Emerging from prison Ruthven adopts a new identity and travels to Italy to begin a life of crime, because

he told himself always that the mental suffering, the intolerable scorn he had faced, had shown him the world as it is, and not as it pretends to be. He postulated a deceitful, hypocritical world with a smile on its face for the man of wealth, and a frown and a brick for the poor devil who had the will to enjoy and not the means to gratify his longings.

Before his disgrace he had hated only one man—afterwards he hated all men, and at least one woman—she who preferred Gay Marven, fortune's favourite, to himself, fortune's scapegoat. But in addition to enabling him to appreciate the smiles and frowns of the world at their proper worth he told himself that his experience had made a man of him. It certainly left him a purposeful, resourceful, scrupleless being, with a definite object in existence.

For the majority of the novel, however, Paternoster, passes over Hora's supersized career of crime and shifts his attention to his rival Malvern's son, whom Hora kidnapped in his infancy and raised as his own, chiefly to complete his revenge on Malvern and his wife. With this bit of background, the author concentrates on Guy Hora's criminal acts, his meeting with Malvern's lovely and virtuous ward, their seemingly doomed love for one another, and Guy's determination to atone for his crimes—which is made possible by his generous acts, the intercession of one of his victims, and Lynton Hora's murder by a miscellaneous underworld thug. Along with the attenuated struggles of virtue and love versus crime and revenge, Paternoster introduced a detective (albeit an ineffectual one) to produce yet another threat and complete his melodrama.

MAX PEMBERTON

The same year that Paternoster published *The Master Criminal* Max Pemberton came out with *The Diamond Ship* (1907). From reading it, it comes as no surprise that Pemberton was editor of the boy's magazine *Chums*. There are the toys: like his *The Motor Pirate* which revolves around a preternaturally fast motor car, *The Diamond Ship* centers on a super steam yacht tricked out with machine guns and a torpedo tube sailing around in pursuit of the diamond ship. It does have a woman with a mysterious past to be rescued and given back her real identity, but more than that it has evil that the wealthy and accomplished hero, Dr. Ean Fobos, must confront and conquer. The immediate manifestation of that evil is the diamond ship, a ship cruising the South Atlantic aboard which are stored the jewels from robberies throughout the world as well as diamonds illicitly smuggled from the mines in Africa. The diamond ship, moreover, represents a world-wide conspiracy. Thus

> I am to prove that there is a conspiracy of crime so well organised, so widespread, so amazing in its daring, that the police of all the civilised countries are at present unable either to imagine or to defeat it.

The chief of this organization is Valentine Imroth. While Pemberton makes Imroth the brains of a multi-national cartel of crime, in the narrative it is more important that he is Jewish. Thus Pemberton puts in an ounce of Shylock's use of prejudice to justify cruelty:

> Here to-night my reward begins. The great Dr. Fobos comes to me upon his knees to beg me the gift of a woman's heart. How many have so come since I was this doctor's age—a young man, spurned by his people, a fool, living honestly, a worshipper in temples made by man? And to all, I have said as I say to him, no, a thousand times, no! Get you gone from me as they have gone. Admit that the Jew is your master after all. Live to remember him—bear the brand upon your heart, the curse which he has borne at your people's will, at the bidding of their faith.

But *The Diamond Ship* hardly has the subtlety of *The Merchant of Venice*, and Imroth's every appearance is occasion for anti–Semitism. Thus his entrance in the novel:

> IMAGINE a man some five feet six in height, weak and tottering upon crazy knees, and walking laboriously by the aid of a stick. A deep green shade habitually covered protruding and bloodshot eyes, but for the nonce it had been lifted upon a high and cone-shaped forehead, the skin of which bore the scars of ancient wounds and more than one jagged cut. A goat's beard, long and unkempt and shaggy, depended from a chin as sharp as a wedge; the nose was prominent, but not without a suggestion of power; the hands were old and tremulous, but quivering still with the desire of life. So much a glare of the furnace's light showed me at a glance.

In spite of this, at the end of the novel Imroth escapes—after capitulating to the hero who has kidnapped his wife.

TYLER DE SAIX

Henry De Vere Stacpoole used the name Tyler de Saix when he wrote detective stories. In *The Man Without a Head (1908)* he gave readers a conundrum story built around multiple bodies with no heads and no clues to lead his little Anglo-German detective, Inspector Gustave Freyberger, to the villain. Forgetting about Professor Moriarty, de Saix begins to define his villain by bouncing off of Sherlock Holmes' supposed preoccupation with material clues:

> "You see," said he, "that in a case like this you are not following the traces of feet, but the working of a brain. Now the common criminal may be taken by the methods of a Sherlock Holmes. The good Sherlock sees mud of a certain character on a man's boots, and concludes that the man has been to Dulwich, or is it Leatherhead? because mud of that description is found there. Our Sherlock is all eyes, nothing escapes him. He is just the sort of person I would choose to follow me if I were a criminal, for I would leave traces behind me that he would be sure to follow and that would eternally confound him. His methods would capture a bricklayer who had murdered his wife, perhaps, but they would not capture me. I doubt if I could capture myself," said Freyberger, chuckling.

The detective soon discovers that the villain responsible for the accumulating crimes is not an ordinary criminal:

> Freyberger, just now, was beginning to feel that, somewhere, lost in the darkness of the world, there existed a mind antagonistic to his own, an appalling mind, a mind of giant stature and dwarf-like subtlety and crookedness.
>
> ...
>
> The face of the man Muller ... speaks to me in the old and long-written language of human expression. It is a terrible face and full of evil, full of logic and subtlety and craft. It is the face of a mathematician, yet the face of a satyr. It is cold as ice.
>
> ...
>
> Though I had never seen any of his work, judging from my recollection of the

man, I would say he was a great genius. He had the brilliancy of eye, the concentration of gaze, which one rarely meets with in commonplace people

While de Saix adds the requisite precision and genius, his master criminal is more deranged serial killer than mastermind or brilliant head of a criminal conspiracy. Thus readers discover at the end that one perfectly executed crime has made a genius into a monster:

> I will tell you what I think in a few words. This Muller accomplished a deeply reasoned out and intricate crime in Paris eight years ago. Well, having done that, his reason withdrew itself, exhausted possibly, but the lust for killing excited by the crime remained and grew and had to be satisfied. He strangled three people.

In the end it is not the detective's insight or expertise that ends the criminal's career, but a heart attack.

OSWALD CRAWFURD

The League of the White Hand: Extracts from Its Secret Annals (1909) serves two purposes. First is the reason why ephemera is called ephemera: only three copies of the book can be found in libraries world-wide. All are inaccessible. The second is that it is a master-criminal/secret society book apparently patterned on Wallace's *Four Just Men*—which suggests the possibility that there may have been other lost secret society/master criminal books written at the time. As far as *The League of the White Hand* goes, all I have had to go on was the following blurb from *The Bookshelf* (June 1909):

A Detective Masterpiece

All who remember the eminently successful "Revelations of Inspector Morgan" will welcome a new volume after the same style by the late Oswald Crawfurd. The book is entitled "The League of the White Hand," and deals in a thoroughly exciting and ingenious manner with the enterprises of a certain secret society having as its aim the administration of justice on all classes of his Majesty's subjects when the resources of Scotland Yard prove impotent. The account of the kidnapping of a Cabinet Minister, by removing him bound and gagged in the empty case of a grand piano, which is placed in a furniture van before the very eyes of policemen and suffragettes, is one of the finest yarns we have read for a long time; and the volume contains other stories equally original, stirring, and entertaining. No one, therefore, who appreciates and enjoys thrilling narrative, ingenuity of plot, and graphicness of style should miss reading this book. It is published by MESSRS. CHAPMAN & HALL.

And this piece from an on-line biography of Crawfurd:

> *The League of the White Hand* (1909) describes the actions of a society devoted to opposing 'that growing and pestilent form of collectivism which chooses to call itself Socialism.' The League's agenda is aristocratic, anti-millionaire, anti-union, and pro-suffragette; its tactics include kidnapping [http://oxfordindex.oup.com/].

ALBERT DORRINGTON

Albert Dorrington used two contemporary issues—the discovery of Radium (isolated as an element in 1910) and the accelerating anti–Asian xenophobia focused by the Russo-Japanese War (1904–1905)—in *The Radium Terrors* which first ran as a serial in *The Scrap Book* in 1911. His plot, however, hardly even measures up to standards of dime novels or penny dreadfuls. In *The Radium Terrors* the villain exposes wealthy individuals to radium so that they will have to pay extortionate prices to be cured of radiation poisoning. There is a private detective, Gifford Renwick, who chases around trying to put an end to all of this, but who is repeatedly side-tracked by his chivalrous ministrations to three women involved in the case. Dorrington locates the center for all of the mischief in the novel in Dr. Teroni Tsarka whom he identifies as a master criminal:

> The little doctor interrupted his swift thoughts by rising from the ottoman and assuming a Napoleonic attitude beside the brass reading lamp.
> There was malice in the last word, and in the brief pause that followed Gifford studied the capacious brow and rather well-formed features under the creaseless skull-cap. He felt instinctively that he was under the surveillance of a master criminal, a man frail of body, but whose very presence exuded the Titanic energies of his mind. Yet the Englishman, impressed as he was by Doctor Tsarka's personality, could scarcely repress a smile at his diminutive figure and mock serious pose.

While money partly motivates Tsarka's and his brutal associate Horubu's (a veteran of the Japanese Manchurian campaign) evil schemes, capitalists and Westerners lie at its core:

> "From boyhood I worked under the lash," he continued. "Poor, neglected, I grew to manhood with a desire in my heart to wreak a terrible retribution upon society. On every side I was met by greed and avarice even among my own countrymen. The feeling of anarchy left me as I grew older. With my brain harnessed for a conflict with the rich of England and America I struggled through the eighteen Gehennas of Mencius into the white light of Reason. And," he paused to moisten his lips, "in the name of Reason and Justice I have brought the weapon of science to bear upon the beast of sloth—the idle rich and the leering aristocrat."

But after the opening chapters of the novel all of this disappears in a jumble of hide and seek, romance, and racism.

JOHN BUCHAN

In 1913 John Buchan published *The Power-house* in *Blackwood's Magazine*—a publication a universe removed from *The Scrap Book,* the magazine which published *The Radium Terrors*. Like its predecessor, *Prester John* (1910), and its successor, *The Thirty-Nine Steps* (1915), in *The Power-house* Buchan tells the tale of a principled but innocent individual who accidentally becomes involved with and then threatened by a gigantic evil, which, in the end, his ingenuity and pluck (as well as coincidence) enable him to defeat. Perhaps because of its brevity, however, *The Power-house* lacks the palpable threats (a native uprising in Africa and a German invasion of Britain) Buchan used to make *Prester John* and *The Thirty-Nine* steps work. For part of the narrative, the hero seeks to save a friend from physical danger, the source of which he accidentally discovers on a vacation ramble. When he meets Andrew Lumley, the hero, Edward Leithen, knows a master criminal when he sees one:

> The man had a curious terror for me, a terror I cannot hope to analyse and reproduce for you. My bald words can give no idea of the magnetic force of his talk, the sense of brooding and unholy craft. I was proposing to match my wits against a master's, one, too, who must have at his command an organization far beyond my puny efforts.... I was a boy's mechanical toy arrayed against a Power-House with its shining wheels and monstrous dynamos.

In a conversation between Leithen and Lumley, the hero gets a vague picture of an organization wreaking occasional chaos as part of a plan to redo civilization:

> "Even now the knowledge which makes possible great engines of destruction is far beyond the capacity of any defence. You see only the productions of second-rate folk who are in a hurry to get wealth and fame. The true knowledge, the deadly knowledge, is still kept secret. But, believe me, my friend, it is there."
>
> He paused for a second, and I saw the faint outline of the smoke from his cigar against the background of the dark. Then he quoted me one or two cases, slowly, as if in some doubt about the wisdom of his words.
>
> It was these cases which startled me. They were of different kinds—a great calamity, a sudden breach between two nations, a blight on a vital crop, a war, a pestilence. I will not repeat them. I do not think I believed in them then, and now I believe less. But they were horribly impressive, as told in that quiet voice in that sombre room on that dark June night. If he was right, these things had not been the work of Nature or accident, but of a devilish art. The nameless brains that he spoke of, working silently in the background, now and then showed their power by some cataclysmic revelation.

Leithen leaves Lumley's country house determined to both save his friends and expose the conspiracy. Shadowed and threatened in London, the hero finally achieves his purpose and reads in the papers that Lumley has died of heart failure.

SAX ROHMER

The stories that would become *The Mystery of Fu Manchu* first appeared in *The Story Teller* in 1912 (and in *Collier's* in the U.S. the next year). In them, Sax Rohmer (Arthur Henry Sarsfield Ward) mixed in some of the most familiar elements of the last twenty years of popular fiction. There is Sherlock Holmes aplenty. The hero-worshipping Dr. Petrie narrates adventures of super detective Denis Nayland Smith in his search for Fu Manchu. Indeed, the opening episode in the novel reproduces Conan Doyle's "The Speckled Band," and is the first of a series of locked room mysteries upon which the first half of the book is constructed. Rohmer, however, was hardly interested in the rational side of the detective elements in the book—he was a lot more concerned about things gothic. Gothic terms pepper Petrie's narration: uncanny, bizarre, weird, strange, horrible, chill, shudder, devilish, cruel, awful, fiendish, ghastly, dreadful, danger, inhuman, unnatural, repulsive, uncanny, and dread, for example, repeatedly describe the way things feel. Action takes place mostly at night, often in eerie places—like the rotting ship hulk that Fu Manchu takes as one of his hide outs. The foreign and the exotic have much to do with all of this, from the Burmese Dacoits creeping around to the Indian Thug who tries to strangle Nayland Smith. Reflecting a literary trend going back at least as far as Mackay's *The Yellow Invasion* (1895) and M.P. Shiel's (another late Victorian gothic writer) *The Yellow Danger* (1899), xenophobia directed at Asians, particularly at China and the Chinese, looms very large in *The Mystery of Fu Manchu*. Thus, for example,

> to Smith and me, who knew something of the secret influences at work to overthrow the Indian Empire, to place, it might be, the whole of Europe and America beneath an Eastern rule, it seemed that a great yellow hand was stretched out over London.

And Dr. Fu Manchu embodies that "great yellow hand":

> From the time when Nayland Smith had come from Burma in pursuit of the advance-guard of a cogent Yellow Peril, the face of Dr. Fu Manchu rarely had been absent from my dreams day or night. The millions might sleep in peace—the millions in whose cause we labored!—but we knew the reality of the danger, knew that a veritable octopus had fastened upon England—a yellow octopus whose head was that of Dr. Fu Manchu and whose tentacles were dacoity, thuggee, modes of death, secret and swift, which in the darkness plucked men from life and left no clew behind.

Rohmer's xenophobia piggy-backs on the accumulated features of the master criminal character type. Indeed, Petrie and Nayland Smith repeat that Fu Manchu "is no ordinary criminal. He is the greatest genius the powers of evil have put on earth for centuries." He shares the identification with super science common to his predecessors. The characters most often add his professional title to his name, thus it's "Dr. Fu Manchu." And readers learn that

> he was a scientist trained at a great university—an explorer of nature's secrets, who had gone further into the unknown, I suppose, than any living man.

They learn that he is a "profound chemist," and that he has a menagerie of strange and dangerous creatures. Indeed he possesses most of the other master criminal criteria: he works through minions, he avoids or is exempt from the power of the police and the law, he has inaccessible lairs, he has inexhaustible financial resources, plus he seems to be omnipresent and, unless checked, potentially omnipotent. These features continued to form the basis for the popularity of Fu Manchu through twelve additional novels and a number of films beginning with a film version of *The Mystery of Fu Manchu* in 1923.

Reprise

After reading through the miscellany surveyed above, it becomes clear that some of the books were principally directed at adults and the others directed at adolescents. Thus one finds books based on social commentary like *The Robberies Company Ltd.* in the same category as simplistic moral exempla like *The Master Criminal* and hide and seek romps like *The Diamond Ship*. In neither case, however, are they to be confused with detective stories—even if they have amateur or professional detectives in them. For one thing, they come from different literary traditions. Forget about Sherlock Holmes, master criminal books grew in part from gothic fiction modified by the sensation novel and then modified again by the dystopian leanings of early science fiction. The other source was contemporary adventure yarns, both the "young adult" fiction of the dime novel and *Boys' Own Paper* and imperial romances like Rider Haggard's *She*. Rather than being based on solving problems like detective stories, master criminal stories employed different kinds of plots. Since the principal aim of the master criminal story was to demonstrate that the antagonist was in fact a master criminal, writers found that that was accomplished best by episodic plots that demonstrated coup after coup of the criminal and frustration after frustration of the hero. Additionally, just as the essence of the antagonist dictated the plot of the master criminal story, it also influenced the character of the hero. Here it needs to be noted that from the origins of the form, detecting is only a means to an end: for Walter Hartright in *The Woman in White* detecting and romantic fulfillment intertwine and, as for Sherlock Holmes, unlike Conan Doyle's other stories, in "The Final Problem" Holmes' most outstanding characteristic is not his powers as a detective but his sacrifice of self to rid his world of Moriarty's evil. It's also the reason the initiation theme looms so large with heroes from Boothby's Richard Hattaras to Nelson's Lloyd's Herberton Wade and Buchan's Edward Leithen: in master criminal stories it's not expertise that saves the world, but grit, pluck, and all of the other virtues taught by late Victorian society.

Part of this came from the fact that the scope of master criminals' motives matched the dimensions of their crimes. While contemporary detective stories may have included a plot or two depending on religious mania, or kleptomania, or somnambulism, they largely depended upon a limited number of personal motives (gain, jealousy, etc.) and give psychological and political motives a wide berth. Master criminal stories, on the other hand, needed to explain why intelligent, successful, and highly educated people very consciously contemplated, organized, and set into motion large-scale criminal enterprises. For some writers the answer was in megalomania. The term, first used in 1885 (OED) and employed by both Lombroso and Freud, became a convenient explanation for why people undertake such epic antisocial activity. Some writers combined megalomania with the notion of revenge—with villains inflicting retribution on an entire culture for real or imagined slights suffered as individuals. Others, like Sax Rohmer, Max Pemberton, and Alfred Dorrington depended upon racism. And finally, after the turn of the century, politics enters as a motivation of master criminals—in some cases this has to do with the perceived inefficiency of current governments (as in *The Four Just Men*), and in others it has to do with the inequality of the distribution of wealth (as in *The Robberies Company, Ltd.*). The principal focus of most master criminal books, however, rests not just on why but on what they do and how they are finally stopped.

While master criminal stories depend upon detectives (or someone acting as a detective), they and their heroes have more in common with traditional literature than did the new puzzle oriented detective story. After Conan Doyle's introduction of Professor Moriarty to be his last bow, master criminals became more than simply antagonists to show the detective's brilliance—their motivation (an element present but rarely if ever exploited in detective stories) as well as the epic consequences of their plots became things some writers wanted to exploit. Vile and repugnant many of them may be, but master criminal stories do have themes other than puzzle solving—or perhaps it's more accurate to say that they have a theme, the idea that individuals have no control over things that are scary, big and bad, things like organized crime, racial or ethnic minorities, socialists, capitalists, and psychopaths.

The master criminal story in general and the Fu Manchu books in particular spawned two responses during World War I and afterward. First of all they grew into the xenophobic thriller—exemplified at one end of the spectrum by John Buchan's *The Thirty Nine Steps* (1915) with "Blackstone" and the threat of war with Germany, and at the other end of the spectrum by Sapper's *Bulldog Drummond* (1920) with Carl Peterson as the master criminal and the threat of everything not British. Partly because they had nominal detectives in them, these books and their ilk became anathema to writers of standard detective fiction. Given that the popularity of the revised and revising form of detective fiction at the turn of the century lay in its avoidance of disturbing and controversial topics and its focus on games, logic and reason, master criminal stories and thrillers of any sort are one of reasons that gave rise to the sets of "fair play" rules of the 1920s, one of which was the "no Chinamen must appear in the story."

Final Thoughts

Looking back at the detective story in the twenty three years between 1891 and 1914, what happened? Briefly, the detective story changed, prospered, spun off parts that developed on their own into different kinds of fiction, and then matured after the war into the forms of the modern detective story.

Detective stories flourished in the 1890s in part because of the intersection of publishing, reading, and advertising. Due to radical advances in printing technology, by the end of the nineteenth century publishers had the means to print whatever they wished, and to print it in large, very large quantities. By the late eighteen eighties they could also both quickly print tens of thousands of copies of whatever there was to print—and print it with illustrations. And they did, copiously, not in the form of books as much as in the form of magazines and newspapers, media a lot more readers could afford to buy and had the time to read. By the end of the century the number of adults (and children) able to read grew exponentially on both sides of the Atlantic. After the Civil War, many states in the U.S. followed Massachusetts in making elementary education compulsory. In Britain the same requirement was put in place by the Education Act of 1870. Thus by 1890 there were many more literate citizens in both countries than there had been at the middle of the century. While these things were going on, the beginning of modern advertising, printing and detective stories came together in the person of Robert E. Bonner, publisher of *The New York Ledger*. Bonner never did anything in a small way. He flooded cities with tens of thousands of free sample copies of his story paper. Even though he did not accept ads (nor did George Newnes in *Tit-Bits*), Bonner advertised in others' papers by letting them print chapters (but not the entirety) of his serials and by taking out what for the times were gargantuan and inventive ads—ads such as one sentence printed over and over hundreds of times filling an entire page of newsprint. In addition to spending an astronomical sum on ads, Bonner helped to change the relationship between writer and publisher. Instead of writers going to publishers to have their work published, Bonner (as was customary in newspapers) hired most of his writers to produce the kind of fiction he wanted, and one of the things he wanted was detective stories both long and short. But he also sought out well known writers, paid them enormous sums, and then used their work as endorsements of his story paper—the most egregious case of this was Bonner's payment of £1,000 to Dickens in 1859 to write his crime and detection story "Hunted Down" for *The Ledger*. Bonner served as a model for the next generation of publishers, publishers like Joseph Pulitzer, William Randolph Hearst, and, in Britain, George Newnes and Alfred Harmsworth. Each, in his own ways, changed what was published and what people read. In 1915 P.G. Wodehouse summed up the world of popular publishing and the role of detective stories in it in his novel *Something Fresh*:

> The Mammoth Publishing Company, which controls several important newspapers, a few weekly journals, and a number of other things, does not disdain the pennies of the office-boy and junior clerk. One of its many profitable ventures is a series of paper-covered tales of crime and adventure. It was here that Ashe found his niche. Those "Adventures of Gridley Quayle, Investigator," which are so popular with a certain section of the reading public, were his work. Until the advent of Ashe and Mr. Quayle, the "British Pluck Library" had been written by many hands, and had included the adventures of many heroes.

But the rage for detective stories at the turn of the century did not just depend on the thirst for thrills by office boys and junior clerks. By the 1880s contests had become a usual part of the promotion of newspapers and magazines in both Britain and the U.S. There were contests for writers and different kinds of contests for readers, both of which usually offered a cash prize. The prize contest for the best adventure, detective, sea, or sport story may have served to advance the cause of the short story among aspiring writers, but it hardly served publishers' main purpose—significantly increasing the number of readers and readers' commitment to a particular magazine or newspaper. But the puzzle and the puzzle story contest, from the publisher's view, was designed to do just that—attract and keep committed readers. Puzzle contests involved following clues and either finding something or arriving at a conclusion predetermined by the publisher's writer or writers. George Newnes and Greenhaugh Smith were both deeply involved with prize puzzles during their *Tit-Bits* days—including clues for a treasure hunt for 500 buried sovereigns featured in the magazine. That particular bit of promotion has an almost smoking gun connection with the detective story, for it was Arthur Morrison (the writer later chosen for the replacements for the Sherlock Holmes stories for *The Strand* in 1893) that Newnes sent out to bury the treasure (see Hulda Friederichs, *The Life of Sir George Newnes*, 1911). It is not a great leap from the clues in a prize contest to a detective story. And contemporary critics were quick to make the connection between the puzzle and the detective story. The success of the Sherlock Holmes stories in the early 1890s, in fact, demonstrated to publishers and writers that narratives showing someone cleverly solving an interesting and complicated puzzle attracted as many or more readers than occasional puzzle contests. And most didn't cost as much.

Fictional detectives before Sherlock Holmes came in two types, hunter-trackers who followed clues that others had not found or noted, and Poe's genius who solved mysteries by interpreting clues that others could not understand. They are basically not complex character types, one readers follow with interest and the other readers follow with awe. Hunter-tracker, professionals, like Dick Donovan, from notebook fiction, were the star detectives before Sherlock Holmes gained traction in 1891, after which they, and police detectives in general, become a definite minority. What Conan Doyle did to supplant them was to remove his detective from the police who, what with the Turf Fraud Corruption case in 1877, and Jack the Ripper and Fenian bombings in the 1880s, were not in the best repute. More importantly, he humanized Poe's grouchy, aloof, genius, largely by giving him attributes of a physician—he freely admitted that Dr. Joseph Bell was his model for Holmes, Holmes is a consultant (parallel to the medical specialist to whom G.P.s like Conan Doyle referred stubborn or puzzling cases), and Baker Street is several blocks from Harley Street where high priced physician/consultants saw patients. What writers and editors were on the lookout for after 1893 when the Sherlock Holmes stories apparently ended was a detective who was not the determined police officer, who was really smart, but was not Sherlock Holmes. In 1893, therefore, the new detectives were Sexton Blake, a hero out of the outdated French tradition, Sebastian Zambra, supposedly linked to the camera, L.T. Meade's first physician, and female detective Loveday Brooke. Over the rest of the decade Holmes look-alikes John Pyn, Martin Hewitt, and Paul Beck were joined by other women (Dorcas Dene and Dora Myrl), an Indian seer (Kala Persad), a Russian detective (Michael Danevitch), C. Cutcliffe Hyne's lawyer, a pawn shop keeper (Hagar Stanley), Shiel's recluse aristocrat, and a couple of ghost busters from Meade and Eustace and the Hesketh-Prichards. While Holmes clones continued in the likes of the Thinking Machine and Hamilton Cleek, after the turn of the century the diversity of detectives increased. They became really eccentric like the Old Man in the Corner or Canon Whitechurch's goofy health food enthusiast. There were real scientists from Butler, Freeman, and Reeve. There were more women (Lady Molly, Claire Kendall, Madelyn Mack), a kid (Barney), a priest (Father Brown), and another ghost buster (Carnacki). And there were heroes deprived of normal senses from the deaf hero of Mary Braddon's *Trail of the Serpent* reprinted in 1901 in *Tit Bits*, to the wheelchair bound Napoleon Prince, to the two blind detectives Stephen Garth and Max Carrados.

Regardless of gender, ethnicity, handicap, age, social class, personality, dress, or personal hygiene, all of these detectives did the same thing—they solved problems that others had not been able to solve. In the 1840s and 50s it may have been important for the detective's actions to demonstrate to readers that through the proper use of evidence crimes were and are solved and justice prevailed and prevails. To do this writers had on their side the belief in a providential universe as well as in certain physical traits and a biologically determined criminal class verified by Professor Lombroso. In the 1890s the point of the problems in detective stories changed. Stories rarely gloat over the triumph of justice and seldom reveal details of the punishment of the wicked—the wicked who are often shoved off stage with the police, or one last bullet, or one last dose of cyanide. Theology and biology were taken off the table—along with politics, sex crimes, and mass murder which had never been on it—as the underlying matter of detective fiction. While some of the new detective stories turn on explaining newly discovered forensic methods of gathering evidence, most of them were a lot less about justice than they were about process and the presentation of puzzles. There was a new emphasis on the clues embedded in the narratives. While they were technically supposed to be found by the readers, clues were so vital to the surprise that was the heart of the new detective story that some became esoteric, or obliquely presented so that only the detective could reveal them at the close of the story.

Writing the 8,000-word short story (the new normal) which had to contain a problem, hidden clues to its solution, a surprise ending, and a memorable main character, presented various challenges to writers. This was even more the case with detective stories in the 1890s once the serious themes associated with crime moved off stage, to be assumed rather than discussed because to do so would ruin the principal puzzle purpose of the story and spoil the entertainment which readers and publishers were seeking. Thus, along with theme, short detective stories of the era had little or no room for traditional elements of fiction, including setting, tone, and character. Due to Poe and Conan Doyle, even point of view became standardized and Watsons multiplied throughout the 90s. Because of the popularity of Sherlock Holmes, however, writers had license to develop the hero of their stories. And, as seen above, they did so with a vengeance. Even if it was a difficult thing to do, however, after the turn of the century some writers tried to make the detective short story formula a vehicle for something other than the gratification of puzzles. This can be seen best looking at writers in the U.S. where some used the detective story to attack corporate greed or the beef trust or the railroad trust or the corruption of City Hall. Chesterton and Melville Davisson Post exemplify another unorthodox use of the formula with the focus of Father Brown and Uncle Abner on sin and its effects on individuals. And then some writers began with the detective story in mind and ended up with something else. Thus the ghost buster tales of Hesketh-Pritchard and Hobson start with detectives and end in another dimension. Taking a cue from Professor Moriarty in "The Final Problem" and Conan Doyle's solution to too much Holmes, some writers turned to stories about master criminals which inevitably became episodic thrillers that departed for yet another reality and left ratiocination in the dust. Finally, at the turn of the century writers with past or future detective story credentials took up the gentleman burglar tale as an alternate way of telling a story about a clever, exciting, and suave solution to a complex puzzle.

When it came to detective stories, at the turn of the last century writers encountered the Goldilocks dilemma. As it had been written in the 1850s and 1860s, the triple decker detective novel was too long. In fact it wasn't really a detective novel but a novel about sentiment with a detective story as one of its elements. Besides, reviewers were beginning to complain about detective novels, when they came up in journals, being too long. On the other hand, the short story, the form preferred by the publishers of the hot new magazines at the turn of the century, was too short, too short even to articulate a real puzzle that engaged readers with multiple suspects, along with knotty problems presented by space and time that could be illustrated in a time-table and a room drawing for readers to ponder. The alternative to these was the short novel. This was the answer provided by E.C. Bentley's *Trent's Last Case* in 1913 which led the way to Agatha Christie, Ronald Knox, Dorothy Sayers, Margery Allingham, and all the other writers in Britain and the United States who made the 1920s and 1930s the Golden Age of the detective story.

Appendix

Biographical Notes

"Above" indicates that the person and his or her work is discussed in the text.

Samuel Hopkins Adams (1871–1958): American journalist, writer, instrumental in the passage of the U.S. Pure Food and Drug Act (1906); above *Average Jones* (1911).

Grant G.B. Allen (1848–1899): Canadian journalist, writer; above *An African Millionaire* (1897), *Miss Cayley's Adventures* (1898), and *Hilda Wade* (1900).

Edwin Balmer (1883–1959): American journalist, editor, and novelist; collaborator with Philip Wylie and William B. McHarg; above *The Achievements of Luther Trant* (1910).

Robert Barr (1849–1912): Scottish-Canadian educator, journalist, publisher, writer; above *The Triumphs* of *Eugene Valmont* (1906).

Robert Eustace Barton. M.D. (1854–1943): English physician, writer; collaborator with L.T. Mead, Edgar Jepson, and Dorothy L. Sayers; above *The Master of Mysteries* 1898; *The Brotherhood of the Seven Kings* (1898) *The Oracle of Maddox Street* (1902); *The Sorceress of the Strand* (1902).

Harry Blyth (1852–1898) [wrote as *Hal Meredeth*]: English journalist, publisher, writer; above "The Missing Millionaire" (1893).

Matthias McDonnell Bodkin (1850–1933): Irish lawyer, journalist, politician, writer; above *Paul Beck the Rule of Thumb Detective* (1898), *Dora Myrl, Lady Detective* (1900)

Guy Newell Boothby (1868–1905): Australian writer; above *Dr. Nickola* (1895); *A Prince of Swindlers* (1897).

Ernest Bramah [Smith] (1868–1942): English writer, editor; above *Max Carrados* (1913).

George Ira Brett [pseudonym of Oswald F. Crawfurd] (1834–1909): English diplomat, publisher, writer; above *The Long Arm and Other Detective Stories* (1895).

John Buchan, 1st Baron Tweedsmuir (1875–1940): Scottish politician, historian, writer, governor general of Canada; above *The Powerhouse* (1913).

Frank Gelett Burgess (1866–1951): American artist, poet, humorist, writer; above *The Master of Mysteries* (1912).

George Franklin Butler, M.D. (1857–1921): American; professor of medicine, writer; above *The Exploits of a Physician Detective* (1908).

Sir Gilbert Campbell (1838–1899): English writer, editor, publisher, convicted felon; above *New Detective Stories* (1891).

Scott Campbell [pseudonym of Frederick W. Davis 1858–1933]: above *Below the Dead Line* (1906).

Charles Edward Carryl (1841–1920): American stockbroker, poet, writer; above *The River Syndicate and Other Stories* (1899).

R.T. Casson: no biographical material available.

George Randolph Chester (1869–1924): American journalist, writer; above *Get-Rich-Quick Wallingford: A Cheerful Account of the Rise and Fall of an American Business Buccaneer* (1907).

Gilbert Keith Chesterton (1874–1936): English poet, dramatist, journalist, orator, literary and art critic, biographer, and Christian apologist; above *The Innocence of Father Brown* (1911).

Dick Donovan [pseudonym of James Edward Preston Muddock] (1843–1934): English journalist and writer; above *The Man-Hunter: Stories from the Note-Book of a Detective* (1888), and *The Chronicles of Michael Danevitch* (1897).

Albert Dorrington (1874–1953): Anglo-Australian journalist and writer; above *The Radium Terrors* (1911).

May Edginton (1883–1957): English dramatist, writer; above *The Adventures of Napoleon Prince* (1913).

Joseph Smith Fletcher (1863–1935): English poet, journalist, writer; above *The Adventures of Archer Dawe, sleuth-hound* (1909).

J. Malcolm Fraser: see B. Fletcher Robinson.

Mary E. Wilkins Freeman (1852–1930); American writer; above *The Long Arm and Other Detective Stories* (1895).

Richard Austin Freeman, M.D. (1862–1943): English physician, writer; above *Dr. Thorndyke's Cases* (1909); with John J. Pitcairn as Clifford Ashdown *The Adventures of Romney Pringle* (1902) and *From A Surgeon's Diary* (1904).

Jacques Futrelle (1875–1912); American journalist, writer; above *The Thinking Machine* (1907).

Anna Katharine Green (1846–1935); American poet, writer; above *A Difficult Problem, The Staircase at Heart's Delight and other stories* (1900); *Masterpieces of Mystery* (1913).

Arthur Griffiths (1838–1908); English prison administrator, writer; above *In Tight Places: Adventures of an Amateur Detective* (1897).

Augusta Groner (1850–1929); Austrian writer; above *Joe Muller, Detective* (1910).

Clifford Halifax, M.D. [pseudonym of Edgar Beaumont] (1860–1921): English physician, writer, collaborator with L.T. Meade; above *Stories from the Diary of a Doctor* (1893).

Thomas Hanshew (1857–1914): American actor, writer; above *The Man of Forty Faces* (1910).

Julian Hawthorne (1846–1934): American engineer, journalist, writer, editor, critic; above *The Lock and Key Library* (1909).

Henry Augustus Hering: no biographical material available.

Hesketh Vernon Hesketh-Prichard (1876–1922): English adventurer, cricketer, journalist, writer; above *Ghosts; Being the Experiences of Flaxman Low* (1899); *November Joe: Detective of the Woods* (1913).

Headon Hill [pseudonym of Francis Edward Grainger] (1867–1927): English writer; above *Clues from a Detective's Camera* (1893); *The Divinations of Kala Persad, and Other Stories* (1895).

William Hope Hodgson (1877–1918): English writer; above *Carnacki the Ghost-Finder* (1913).

Harrison Jewell Holt (1875- ?): American journalist, businessman, writer; above "The Disappearance of the Japanese Envoy" (December 1912).

Ernest William Hornung (1866–1921): English poet, writer; above *Raffles: The Amateur Cracksman* (1898), *The Crime Doctor* (1914).

Fergus Hume (1859–1932): Australian dramatist, writer; above *The Green-Stone Chamber and Other Stories* (1896); *Hagar of the Pawn Shop* (1897).

Charles John Cutcliffe Wright Hyne [aka Weatherby Chesney] (1866–1944); English writer; above "The Tragedy of the Third Smoker" (1898).

Herbert Keen: no biographical material available.

Alfred Henry Lewis (1855–1914): American lawyer, journalist, editor, writer; above *Confessions of a Detective* (1906).

Francis Lynde (1856–1930): American journalist, writer; *Scientific Sprague* (1912).

Thomas P. MacNaught: no biographical material available.

Richard Marsh (1857–1915) [pseudonym of Richard Bernard Heldmann]: English editor, writer; above *The Aristocratic Detective* (1898).

James Brander Matthews (1852–1929): American professor of dramatic literature, scholar, critic, writer; above *The Long Arm and Other Detective Stories* (1895).

William B. McHarg (1872–1951): American journalist, writer, collaborator with brother-in-law Edwin Balmer; above *The Achievements of Luther Trant* (1910).

L. T. Meade [pseudonym of Elizabeth Thomasina Meade Smith]: Irish editor, writer, feminist; above (with Clifford Halifax) *Stories from the Diary of a Doctor* (1893), (with Robert Eustace) *The Master of Mysteries* (1898); *The Brotherhood of the Seven Kings* (1898); *The Oracle of Maddox Street* (1902), *The Sorceress of the Strand* (1902).

Miriam Michelson (1870–1942): American journalist, writer; above *In the Bishop's Carriage* (1903).

John A. Moroso (1874–1957): American writer; above "Cuttlefish Farington."

Arthur George Morrison (1863–1945): English journalist, writer; above *Martin Hewitt Investigator* (1894), *The Dorrington Deed Box* (1897).

David Christie Murray (1847–1907): English journalist, writer; above *The Investigations of John Pym* (1895); *A Rogue's Conscience* (1899).

James Hume Nisbit (1849–1923): Scottish-Australian artist, poet, writer; above *Comrades of the Black Cross* (1899).

Harvey J. O'Higgins (1876–1929): Canadian journalist, writer; above *The Adventures of Detective Barney* (November 9, 1912).

Edward Phillips Oppenheim (1866–1943): English writer; above Peter *Ruff and the Double Four* (1911).

Baroness Emma Orczy (1865–1947): Hungarian-English playwright, artist, writer; above *The Case of Miss Elliot* (1905), *The Old Man in the Corner* 1909, *Lady Molly of Scotland Yard* (1910).

Rodrigues Ottolengui (1861–1937): American dentist, writer; *An Artist in Crime* (1892), *Final Proof, or, The Value of Evidence* (1898).

Frank Lucius Packard (1877–1942): Canadian engineer, writer; above *The Adventures of Jimmy Dale* (1917).

G. Sidney Paternoster (1866–1925): English journalist, writer; above *The Motor Pirate* (1903), *Master Criminal* (1907).

Max Pemberton (1853–1950): English journalist, editor, writer; above *Jewel Mysteries I Have Known: From a Dealer's Note Book* (1895), *The Diamond Ship* (1907).

Charles Felton Pidgin (1844–1923): American statistician, writer; above *The Chronicles of Quincy Adams Sawyer, Detective* (1912).

Catherine Louisa Pirkis (1841–1910): English writer, animal activist; above *The Experiences of Loveday Brooke, Lady Detective* (1893).

John J. Pitcairn (1860–1936): above *Romney Pringle* (1902); *From A Surgeon's Diary* (1904)

Melville Davisson Post (1869–1930): American lawyer, writer; above *The Strange Schemes of Randolph Mason* (1896), *Monsieur Jonquelle* (1913), *Uncle Abner, Master of Mysteries* (1919).

Arthur B. Reeve (1880–1936): American lawyer, editor, journalist, writer; above "The Case of Helen Bond" (1910), *Constance Dunlap* (1913), *Clare Kendall* (1913).

Mary Roberts Rinehart (1876–1958): American writer; above *The Circular Staircase* (1908).

Bertram Fletcher Robinson (1870–1907): English editor, writer; above *Chronicles of Addington Peace* (1905) and with J. Malcolm Fraser *Trail of the Dead* (1904).

Sax Rohmer [pseudonym of Arthur Henry Sarsfield Ward] (1883–1959): English writer; above *The Insidious Fu Manchu* (1914).

Tyler de Saix [pseudonym of Henry De Vere Stacpoole M.D.] (1863–1951): Irish physician, writer; above *The Man Without a Head* (1908).

Harvey Scribner (1850–1913); American lawyer, writer; above *My Mysterious Clients* (1900).

Matthew Phipps Shiel [Matthew Phipps Shiell] (1865–1947): West Indian writer; above *Prince Zaleski* (1895).

George R. Sims (1847–1922): English journalist, poet, dramatist, writer; above *Dorcas Dene, Detective, Her Life and Adventures* (1897).

Herbert Greenough Smith (1855–1935): English editor; above "The Case of Roger Carboyne" (1892).

Lincoln Steffens (1866–1936): American journalist, writer; above *The Shame of the*

Cities (1904), above "Mickey Sweeney, Detective of Detectives" (1908).

Arthur J.A. Stringer (1874–1950); Canadian poet, writer; above *The Wire Tappers* (1906).

Roy Tellet [pseudonym of A. Eubule Evans] (1839–1896): English clergyman, editor, translator, writer; above *The Long Arm and Other Detective Stories* (1895).

Arthur C. Train (1875–1945): American lawyer, writer; above *McAlister and His Double* (1905).

Elizabeth Phipps Train (1856–1903): American writer; above *The Social Highwayman* (1896).

Louis Joseph Vance (1879–1933): American writer; above *The Lone Wolf* (1914).

Florence Walden [pseudonym of Alice Price James] (1857–1929): English actress, writer; above *House on the Marsh* (1884).

Richard Horatio Edgar Wallace (1875–1932): English journalist, writer; above *4 Just Men* (1905).

Hugh C. Weir (1884–1934): American journalist, editor, screenwriter, writer; above *Miss Madelyn Mack, Detective* (1914).

Carolyn Wells (1862–1942): American librarian, poet, writer; above *The Clue* (1909).

Frederick Merrick White (1859–1935): English writer; above *The Master Criminal* (1897).

Victor Lorenzo Whitechurch (1868–1933): English clergyman, writer; above *Thrilling Stories of the Railway* (1912).

Neil Wynn Williams: no biographical material available.

Israel Zangwill (1864–1926); English dramatist, political activist, writer; above *The Big Bow Mystery* (1892).

Works Cited

Adams, Samuel Hopkins. *Average Jones.* New York: Grosset Dunlap, 1911.

Albright, Evelyn May. *The Short-Story, its principles and structure.* London: Macmillan, 1907.

Allen, Grant. *An African Millionaire.* New York: Arnold, 1897.

_____. *Hilda Wade: A Woman of Tenacity and Purpose.* New York: Putnam, 1899.

_____. *Miss Cayley's Adventures.* London: Richards, 1899.

Ashdown, Clifford. See Freeman, R. Austin and John Pitcarin.

Balmer, Edwin, and William B. McHarg. *The Achievements of Luther Trant.* Boston: Small Maynard, 1910.

Barr, Robert. "Detective Stories Gone Wrong: The Adventures of Sherlaw Kombs." *The Idler*, May, 1892.

_____. *The Triumphs of Eugene Valmont.* New York: Appleton, 1906.

Barrett, Charles R. "Short Stories Classified." *The Editor*, August 1908.

_____. *Short Story Writing.* Garden City, NY: Doubleday, 1900.

"The Bellman's Bookshelf." *The Bellman.* December 22, 1917.

"Book Notes." *The Yale Literary Magazine.* October 1894.

"Bookishness." *Life.* Oct 25, 1885.

Bodkin, Matthias McDonnell. *Dora Myrl, Lady Detective.* London: Chatto Windus, 1900.

_____. *Paul Beck the Rule of Thumb Detective.* London: Pearson, 1898.

"Bookstall Books." *The Speaker.* October 7, 1893.

Boothby, Guy. *A Bid for Fortune.* New York: Appleton, 1899.

_____. *Dr. Nikola's Experiment.* New York: Appleton, 1899.

_____. *The Viceroy's Protégé, or A Prince of Swindlers.* New York: New American Book Company, 1903.

Boutelle, Clarence. *The Man Outside. Frank Leslie's Popular Monthly.* April 1887.

Bramah, Ernest [Ernest Brammah Smith]. *Max Carrados.* London: Methuen, 1914.

"Briefer Notices." *The American.* April 12, 1890.

Buchan, John. *The Powerhouse.* Boston: Houghton Mifflin, 1916.

Burgess, Frank Gelett. *The Master of Mysteries.* Indianapolis: Bobbs-Merrill, 1912.

Burton, William Edward. "The Cork Leg." *Burton's Gentleman's Magazine.* March 1838.

_____. "The Secret Cell." *Burton's Gentleman's Magazine.* September 1837.

Butler, George F. *The Exploits of a Physician Detective.* Chicago: Abbot, 1911.

Campbell, Gilbert. *New Detective Stories.* London: Ward Lock, 1891.

Campbell, Scott. *Below the Dead Line.* New York: Dillingham, 1904.

Carryl, Charles. *The River Syndicate and Other Stories.* New York: Harper, 1899.

Casson, R.T. *Sam Smart, A Detective's Reminiscences: From the Diary of Sam Smart.* London: British Library, Historical Print Editions, 2011.

_____. *Strange Cases from a Detective's Diary.* London: British Library, Historical Print Editions, 2011.

Chester, George Randolph. *Get Rich Quick Wallingford*. New York: Burt, 1907.

Chesterton, G.K. "A Defense of Detective Fiction." *The Booklovers Magazine*. January 1903.

_____. *The Innocence of Father Brown*. New York: Lane, 1910.

_____. "Why Books Become Popular." *The Bibliophile*. September 1908.

Cody, Sherwin, ed. *The Best Tales of Edgar Allan Poe*. Chicago: McClurg, 1903.

Conan Doyle, Arthur. *Memories and Adventures*. London: Hodder and Stoughton, 1924.

"Conan Doyle's First Novel." *Medical and Surgical Reporter*. March 7, 1896.

"Crime in Fiction." *Blackwood's Magazine*. August 1890.

"Current Literary Topics." *The Writer*. December 1905.

"Current Literary Topics." *The Writer*. October 1907.

Curties, Henry. *The Queen's Gate Mystery*. Boston: Estes, 1908.

De Saix, Tyler, *The Man Without a Head*. New York: Moffet Yard, 1908.

"Detective Fiction." *The Saturday Review*. December 4, 1886.

Donovan, Dick. *Caught at Last: Leaves from the Note-book of a Detective*. London: Chatto and Windus, 1889.

_____. *The Chronicles of Michael Danevitch of the Russian Secret Service*. London: Chatto Windus, 1897.

Dorrington, Albert. *The Radium Terrors*. Garden City: Doubleday Page, 1912.

Edginton, May. *The Games of Napoleon Prince*. New York: Cassell, 1912.

Edwards, Annie. *Archie Lovell*. *The Galaxy*. September 15, 1866.

"Fiction." *The Literary World*. April 7, 1894.

"Fiction." *The Review of Reviews*. January 1892.

"Fiction." *The Speaker*. November 26, 1892.

"Fiction." *The Speaker*. July 21, 1894.

Fletcher, J.S. *The Adventures of Archer Dawe, sleuth-hound*. London: Digby, 1909.

Freeman, R. Austin. *John Thorndyke's Cases*. London: Chatto, 1909.

_____. *The Red Thumb Mark*. London: Collingwood, 1907.

_____. *The Singing Bone*. London: Hodder Stoughton, n.d.

Freeman, R. Austin, and John Pitcarin. *The Adventures of Romney Pringle*. London: Ward Lock, 1902.

_____, and _____. *From A Surgeon's Diary*. Philadelphia: Oswald Train, 1977.

Friederichs, Hulda. *The Life of Sir George Newnes, Bart*. London: Hodder and Stroughton, 1911.

Futrelle, Jacques. *The Thinking Machine*. New York: Dodd, 1907.

_____. *The Thinking Machine on the Case*. New York: Appleton, 1908.

Green, Anna Katharine. *A Difficult Problem, The Staircase at Heart's Delight and other stories*. New York: Lupton, 1900.

_____. *Masterpieces of Mystery*. New York: Dodd Meade, 1913.

_____. *The Old Stone House and Other Stories*. New York: Putnam, 1891.

Griffiths, Arthur. *In Tight Places: Adventures of an Amateur Detective*. London: Jarrold, 1900.

Groner, Augusta. *Joe Muller, Detective: Joe Muller, Detective: Being the Account of Some Adventures in the Professional Experience*. New York: Duffield, 1910.

Gullifer, Helena. *A Fool for His Pains*. London: Samson Low, 1883.

Hanshew, Thomas. *Cleek: The Man of Forty Faces*. New York: Cassell, 1913.

_____. *Cleek of Scotland Yard*. Garden City, NY: Doubleday Page, 1914.

Harte, Bret. *Condensed Novels* (second series). *New Burlesques*. Boston: Hougton Mifflin, 1902.

Hawthorne, Julian, ed. *The Lock and Key Detective Library*. Vol 9. New York: Review of Reviewers, 1907.

Hering, Henry A. *The Burglar's Club: A Romance in Twelve Chronicles*. New York: 1906.

Hesketh-Pritchard, Hesketh Vernon. *Ghosts: Being the Experiences of Flaxman Low*, London: Pearson, 1899.

_____. *November Joe: Detective of the Woods*. Boston: Houghton Mifflin, 1913.

Hill, Headon. *Clues from a Detective's Camera*. London: Arrowsmith, 1893.

_____. *The Divinations of Kala Persad, and Other Stories*. London: Ward Lock, 1895.

_____. *Zambra, the Detective: Some Clues from his NoteBook*. London: Chatto, 1894.

Hodgson, William Hope. *Carnacki the Ghost-Finder*. London: Nash, 1913.

Holt, Harrison Jewell. "The Disappearance of the Japanese Envoy." *Pearson's Magazine*. December 1912.

Hornung, E.W. *The Amateur Cracksman*. London: Methuen, 1899.

_____. *The Crime Doctor*. Indianapolis: Bobbs Merrill, 1914.

Hume, Fergus. *The Dwarf's Chamber and Other Stories*. London: Ward Lock, 1896.

_____. *Hagar of the Pawn Shop*. New York: Buckles, 1899.

James, Florence Alice Price. *The House on the Marsh*. New York: Appleton, 1884.

Keen, Herbert. "The Chronicles of Elvira House." *The Idler*. February 1896.

Kilmer, Joyce. "On Detective Stories." *The Editor*. January 29, 1916.

King, Robert M. *School Interests and Duties*. New York: American Book Company, 1894.

Lewis, Arthur Henry. *Confessions of a Detective*. New York: Barnes, 1906.

"Literary News and Notes." *The Author*. May 15, 1891.

Lloyd, Nelson. *The Robberies Company, LTD*. New York: Scribners, 1906.

The Long Arm and Other Detective Stories. London: Chapman Hall, 1895.

Lynch, Lawrence [pseudonym]. *No Proof*. London: Ward Lock, 1895.

Lynde, Francis. *Scientific Sprague*. New York: Scribner, 1912.

"Lyre and Lancet." *Punch*. July 21, 1894.

"The Maulverver Murders." *Saturday Review*. August 24, 1907.

McEuen, Carroll. "The Romance of Detective Stories." *The Yale Courant*. February 1907.

Meade, L.T., and Clifford Halifax. *Stories from the Diary of a Doctor*. London: Newnes, 1894.

Meade, L.T., and Robert Eustace. *The Brotherhood of the Seven Kings*. London: Ward Lock, 1899.

_____, and _____. *A Master of Mysteries*. London: Ward, 1898.

_____, and _____. *The Oracle of Maddox Street*. London: Ward, 1904.

_____, and _____. *The Sorceress of the Strand*. London: Ward, 1903.

Michelson, Miriam. *In the Bishop's Carriage*. New York: Grosset Dunlap, 1903.

"Miss Green's Detective Stories." *The Literary News*. January-February 1880.

"The Moonstone." *The Nation*. September 17, 1868.

Moroso, John A. "Cuttlefish Farrington." *Pearsons*. April 1914.

Morrison, Arthur. *The Dorrigton Deed Box*. London: Ward Lock, 1897.

_____. *Martin Hewitt Investigator*. New York: Harper, 1907.

Murray, David Christie. *The Investigations of John Pym*. London: Lane, 1895.

_____. *A Rogue's Conscience*. London: Buckles, 1899

"New Books and New Editions." *Albany Law Journal*. June 23, 1900.

"New Novels." *The Academy*. March 23, 1889.

"New Novels and New Editions." *The Literary World*. August 25, 1893.

Nisbit, Hume. *Comrades of the Black Cross*. London. White, 1899.

O'Higgins, Harvey. *The Adventures of Detective Barney*. New York: Grosset Dunlap, 1912.

"Old Puzzle Cards." *The Strand*. December 1899.

"On Certain Recent Short Stories." *Cosmopolitan*. September 1891.

Oppenheim, E. Phillips. *Peter Ruff and the Double Four*. New York: Collier, 1912.

Orczy, Emmuska M. R. M. J. B. *The Case of Miss Elliott*. London: Greening, 1909.

_____. *The Old Man in the Corner*. London: Hodder Stoughton, 1908.

_____. *Lady Molly of Scotland Yard*. London: Cassell, 1910.

"Our Booking Office." *Punch*. July 24, 1907.

Ottolengui, Rodriguez. *An Artist in Crime*. New York: Putnam, 1892.

_____. "The Azteck Opal." *The Idler*. April 1895.

_____. *Final Proof, or, The Value of Evidence.* New York: Putnam, 1898.

"Our Booking Office." *Punch.* April 27, 1889.

Packard, Frank L. *The Adventures of Jimmie Dale.* New York: Burt, 1917.

Partridge, Emelyn. "The Short Story." *The Suburban.* October 27, 1906.

Paternoster, G. Sidney. *The Master Criminal.* New York: Cupples, 1907.

_____. *The Motor Pirate.* London: Page, 1904.

Peck, Harry T. *Studies of Several Literatures.* New York: Dodd Mead, 1909.

Pemberton, Max. *The Diamond Ship.* London: Cassell, 1907.

_____. *Jewel Mysteries I Have Known: From a Dealer's Note Book.* New York: Fenno, 1904.

Pidgin, Charles Felton. *The Chronicles of Quincy Adams Sawyer, Detective.* New York: Grosset Dunlap, 1912.

Pirkis, Catherine Louisa. *The Experiences of Loveday Brooke, Lady Detective.* London: Hutchinson, 1894.

"Popularising Science." *Nature.* July 26, 1894.

Post, Melville Davisson. *Monsieur Jonquelle Prefect of the Paris Police.* New York: Mc-Clelland Stewart, 1923.

_____. *The Strange Schemes of Randolph Mason.* New York: Putnam, 1896.

_____. *Uncle Abner Master of Mysteries.* New York: Appleton, 1919.

"Prize Competitions." *Cassell's Family Magazine.* January 1894.

"Recent English and Canadian Fiction." *The Dial.* November 16, 1892.

"Recent Fiction." *The Critic.* January 19, 1889.

"Recent Fiction." *The Overland Monthly.* April 1885.

Reeve, Arthur B. *Constance Dunlap.* New York: Grosset Dunlap, 1913.

_____. *The Silent Bullet.* New York: Grosset Dunlap, 1910.

"Review, Fergus Hume's *The Red Headed Man.*" *The Literary World.* December 1899.

"Review of *In the Shadow of the Rope.*" *Pacific Monthly.* November 1902.

"Reviews." *The Literary Era.* January 1894.

"Reviews and Notices of New Books." *The Antiquary.* January 1890.

Rinehart, Mary Roberts. *The Circular Staircase.* New York: Grosset Dunlap, 1908.

Robinson, Bertram Fletcher. *The Chronicles of Addington Peace.* New York: Harper, 1905.

Robinson, Bertram Fletcher, and J. Malcolm Fraser. *Trail of the Dead.* London: Ward, 1904.

Scribner, Harvey. *My Mysterious Clients.* New York: Clarke, 1900.

"The Search." *The Living Age.* December 1906.

Shiel, M.P. *Prince Zaleski.* London: Lane, 1895.

Sims, George R. *Dorcas Dene, Detective, Her Life and Adventures.* London: White, 1897.

Smith, Herbert Greenhaugh. "The Case of Roger Carboyne." *The Strand.* July 1892.

Smith, Matthew. *Bulls and Bears of New York.* Hartford, CT: Burr, 1874.

Snyder, Carl. "What do the American People Read." *The American Journal of Politics.* April 1894.

"Some New Novels." *The Book Buyer.* September 1885.

Steffens, Lincoln. "Mickey Sweeney, Detective of Detectives." *American Magazine,* July 1908.

Stevenson, Burton. *The Marathon Mystery.* New York: Holt, 1904.

_____. "Supreme Moments in Detective Fiction." *The Bookman.* March 1913.

"Story Paper Literature." *The Atlantic Monthly.* September 1879.

Stringer, Arthur. *The Wire Tappers.* New York: McKinley, Stone, MacKenzie, 1906.

"The Thief and Detective." *Scientific American.* May 30, 1896.

Tracy, Louis B. *A Mysterious Disappearance.* New York: Clode, 1905.

Train, Arthur. *McAlister and His Double.* New York: Scribners, 1905.

Train, Elizabeth Phipps. *A Social Highway Man.* Philadelphia: Lippincott, 1896.

Twain, Mark. *A Double Barrelled Detective Story.* New York: Harper, 1902.

"Two Lively Indoor Games." *The American Agriculturist,* 1865.

Vance, Louis Joseph. *The Lone Wolf: A Melodrama.* New York: Burt, 1912.

Vidocq, Eugene Francois. "*The Bill of Exchange.*" *Burton's Gentleman's Magazine,* December 1838.

_____. "*The Conscript's Revenge.*" *Burton's Gentleman's Magazine, May 1939.*

_____. "*Doctor D'Arsac.*" *Burton's Gentleman's Magazine.* October 1838. http://www2. mcdaniel.edu/WestminsterDetectiveLibrary/stories/Doctor DArsac/Doctor DArsac p1.html

_____. "*The Gambler's Death.*" *Burton's Gentleman's Magazine, February 1839.*

_____. "*Jean Monette.*" *Burton's Gentleman's Magazine.* April 1839.http://www2. mcdaniel.edu/WestminsterDetective Library/stories/Jean Monette/Jean Monette p1.html

_____. "*Marie Laurent.*" *Burton's Gentleman's Magazine, September 1838.*

_____. "*Pierre Louvois.*" *Burton's Gentleman's Magazine, March 1839.*

_____. "*The Seducer.*" *Burton's Gentleman's Magazine. March 1839.*

_____. "*The Strange Discovery.*" *Burton's Gentleman's Magazine. January 1839.*

Wallace, Edgar. *The Four Just Men.* London: Tallis, 1905.

Ward, Arthur Henry Sarsfield. *The Mystery of Fu Manch*u. London: Methuen, 1913.

Waters, Thomas [pseudonym]. *Recollections of a Policeman.* New York: Cornish and Lamport, 1858.

"Weekly Record of New Publications." *The Publishers' Weekly.* March 28, 1885.

"Weekly Record of New Publications." *The Publishers' Weekly.* January 14, 1891.

Weir, Hugh C. *Miss Madelyn Mack, Detective.* Boston: Page, 1914.

Wells, Carolyn. *The Clue.* New York: Burt, 1909.

_____. "Over the Book Counter." *The Reader,* October 1903

_____. *The Technique of the Mystery Story* Springfield, MA: The Home Correspondence School, 1913.

White, Frederick Merrick. *The Master Criminal.* London: Castrovilli, 1898.

Whitechurch, Victor Lorenzo. *Thrilling Stories of the Railway.* London: Pearson, 1912.

"Wilkie Collins." *The Eclectic Magazine.* December 1889.

Williams, Neil W. *The Electric Theft.* Boston: Small Maynard, 1906.

The Writer. Untitled review. January 1892.

Zangwill, Israel. *The Big Bow Mystery.* Chicago: Rand McNally, 1895.

Index